Preface books

A series of scholarly and critical studies of major writers intended for those needing modern and authoritative guidance through the characteristic difficulties of their work to reach an intelligent under-standing and enjoyment of it.

General Editor: MAURICE HUSSEY

Available now:

A Preface to Wordsworth	JOHN PURKIS
A Preface to Donne	JAMES WINNY
A Preface to Milton	LOIS POTTER
A Preface to Coleridge	ALLAN GRANT
A Preface to Jane Austen	CHRISTOPHER GILLIE
A Preface to Yeats	EDWARD MALINS
A Preface to Hardy	MERRYN WILLIAMS
A Preface to Dryden	DAVID WYKES

Other titles in preparation:

A Preface to Spenser	HELENA SHIRE
A Preface to Dickens	ALLAN GRANT

A Preface to Pope

I.R.F. Gordon

Longman London and New York

LONGMAN GROUP LIMITED
London and New York

Associated companies, branches and
representatives throughout the world

Published in the United States of America by Longman Inc. New York

This edition © Longman Group Ltd. 1976

This edition first published 1976
Second impression 1977

ISBN 0 582 31505 0 Cased
ISBN 0 582 31506 9 Paper

Printed in Hong Kong by Dai Nippon Printing Co. (H.K.) Ltd.

Library of Congress Cataloging in Publication Data

Gordon, I.R.F.
   A preface to Pope.

   (Preface books)
   Bibliography: p.
   Includes index.
   1. Pope, Alexander, 1688-1744. I. Title.
PR3633.G6   821'.5   75-25572
   ISBN 0 582 31505 0
   ISBN 0 582 31506 9 pbk.

To the memory of Douglas Brown

I.R.F. GORDON took his M.A. at Queens' College, Cambridge, and
his Ph.D. from the University of California at Los Angeles. He was
Assistant Professor of English at the University of Western Ontario,
and is now Senior Lecturer in English at the Cambridgeshire College
of Arts and Technology. He has edited two anti-Walpole pamphlets
for the Augustan Reprint Society.

Contents

List of Illustrations

Foreword

Alexander Pope, unquestionably the leading English poet of the first half of the eighteenth century, was an intriguing and paradoxical character: a man of wrath, full of recrimination and accusation, and at the same time a poet of the virtues of friendship, reasonableness, good sense and social responsibility. Ian Gordon's *Preface* pulls out, one by one, the strands in that artistic and social temperament, and offers a biographical and intellectual portrait of a man, cultivating his famous grotto and garden down by the Twickenham riverside, who remained at the centre of metropolitan culture and wit: a man whom the Whigs reviled and the Tories admired, both to an exorbitant degree.

That other arts than literature should play a large part in a survey such as this will occasion no remark, but the reader unfamiliar with its subject may be surprised by the importance attached in literature between the times of Pope and Jane Austen to landscape gardening. In this pursuit lies the blend of the aesthetic with the practical, an art much lower than architecture but ideally planned together with it in the same perspective. As we discover from pp. 142–47 Pope accused the landlord figure he calls Timon of exceeding all good taste, not least in the size of his operations that 'bring all Brobdingnag before your thought'. Yet, on the other hand, he supports the planning projects, also vast, of his friend Burlington:

> Let his plantations stretch from down to down,
> First shade a Country, and then raise a Town.

> *Moral Essays*, IV

He goes further and imagines whole navies, harbours, temples, the entire solid texture of a community. The distinction between these two men is important. What Timon's building lacks is an ideal dimension, an attempt to reduce the wildness of nature to provide the context for a civilized city. Such a vision is at the core of Pope's art as a way of stemming the onrush of dullness, madness, corruption and universal darkness which were his obsessions in the years when he was completing *The Dunciad*. Such an art, replete with social responsibility, provides the modern searcher with a perfect model of a literary art in close touch with the ultimate problems of its day, a relevance, and a justification.

As expressed in his *Essay on Man*, which Dr Gordon analyses in chapter 5, Pope's ideas assumed a more systematic though not original form. He can always produce the epigrammatic statement and build a series of them into a credible, if encapsulated, species of dogma. To hold an entire poetic structure in our imagination and respond to it adequately, so as to appreciate the overall design, may be for some readers a most demanding activity, especially where the freer forms and more glowing images of romantic poetry still cling to the mind. Yet it is, as Dr Gordon's readers will discover, a poetic vision, much crisper though less emotionally intense, and probably no less exciting when we come across such a couplet as:

> The spider's touch, how exquisitely fine!
> Feels at each thread, and lives along the line;
>
> *Essay on Man*, I

The passages chosen for the Critical Survey are examined in depth as all Pope's verse should be. A single canto or epistle at a time is as much as the new reader should undertake. Here, informed by the author's experience in teaching Pope's poetry to several types of student, readers are equipped with the ideas and skills desirable to promote their own expanding enjoyment of a major poet.

MAURICE HUSSEY
General Editor

Introduction

This book is designed to help the reader who is coming to Pope's poetry for the first time. Such a person will probably find that Pope's poems make demands on him very different from those he is used to in reading poetry. To take a very simple example, Pope's poems are long, much longer perhaps than most modern students have come to expect. The aim of this *Preface* is to provide sufficient background understanding to enable the student to appreciate and enjoy Pope's poetry for himself. The emphasis is therefore not so much on telling the reader what to think of Pope, though the author's own views have inevitably emerged strongly at places, as on giving the reader the necessary information to make that judgment for himself.

Part One attempts to place Pope in his own time and to give the reader a sense of the historical, intellectual, and cultural climate in which his poetry developed. The first chapter is a short biography that pays special attention to those bonds of friendship and duty that shaped his life. Chapter 2 deals with the theme of town and country and the way it takes on allusive significance at the same time as it gives a sense of concrete reality to his poetry. Chapter 3 shows how an understanding of Pope's relationship to the kindred arts of his day enriches our appreciation of his work, while chapter 4 deals with literary criteria and expectations that Augustan readers took for granted, but that we no longer do. The fifth chapter explores the intellectual background to Pope's thought and the way it affected his writing.

Part Two offers close readings of some key passages in his poetry, chosen to represent both the range of his achievement and the development of his art. Part Three is a reference section intended as a tool to help those readers who feel discouraged by the frequent naming of contemporary persons and places in Pope's poetry. We can never entirely regain the full trenchancy of a poetry that was written to be topical, but we can go a long way towards doing so at the same time as we extend our knowledge of early eighteenth-century social and political history.

Pope's poetry attracts our admiration in a variety of different ways. Sometimes it is the wit of its rhetorical and imaginative structures that strikes us most forcefully; at other times it is the ease and eloquence of its numbers; and on still other occasions it is the cutting compactness of its language that has the strongest effect. But above all it is the poet's passionate concern for the state of society and his commitment to the moral norms of civilized life that compels our continuing respect and attention. Pope's pointed couplets and poised rhythms confront the reader with critical choices that force him to re-examine his own position with regard to the world he lives in. As Dr Johnson says in his *Life of Pope*, 'he did not court the candour, but dared the judgement of his reader'.

Acknowledgements

This book owes much to the enthusiasm for Pope's poetry conveyed to me over the years by my several teachers. I recall with great pleasure the teaching of Douglas Brown, to whose memory this book is dedicated, and the rich appreciation for literature that he imparted to all his pupils. I am greatly indebted to Ralph Cohen and Maximillian Novak, who gave generously of their time and encouragement while supervising my dissertation at the University of California, and to F.E.L. Priestley with whom I had the privilege of collaborating as a teacher at the University of Western Ontario. I should like to make particular mention of the work of Maynard Mack, whose writings on Pope are invaluable to every student of the eighteenth century, and who has answered all my enquiries with the greatest courtesy.

My thanks are especially due to Maurice Hussey, the general editor of this series, whose indefatigable patience and good nature have been sorely tried, and to David Baxter with whom I have spent many stimulating hours exchanging ideas about the eighteenth century. I should also like to thank Elizabeth Maskell who typed my manuscript, and Whit and Lynn Hieatt who read the typescript and made valuable suggestions for its improvement. Finally I owe the largest debt of gratitude to the encouragement and help of my wife, Felicia, who has read this book throughout its various stages and been my most severe, as well as my most generous, critic.

The author and publisher are grateful to the following for permission to reproduce photographs:

D. Baxter, pages 22 and 148; British Museum, pages 50 and 67; Mrs. Brown-Swinburne, page 14; Derek Clifford, page 70; Earl of Harrowby, page 15; Huntingdon Library, California, page 129; O.G. Jarman, page 178; London Borough of Richmond Upon Thames, pages 4 and 59; Mansell Collection, pages 106 and 164; National Gallery of Scotland, page 11 *top*; National Portrait Gallery, pages 10,120,173 and *frontispiece*; Penguin Books Ltd., page 62 *top*; Radio Times Hulton Picture Library, page 44; Trinity College, Dublin, page 11 *bottom*; University Library, Cambridge, pages 62 *bottom*, 65, 68, 71 and 79.

The painting of The Thames near Marble Hill, Twickenham by Richard Wilson reproduced on the cover is by courtesy of the Tate Gallery.

Part One
The Poet in his Setting

1 Alexander Pope, the Man and his Life

Lord Bolingbroke's usual health after dinner is 'Amicitiae et Libertati'. I should like to have it for a motto to my door, with an 's' added after it.*

Pope to Spence, April 1742

I believe, if any one, early in his life should contemplate the dangerous fate of authors, he would scarce be of their number on any consideration. The life of a Wit is a warfare upon earth; and the present spirit of the learned world is such, that to attempt to serve it (any way) one must have the constancy of a martyr, and a resolution to suffer for its sake.

When Pope wrote these words in the Preface to the first edition of his collected *Works* in 1717 he was not overdramatizing the vulnerability of the poet's position, nor was he exaggerating the degree of forbearance necessary to serve the learned world. 'The life of a Wit', in post-Restoration England, truly was 'a warfare upon earth'. Dryden had received similar, if not as savage, treatment a generation earlier, and both Swift and Gay had to come to terms with it during Pope's own time. Each of these writers found themselves attacked for reasons that only too often had little or nothing to do with their published work. The Augustan man of letters' private life became a public concern, much as a politician's does in our own day. Any scandal that could be dredged up, whether fictional or factual hardly mattered, was useful ammunition in the continual warfare that attended the Augustan literary scene. As a result factual accounts of early eighteenth-century writers' lives were frequently deliberately distorted or confused. Swift, we are told, was mad, whereas Pope was seen as having a warped mind in a warped body. Such impressions, however partisan they may originally have been, tend, like mud, to stick, and we can find Pope described as recently as 1925 and by Lytton Strachey as a 'fiendish monkey'.

Furthermore the beginning of the eighteenth century was a period in which political parties were establishing themselves in England, and literature found itself closely connected with such a development. Writers were in heavy demand as purveyors of propaganda and, even if an author managed to avoid becoming a paid party hack, the author's duty to the public was so strongly felt that he was more or less forced to commit himself to either a Whig or Tory position. Either way he was bound to make enemies

*The 's' after it would make the meaning 'Sacred to Friendship and Liberty'.

as well as friends, and although Pope strove hard for a number of years to maintain Party independence his essential Tory sympathies were bound to create enemies for him. Such persons leapt at the slightest chance to vilify him (see chapter 2), and though his conduct was by no means spotless (he was certainly capable of giving at least as good, and generally better, than he got) it was far more attractive and praiseworthy than common literary lore has held it to be. It seems to be worthwhile, therefore, beginning this introduction to his work with an accurate account of the major events of his life.

Early life and education, 1688-1708

Alexander Pope was born, of Catholic parents, in Lombard Street in the City of London on 21 May 1688. He was the only child of his parents' marriage and was born when his mother was already forty-six and his father forty-two. His lifelong devotion to his elderly parents, whom he cared for till the time of their respective deaths, is one of the most moving and significant aspects of his life. Nowhere is this admiration and love more poignantly expressed than in the final forty lines of *An Epistle to Dr Arbuthnot*, composed just before his mother's death in 1733, where he celebrates his parents' virtue, gentleness and independence.

The Pope family lived in Lombard Street until Alexander was five years old. By all accounts he was a very healthy and happy child of a particularly sweet temper who showed no signs of the illness that later disfigured him. Spence tells us that a portrait of him painted when he was about ten years old shows his face as 'round, plump, pretty, and of a fresh complexion. I have often heard Mrs Pope say that he was then exactly like that picture . . . and that it was the perpetual application he fell into about two years afterwards that changed his form and ruined his constitution.'

His father had been a successful linen merchant for almost twenty years prior to his son's birth, but had been forced to retire early in life owing to the anti-Catholic laws passed after the arrival of William III. In the same year as Alexander was born an Act of Parliament came into being which prohibited Catholics from living within ten miles of the City of London. This Act, which received renewed prominence from royal proclamations issued in 1696, 1715, and 1744, became a major factor in determining the course of Pope's life. We do not know for certain where the Pope family lived from the time they left Lombard Street in 1693 to the time they moved to Binfield in Berkshire about 1700. There is some indication they lived at Hammersmith, which although not far enough out of the city of London legally to satisfy the anti-Catholic laws, would probably have been far enough out to indicate the right intention.

Engraved by W. Evans

MRS POPE,

Daughter of Samuel Cooper, Painter;
and Mother of Alexander Pope.

Editha Pope, the poet's mother

4

Pope received his first education when he was about eight years old from a priest named John Banister who instructed him in Latin and Greek. He then went to Twyford School, near Winchester, which was the best school available for Catholic boys at the end of the seventeenth century. He only stayed there for one year, however, being expelled at the end of that time for writing a satire on one of the masters – an omen, perhaps, of things to come. When Pope was twelve his father complied with the anti-Catholic legislation and moved his family from London. He purchased Whitefield House, together with seventeen acres of land in Windsor Forest, at Binfield in Berkshire.

The move to Binfield brought Pope's formal education to a close and henceforth he largely educated himself. In June 1739 he told Spence that:

When I had done with my priests I took to reading by myself, for which I had a very great eagerness and enthusiasm, especially for poetry. In a few years I had dipped into a great number of the English, French, Italian, Latin and Greek poets. This I did without any design but that of pleasing myself, and got the languages by hunting after the stories in the several poets I read, rather than read the books to get the languages. I followed everywhere as my fancy led me, and was like a boy gathering flowers in the woods and fields just as they fall in his way. I still look upon these five or six years as the happiest part of my life.

They may have seemed in retrospect the happiest years of his life but they were also the years that saw the beginning of what he referred to, in *An Epistle to Dr Arbuthnot*, as 'this long Disease, my Life'. Until the move to Binfield Pope was a perfectly healthy child, but about the age of twelve he contracted a tubercular disease of the bone which became known later as Pott's disease (after Dr Percival Pott, 1714–88, whose observation and treatment of it were famous in the eighteenth century). This disease, which was contracted through milk and was widespread in the days before pasteurization, gradually reduced Pope to a humpbacked condition and dwarfed his growth, so that at his most fully grown he never attained a height greater than four foot six. It finally left him a permanent cripple in need, as Dr Johnson tells us, of wearing stays in order to be able to stand.

Marjorie Nicolson and G.S. Rousseau, who have made by far the most detailed study of Pope's illness, point out in *This Long Disease, My Life* that as a result of this weakness 'he felt the cold severely, and wore three pairs of hose and heavy under garments, sometimes of fur'. Pope remained a chronic invalid and eventually

5

required constant attention from maid-servants in dressing and undressing. The fragility of his 'little, tender, and crazy carcase', as William Wycherley affectionately referred to it, brought other weaknesses with it. Pope suffered continually from severe headaches, coughing, and fevers, and, towards the close of his life, from a whole series of compound illnesses.

But it would be a mistake to end this discussion of Pope's health with the impression that his illness affected his life in a totally negative way. It is true that he could never escape it, and true that occasionally it reduced him to a state of intense gloom, but one of the most striking things that any reader of Pope's *Correspondence* must feel is the power of his struggle to overcome these difficulties and his determination to travel as much as he could and lead as full a life as possible within the limitations forced on him by his body.

About 1704, when Pope was sixteen and already suffering from the tubercular affliction just described, his perpetual application to his studies began to reduce him to so bad a state of health that he believed he was going to die. He sat down and wrote last farewells to his friends, including the Abbé Southcote. The Abbé immediately went to Dr John Radcliffe, the most eminent physician of his time, told him about Pope's illness, and then rode down to Binfield with Radcliffe's directions. The chief part of Radcliffe's advice was that Pope should take more exercise and should ride every day. This advice not only restored him but seems to have been the origin of the horseback rambles through Windsor Forest which he took with his father's neighbour, Sir William Trumbull.

Sir William was a retired diplomat with a great interest in literature, and was over sixty years old when Pope first knew him. Pope was only sixteen or seventeen at the time, but the two men, despite these disparities in age, felt immediate respect for one another. They rode through the Forest together, while the older man listened with great patience to the early efforts of the young poet. As Pope says in the opening lines of his *Pastorals*, written in 1704:

> First in these Fields I try the Sylvan Strains
> Nor blush to sport on *Windsor's* blissful Plains.

The *Pastorals* were Pope's first published poems, but he had been experimenting in poetry long before their publication in 1709. There is perhaps some slight exaggeration in the claim which he later made in *An Epistle to Dr Arbuthnot* that,

> As yet a Child, nor yet a Fool to Fame,
> I lisp'd in Numbers, for the Numbers came.

but only the most literal minded would object. It is quite clear that he began being interested in poetry at a very early age: he told Spence in March 1743 that 'I began writing verses of my own invention farther back than I can remember'. His mother gave Spence similar testimony:

> Mr. Pope's father . . . was no poet, but he used to set him to make English verses when very young. He was pretty difficult in being pleased and used often to send him back to new turn them. 'These are not good rhymes' he would say, for that was my husband's word for verses.

Pope's precocity in poetry is perhaps best illustrated by his attempt to write an epic poem when he was only twelve. The subject was Alcander, Prince of Rhodes, and he later told Spence that he wrote four books towards it, of about one thousand verses each.

During these years of growing up at Binfield, the young poet was not only extending his reading and trying out his poetry, he was also developing his literary acquaintance. At a remarkably early age he got to know the literary wits at Will's Coffee House, who had formed Dryden's circle. There is even a record of Pope being taken, when he was only twelve years old, to see Dryden. The particular members of the Will's group that Pope got to know apart from Trumbull, who has already been mentioned, were the critic William Walsh; the poet Samuel Garth; the dramatists William Wycherley and William Congreve; and the actor Thomas Betterton. These were all older and distinguished literary men by the time Pope knew them and it was obviously not mere coincidence that they should all share an enthusiasm for the young man's ability and company. There is certainly something a little self-conscious in the correspondence Pope wrote to these worldly men of letters, but that is hardly surprising in a young man anxious to make a good impression.

With Wycherley and Walsh Pope struck up particularly close friendships. He helped the old playwright prepare his verse for publication and maintained a long correspondence with him. He visited Walsh at his seat at Abberley in Worcestershire in 1707 and it was from him that he received the famous advice to make correctness his study and aim:

> When about fifteen, I got acquainted with Mr Walsh. He encouraged me much, and used to tell me that there was one way left of excelling, for though we had had several great poets, we never had any one great poet that was correct — and he desired me to make that my study and aim.

The notion of correctness as a literary virtue is improperly understood today. It is by no means the same thing as correction. The first involves the principle of proper literary decorum (see chapter 4), while the second involves the more mechanical matter of revision. Both Pope and Walsh were only too well aware of the dangers of too much of the latter, and I shall end this first section of Pope's life by quoting from a letter he wrote to Walsh on 2 July 1706 saying just this:

> I am convinc'd as well as you, that one may correct too much; for in Poetry as in Painting, a Man may lay colours one upon another, till they Stiffen and deaden the Piece. Besides to bestow heightening on every part is monstrous; Some parts ought to be lower than the rest; and nothing looks more ridiculous, than a Work, where the Thoughts, however different in their own nature, seem all on a level: 'Tis like a Meadow newly mown, where Weeds, Grass, and Flowers are all laid even, and appear undistinguish'd. I believe too that sometimes our first Thoughts are the best as the first squeezing of the Grapes makes the finest and richest Wine.

The experimenting poet, 1709-1717

The eight years from the time of Pope's first published work, the *Pastorals* (May 1709), to the time of the first edition of his collected *Works* (June 1717), form a fairly cohesive unit in his life. This was a period of extraordinary poetic activity which he later described as wandering in 'Fancy's Maze' (*Epistle to Dr Arbuthnot*, l. 340). In these eight years he tried his hand at half a dozen different 'kinds' of poetry (see chapter 4), ranging from pastoral and georgic (*Windsor-Forest*), to didactic (*Essay on Criticism*), to elegiac (*The Elegy to the Memory of an Unfortunate Lady*), to heroic (*Eloisa to Abelard*), to mock epic (*The Rape of the Lock*), to actual epic (the translation of the *Iliad*). To say he tried his hand is perhaps to suggest an unfinished or trial state totally inappropriate to these highly finished and successful poems. The phrase is used here to indicate the sense in which Pope was feeling for his strength during these years and trying out different possibilities. The wide range of his success is a mark of his versatility.

These years were also a time of great expansion in his personal and social life. They mark a period during which Pope spent more time in London than at any other stage in his life, at the same time as he continued to visit his Catholic acquaintances around Binfield. They include the making of the lasting and major friendships with Gay, Swift, Arbuthnot, Bolingbroke and Oxford among his literary and political friends, and with the Carylls, Englefields and Blounts among his Catholic friends. They also include his first meeting with Martha Blount for whom he developed a love which, despite all the barriers it encountered, endured till his death.

The family's move from Binfield to Chiswick in 1716 and the sudden death of his father on 23 October 1717 brought this period, which was so much freer of sober responsibility than most of his life, to a close. There is a strong element of carefree gaiety about the poetry written during these years that is in marked contrast to the more overtly moral mood of his later work:

> Soft were my Numbers, Who could take offence
> While pure Description held the 'place of Sense?
> Like gentle *Fanny's* was my flow'ry Theme,
> A painted Mistress, or a purling Stream.
>
> (*Epistle to Dr Arbuthnot*, 147–50)

Such an element is undoubtedly linked to the relative freedom he enjoyed at the time, though with the death of his father he became solely responsible for his seventy-five year-old mother.

The period begins with the publication of the *Pastorals*. While these were greatly admired by Pope's Tory friends at Will's, they immediately brought him into conflict with London's rival literary group, Addison's 'little Senate' of Whig writers who met at Buttons' coffee-house. Pope's poems were published in a volume of Tonson's *Miscellanies* that also included the *Pastorals* of Addison's friend Ambrose ('Namby Pamby') Philips. Philips was a third-rate poet and his *Pastorals* were clearly inferior to the young Pope's, but Addison's friends Welsted, Tickell and Gildon all highly praised Philips' *Pastorals* in the current periodicals at various times during the next few years, whilst totally ignoring Pope's. Pope was not so much angry as annoyed and when, in 1713, the *Guardian* ran a series of articles on pastoral poetry in general and set Philips along-side Theocritus, Virgil and Spenser, he took the opportunity to expose such critical claptrap for what it was. He anonymously wrote an ironic essay (*Guardian*, no. 40) to conclude the series in which he continued the pattern of praising Philips but, this time, for patently absurd reasons. Philips was furious and threatened to beat Pope with a rod if he ever came near Buttons'. Pope had not only demonstrated an early knack with irony, but had shown that he was quite capable of looking after himself in the eighteenth-century literary jungle. Since Pope's friend Gay further ridiculed Philips's *Pastorals* in his mock-pastoral poem, *The Shepherd's Week*, published a year later in April 1714, scores had been more than evened.

The conflict with Philips and the Buttons' group is told in some detail here in order to give an idea of the sort of jostling for literary standing that was part and parcel of the literary scene in the early part of the eighteenth century. Nearly every publication of Pope's was attended with this sort of critical and personal dispute and the fracas surrounding the publication of the *Pastorals* was mere skirmishing compared with the warfare that surrounded so many of his publications.

Pope's second major publication was *An Essay on Criticism*, first

Bolingbroke, 'My guide, philosopher, and friend.' Essay on Man *IV, 390*

published in 1711 though mostly written at least two years earlier. It was an ambitious undertaking for a young man for in it Pope hoped to compress and refine the wisdom of all past ages concerning criticism and poetry. Such a conception is quintessentially neoclassical, and the poem is consequently a fundamental starting point for anyone wanting to understand eighteenth-century assumptions about literature (see chapter 4). Its reception was quiet at first but then, quite suddenly, a storm broke loose as the critic John Dennis savagely attacked Pope in his *Reflections upon an Essay upon Criticism.* Dennis's attack is full of the most vitriolic and personal abuse imaginable (see chapter 2 for a more extended treatment), and Pope was sensible enough to ignore it for the time being. He retired to friends in the country and particularly to the solace of his new

Arbuthnot, 'Friend to my Life.'
Epistle to Dr Arbuthnot, 27

Swift, 'Dean, Drapier, Bickerstaff,
or Gulliver.' Dunciad *I, 20*

Catholic friend, John Caryll, who lived at Ladyholt, near West Harting in Sussex.

It was during this period that Caryll suggested the subject matter for that most delightful of all Pope's poems, *The Rape of the Lock*. The poem was written, as Pope later told Spence, to 'make a jest' of the estrangement between two Catholic families, the Fermors and the Petres, and 'to laugh them together again'. The incident that Pope was making fun of was the cutting off of a lock of Arabella Fermor's hair by Caryll's cousin the young Lord Petre. He brilliantly ridiculed this episode by giving the events a mock-solemn epic inflation clearly out of all proportion to their trivial significance. The poem was published in its first form, that is without the addition of the Sylphs, in Lintot's collection of *Miscellaneous Poems* of May 1712.

In the following year Pope moved back to London, where he found himself drawn more and more strongly into the circle of writers supporting the Tory Government. His poem, *Windsor-Forest*, published in March 1713 to celebrate the Treaty of Utrecht, was taken by many as a statement of his party commitment despite his own attempts to maintain neutrality,

> In Moderation placing all my Glory,
> While Tories call me Whig, and Whigs a Tory.

as he later put it in his *Imitations of Horace, Satire II, i*, 67–8. For most of the year, however, he lived with the Whig painter Jervas, who had been a pupil of the famous portrait painter Sir Godfrey Kneller. During this year Pope studied painting more closely than at any other time in his life (see chapter 3).

The following spring Pope became involved with the Scriblerus Club. This was a group of six persons—Swift, Parnell, Pope, Gay, Arbuthnot and Robert Harley, Lord Oxford—who met over dinner once a week to talk about literature. They had in common a philosophic belief in conserving the best from the past coupled with a scorn for false taste in learning. The past must be preserved not as a dead but as a living thing. Accordingly they planned to produce the *Memoirs of Martinus Scriblerus* which would burlesque the over-pedantic works of scholars and antiquaries such as Dr Woodward, a well-known contemporary geologist and physician. Various members of the Club wrote different chapters, but the whole thing was brought to an abrupt halt with the dissolution of the Club that resulted from the death of Queen Anne on 1 August 1714. With the Whigs' return to power Arbuthnot was replaced as court physician, Swift left for his voluntary exile in Ireland, and Oxford was put in the Tower. Pope, by retiring to the country, survived the change of Government with nothing worse than the separation of his friends. The *Memoirs* were not published till 1741. The Club is even more important, however, for the many other literary projects which were first discussed at these meetings but which only came to fruition much later.

In the summer of 1713 Pope had found, two years after the event, the opportunity to get even with Dennis in a way that his Scriblerian friends would doubtless have approved. Under the guise of defending Addison, whose play *Cato* Dennis had just attacked, Pope published *The Narrative of Dr Robert Norris*. He invented a fictive episode in Dennis's life in which a Dr Norris was called to cure him of his lunacy. The piece is full of farcical high jinks that completely destroy Dennis, but never in the malignantly vindictive way in which he had attacked Pope.

In October 1713 Pope published his proposals to translate the *Iliad*, and, after the fall of the Tory Ministry in the following summer, he turned his attention almost entirely to Homer. This was to be the major literary occupation of his next six years. It was difficult and tedious work, but it shaped his genius and ensured his financial independence. At first he had grave doubts about his ability to complete such an undertaking. He told Spence, years later, that 'In the beginning of my translating the *Iliad* I wished anybody would hang me, a hundred times. It sat so heavily on my mind at first that I often used to dream of it, and so do sometimes still'. Spence tells us further that 'he used to dream that he was engaged in a long journey, puzzled which way to take, and full of fears that he should never get to the end of it'. But by June 1715 the first four books, in one volume, were published, and from this time forward he proceeded with his task at the rate of four books a year until the poem was completed in May 1720.

One of the most important aspects of Pope's life during the years we are dealing with here was his increasing acquaintance, from November 1711, with the Blount sisters. A month after meeting them he wrote to his friend Cromwell praising 'two of the finest faces in the Universe'. Theresa Blount was the same age as Pope and Martha was two years younger. At first his heart seems to have warmed most to Theresa, but later his affection for Martha grew far closer and stronger. Nothing seems to have given him greater joy in these years than to relax with the two sisters walking around the lovely gardens of their country seat at Mapledurham. In times of trouble or pain it was frequently to the Blount sisters that he turned for comfort. Thus when, in the night of 23 October 1717 his father suddenly died, it was to Martha Blount that he wrote next day: 'My poor Father dyed last night. Believe, since I don't forget you this moment, I never shall'.

The significance of his father's death as an event in Pope's life cannot be too strongly stressed. Five days later he wrote to Caryll saying:

13

Martha and Teresa Blount, 'Two of the finest faces in the universe.'

> You have humanity enough to believe I can be in no disposition
> to write to anybody, or have one thought that can be entertaining,
> when I acquaint you that I lost my father five days ago. My
> poor mother is so afflicted that it would be barbarity to leave
> this winter, which is the only and true reason that I am not now
> at Ladyholt.

For the next sixteen years the conduct of his life was to be largely
shaped by the need to look after his aged and beloved mother who
could not be left alone for long periods of time.

Translator and editor, 1718-1725

Various changes in Pope's life ensued on his father's death. The
elder Pope had left Binfield in 1716, probably to avoid the increased
land taxes which were being levied on Catholics, and had moved
to Chiswick. But now Pope was himself the head of the family and,

Lady Mary Wortley Montagu,
  'The Equal Lustre of the Heavenly mind
  Where every grace with every Virtue's join'd.'

whether it was to get away from the place of his father's death, or because the size of the house was no longer suitable, or for some other reason, he moved in March 1719 with his mother into a small villa which he leased on the bank of the Thames at Twickenham. Except for occasional expeditions into the surrounding countryside, the last twenty-five years of his life were spent at Twitnam, as he affectionately called it. The improvements that he wrought on his house, garden and grotto here became his chief relaxation in life as well as an integral part of his art (see chapter 3). He set out to establish his small estate at Twickenham as a symbol of those cultural and civilized values—literacy, honesty, generosity and hospitality—which he so profoundly believed in and which seemed to be crumbling all about him in Hanoverian England.

His life now took on a much quieter aspect. At first he was fully engrossed in finishing his translation of the *Iliad*. However, when in 1720 that was completed he did not go back, as we might have expected, to writing poetry, but turned instead to editing. He wrote to Caryll in October 1722 saying: 'I must again sincerely protest to you that I have wholly given over scribbling, at least anything of my own, but am become by due gradation of dulness, from a poet a translator, and from a translator a mere editor'. We might feel that anyone who has the attitude to his work that the words 'dulness' and 'mere' here indicate is unlikely to be very successful at it, and we would not be far from wrong. Pope was not a particularly good editor.

His main editorial project was an edition of Shakespeare that would supersede Rowe's, but he also worked on a posthumous edition of his friend Parnell's *Poems* (which was published in 1721), and of the Duke of Buckingham's *Works* (which was published on 24 January 1723 but was seized by the Government three days later on suspicion of Jacobite tendencies in some passages). The Shakespeare edition, in six volumes, finally appeared in March 1725, and though the preface was lively and perceptive the text itself was hastily collated and emended. A year later the leading Shakespeare scholar of the day, Lewis Theobald, published his *Shakespeare Restored, or, a Specimen of the Many Errors Committed . . . by Mr Pope*. Theobald's book was an accurate, if pedantic, explication of Pope's mistakes and was to have consequences for the author more far-reaching than he can possibly have imagined.

The other major piece of work belonging to these years was the translation of the *Odyssey*. Pope was led into this by the extraordinary success of his translation of the *Iliad*. But his heart was no longer in translation and it was undertaken largely as a business venture. He therefore engaged two collaborators, Broome and Fenton, to help him. The idea was that Broome and Fenton would do much of the translation and Pope would revise and polish it. However, the collaboration got him into all sorts of problems about how much should be admitted (the public would be far more likely to pay to read a translation by Mr Pope than to read one by Messrs Pope, Broome and Fenton), and about how much remuneration the collaborators should receive. In the end Broome translated eight books, Fenton four and Pope the remaining twelve. But Pope made over £5,000 on the venture while Broome and Fenton got under £1,000 between them. Unjust as this may seem they could not have made anywhere near that amount without the benefit of Pope's name and his tireless effort to raise a list of subscribers.

Pope's financial independence as an author was now completely assured. Henceforth he would be able to write whatever he wanted to, and not just whatever would sell best. By dint of his own hard work he had made himself the first English author to be able to live off his writings independently of a patron. He was fiercely proud of such independence and clung to it so tenaciously that he twice turned down offers of official government pensions. His description of himself as 'Un-plac'd, un-pensioned, no Man's Heir, or Slave', in his *Imitation of Horace, Satire II, i*, written in 1733, best sums up this justifiable pride. Four years later still he put the same thought slightly differently in his *Imitation of Horace, Epistle II, ii* (68–9):

> But (thanks to *Homer*) since I live and thrive,
> Indebted to no Prince or Peer alive.

The Scriblerian fruition, 1726-1733

Although no particular event occurred in 1726 to cause a sudden change in Pope's life, the completion of his projects as a translator and editor did bring a distinct change of direction in his literary career. The years of experimentation and of journeywork were now over. The poet was free to come fully into his own. Satire, a mode in which he had as yet given only a few glimpses of his genius (*Guardian* no. 40, *The Rape of the Lock*, *The Narrative of Dr Norris*), was to become for the rest of his life the vehicle for its fulfilment.

In 1725 Bolingbroke returned from exile in France and settled near Pope. Together with Swift's two visits to England in 1726 and 1727 (the first for twelve years, and the last of his life) this brought about a kind of Scriblerian revival. Bolingbroke had never been a full member of the Scriblerus Club, but as a leading member of Oxford's Ministry, and as a particular friend of Pope's, he had been closely connected with it. There were reunions at Pope's villa with Gay and Arbuthnot (Parnell had died in 1718, and Oxford in 1724), and there was a revival of spirit in the Tory Opposition with the beginning, in 1726, of Bolingbroke's new anti-Walpole journal, *The Craftsman*. During the next few years the true harvest of the seeds sown at the meetings of the Scriblerus Club in 1714 was reaped. *Gulliver's Travels* was published in October 1726, *The Beggar's Opera* was first produced in January 1728, and the first *Dunciad* came out in May of the same year. In addition, there were other offshoots of the Scriblerus Club published in the four volumes of the Pope–Swift *Miscellanies*, 1727–32, including *Peri Bathous* or *The Art of Sinking in Poetry*. It was, by any standards, a vintage harvest.

The Dunciad has always been a controversial poem. It was of course written as such: Pope meant to annihilate his enemies. Many readers feel, however, that in attacking those persons who had attacked him, Pope sinks to their level. There is undeniably a strong element of personal revenge about *The Dunciad*, but it is important to recognize that the poem grew out of the most profound and deeprooted of all Pope's feelings about literature. At its base is the firmly held belief that bad literature, indeed bad art generally, is immoral, and if allowed to spread unchecked will corrupt and eventually destroy civilization. The artist's duty therefore is a moral duty. He defends the validity of the written word at a time when it is being defiled by those all about him, and in doing so he preserves the living bond between idea and language.

The first *Dunciad* consisted of three books that centred on the crowning of King Tibbald (Lewis Theobald) as King of the Dunces, and came to a climax with a vision of the future in which the Goddess of Dulness held full dominion. In 1728 this is still a vision, or portent of what is to come, but by the time of the revised *Dunciad*, in four books, of 1743, the vision has become actuality. The poem is not easy to read. It is full of dense imagery, classical allusions, names of living persons and topical references. Partly to explain these, although largely to continue the fun, Pope came out in 1729 with a Variorum edition. 'The Dunciad is going to be printed in all pomp . . . ', Pope wrote to Swift in June 1729; 'It will be attended with Proeme, Prolegomena, Testimonia, Scriptorum, Index Authorum, and Notes Variorum'. He doesn't even mention the seven appendices. All this prefatory and reference matter is a continuation of the satire on pedantry, and if much of it is lost upon us today that is because, on the whole, most of our books are less cluttered with such padding.

All this time Pope's health had been deteriorating. In 1728 his ailments had become so bad that in August he agreed to go to Bath to see if the waters would help him. He stayed there for ten weeks but there was no appreciable improvement. 'I do not think I shall ever enjoy any health four days together, for the remaining Sand I have to run', he wrote to Bathurst on 7 November 1728; 'The Bath was tryed after all other remedies, as a last remedy, and that has proved totally ineffectual'. The five years 1728–33 were the most painful Pope had yet had to suffer, partly because of his own weakness and partly because of his mother's failing condition. He lived daily in fear of 'that accident which I dread the most, my Mother's death'. He was afraid to leave Twickenham for more than three days at a time, and when, in the spring of 1731 he was so ill that he had to go on a diet of asses' milk, a highly esteemed cure in the eighteenth century, he travelled all the way back from Bolingbroke's home at Dawley Farm to Twickenham to visit her on several occasions.

Meanwhile he was working on *An Essay on Man*. He wrote to Swift in June 1730: 'Yet am I just now writing, (or rather planning) a book, to make mankind look upon this life with comfort and pleasure, and put morality in good humour'. But the first poem actually to be published after the *Dunciad Variorum* was the *Epistle to Burlington* in December 1731. The publication of this poem, on false taste in gardening and architecture, was attended with enough noise and recrimination to indicate to Pope that the *Dunciad*, far from destroying his enemies, had merely multiplied them. Timon was immediately identified by Grub Street as Lord Chandos, and Pope was accused of the basest ingratitude to an old friend. It was in vain that Pope protested that no particular person was intended in the portrait. Henceforth the plague of scribblers, ('They pierce my Thickets, thro' my Grot they glide'), was to accompany his every publication, and his own efforts to avoid them became correspondingly more devious.

It was for this reason that when the first three epistles of *An Essay on Man* finally appeared in February–May 1733 they did so anonymously. Pope carefully published two other poems at the same time, the *Epistle to Bathurst* in January, and the *Imitation of Horace, Satire II, i: To Fortescue* in February, in order to throw off suspicion of his authorship of *An Essay on Man*. His ruse was totally successful and the poem was so highly acclaimed that when he did finally admit authorship on the publication of the fourth epistle in January 1734 it was difficult for the critics to recant. They then turned to other means of attack and, taking up the cue from the Swiss theologian Jean-Pierre de Crousaz, accused him of Christian heterodoxy, Deism and even Spinozism instead. But this and the defence of his new ally William Warburton belong to the last period of his life, the years that come after the deaths, within six months of each other, of his close friend John Gay and of his dearly beloved mother.

As Pope grew older — he had turned forty in 1728 — so his life took on a mellower and more assured quality. He had no need to impress anyone now. Instead he could make friends according to his own clear beliefs. Over and over again what strikes the reader of Pope's correspondence is the importance of the role that friendship played in his life. Once he had established the bond of friendship he nursed it with almost as much care and affection as he bestowed on his ailing mother. His closest friends — Caryll, Gay, Swift, Arbuthnot, Bolingbroke, Fortescue, Bethel, and later Warburton, Allen, Spence and Marchmont — were clearly the most valuable thing in his life, and when one was ill, or when one died, his grief was immense. 'Good God!' he wrote to Swift on 5 December 1732 the morning after Gay's death, 'how often are we to die before we go quite off this stage? In every friend we lose a part of ourselves, and the best part. God keep those we have left!' The following day he wrote to Martha Blount in just as disturbed terms:

> The world after all is a little pitiful thing, not performing any one promise it makes us, for the future, and every day taking away and annulling the joys of the past. Let us comfort one another, and if possible, study to add as much more friendship to each other, as death has depriv'd us of in him.

Over four months later he was still depressed at the remembrance of Gay's death. He wrote to Swift on 20 April 1733:

> You say truly, that death is only terrible to us as it separates us from those we love, but I really think those have the worst of it who are left by us if we are true friends. I have felt more (I fancy) in the loss of poor Mr Gay, than I shall suffer in the thought of going away myself into a state that can feel none of this sort of losses.

Six weeks after writing this letter his mother died at the age of ninety-one. Her death marked another milestone in the poet's life. For his remaining eleven years he was free, in so far as his health would permit, to leave Twickenham for extended periods of time. A fortnight after he wrote to Caryll saying just this:

> To see you at Ladyholt was the first thought that I had upon this event, but as it is a great and new Æra of my life, and upon which the whole course of it will in a manner change, I must pause awhile to look about me.

The English Horace, 1733-1744

The most obvious change was the great amount of travelling Pope now undertook. He never went to the Continent, as so many eighteenth-century gentlemen did, but he travelled the breadth of southern England in more detail than most of his contemporaries. Nearly every summer and autumn during the last decade of his life was spent in rambling around his friends' country estates. We can reconstruct a typical ramble from his correspondence.

In the summer of 1733, for instance, he set out from Twickenham to visit Lord Cobham in his magnificent house and gardens at Stowe, near Buckingham. From Stowe he went to John Morley's house at Halstead in Essex, and from Essex back across England to Lord Bathurst's estate at Cirencester. He then went down to visit Caryll at Ladyholt in Sussex for three weeks; from there he went to Lord Peterborough at Bevis Mount in Southampton for another three weeks. From Southampton he went to Lord Oxford's house in London for a few days before finally returning to Twickenham. We might add that such invitations, and the letters show how pressing they were, bear remarkable testimony to the affection in which his friends held him.

But if Pope took a new delight in travelling during these last ten years he did not neglect his own house and garden at Twickenham. His grotto, the passage under the road that joined his house to his garden, became the special darling of his fancy and he lavished on it all the attention of his spare hours. There he could retire from the world and relax with his friends:

> Know, all the Distant Din that World can keep
> Rolls o'er my *Grotto*, and but sooths my Sleep.
> There, my Retreat the best Companions grace,
> Chiefs, out of War, and Statesmen, out of Place.
> *Imitation of Horace, Satire II, i*, 123–6.

The example of Horace in retirement at his Sabine Farm is never far in the background. Indeed Horace is the major influence in these years that saw the full flowering of Pope's genius. Reuben Brower has said that Pope's life and literary career 'became progressively an *Imitatio Horatii*', and while this is certainly true it is important to recognize the difference between an imitation and a copy. Pope adapted Horace in these last years, he did not ape him. The Horatian model of conversational ease and amiable urbanity formed a perfect counterpoint to Pope's militant indignation at the corruption which he saw resulting from Walpole's long rule. Every poem written after 1729, with the exception of the revised *Dunciad*, is in some way or another modelled on Horace. In his *Imitations of Horace* the model is explicitly admitted by being printed on the facing page, while in the *Moral Essays* and in *An Essay on Man*, which Pope described to Swift as 'a system of Ethics in the Horatian way', it is implicit in the manner and structure of the poems.

I do not intend to discuss all the poems written in this the richest poetic period of Pope's life, but the *Epistle to Dr Arbuthnot*, published in 1735, just one month before Arbuthnot's death, calls for special mention here because it says so much about his literary career. The poem, 'begun many years since, and drawn up by snatches, as the several occasions offer'd', is perhaps the finest of all his poems in the

An etching of Pope done by Jonathan Richardson for the title page of Pope's
Letters, *1737*

Horatian mould. In it Pope replies to those persons who had for so many years attacked his 'Person, Morals, and Family' (see the Advertisement), by writing a conversational epistle that is largely an *apologia pro sua satura*. What calls for special mention, however, is the discrepancy between the character of Alexander Pope, the living man who writes the poem, and the character of Alexander Pope, the figure he creates who speaks in the poem. Out of the bare bones of his own life Pope has created a 'persona', or dramatic speaker, who is deliberately idealized for the sake of the satiric structure in which vice must be confronted with virtue. The poem is a wonderfully controlled account of his literary development, but in reading it we need always to bear in mind that the whole thing is a carefully contrived piece of image building. It would be a mistake to take the figure of the virtuous poet that emerges from the poem as sole evidence for a biography, though Pope would, no doubt, be quite happy if we did.

The project that occupied most of Pope's time after his mother's death was the publication of his *Letters*. The printing of letters first written for private eyes became one of the most popular of literary productions in eighteenth-century England, and Pope's example had much to do with this. We have only to consider the famous letters of Lord Chesterfield, Horace Walpole, and Lady Mary Wortley Montagu, and the related vogue for epistolary novels and poems, to recognize the importance of the form. One very good reason for such popularity was that the eighteenth-century educated Englishman valued learning and urbanity more than almost anything else, and the letter was a form perfectly suited for wearing one's learning lightly. Pope wanted to have his letters published, but he did not want to seem to do so. Accordingly he felt he must create an excuse for publication. Through an elaborate series of manoeuvres, too complex to trace here, he tricked his old enemy, Edmund Curll, into publishing an edition in May 1735. This was the looked-for justification for publishing his own edition and the 'Authentic' edition of his *Letters* followed two years later in May 1737.

For the publication of his *Letters* Pope did very much what we have already seen him doing in the *Epistle to Dr Arbuthnot*: he carefully shaped his character for public display. Dr Johnson says that he 'may be said to write always with his reputation in his head'. He took the actual letters he had written to his various friends as the basis for his published edition, but he rewrote, rearranged and readdressed them where it suited his purposes. For example, there were too many letters to his friend John Caryll, who was not well known, and too few to Joseph Addison, who was the best known literary figure of the first quarter of the eighteenth century. So Pope simply took some of his letters to Caryll, and, reworking them where necessary, readdressed them to Addison. Critics have been severe on Pope for this, accusing him of hypocrisy and vanity. But it is important to remember that he was using the letter as a literary form, as a vehicle for a special kind of familiar communication, not as a definitive biographical record. He was interested in using the letter form to set up the image of a cultivated and public-spirited man, not, as a twentieth-century writer might use it, to explore his own soul.

At the very least Pope was successful in winning the approval of one famous reader. Ralph Allen, who has been praised as the most benevolent man of his age, and was the original for Squire Allworthy in *Tom Jones*, was so impressed with the character of the man that emerged from Pope's *Letters* that he became a close friend. Indeed Pope's friendship with Allen was perhaps the strongest of all his friendships during the last eight years of his life, and he spent a considerable part of these years staying with Allen at Prior Park, his country estate at Widcombe near Bath.

During the five years from 1733 to 1738 Pope wrote no fewer than fourteen imitations of Horace. These poems have received all too little attention since Pope's time. In them Pope shifts through an extraordinary variety of tones ranging from exasperation to composure, or from poker-faced irony to genial playfulness. At the same time as he was writing these *Imitations* he became deeply involved with the Patriot Opposition to the Whig Government of Robert Walpole. In his earlier years Pope had tried to avoid a rigid party commitment, but he made no attempt at neutrality now. His close friend Bolingbroke, who was in the forefront of the battle to get rid of the 'Great Man', as Walpole was ironically called, must have influenced him strongly. Pope's own effort for the Patriot cause came to a climax with the passionate protestation that imbues the two dialogue poems known together as *The Epilogue to the Satires*, published in May and June 1738. In these two poems Pope entered, in his own words, 'in the most plain and solemn manner he could, a sort of PROTEST against that insuperable corruption and depravity of manners, which he had been so unhappy as to live to see'. The poet's vision of his country had darkened dramatically since the euphoric days of *Windsor-Forest* but, as the last lines of Dialogue II make clear, though Truth stood trembling on the edge of Law, it still guarded the poet and sanctified the line. Universal darkness had not yet buried all.

The year 1739 was notable for the gaining of an unexpected, but not altogether desirable, ally. In 1737 Pope's *Essay on Man* had been attacked for its heterodoxy by Jean-Pierre de Crousaz, and now two years later William Warburton, an ambitious clergyman, published his *Vindication of the Essay on Man*, in which he defended Pope's Christianity. Warburton and Pope met for the first time in April 1740, and from this point on Warburton's influence on Pope steadily increased. He was a ponderous but aggressive man and he soon bullied himself into the role of Pope's literary executor, pushing the far more gentle and sensitive Joseph Spence into the background. In terms of literary pursuit Pope's last few years were largely spent, with one great exception, in working with Warburton on a final edition of his *Works*.

That great exception was his reworking of *The Dunciad*. In 1742 he published the fourth book of the poem under the title *The New Dunciad*. Most readers of Pope have felt that this is his finest sustained piece of poetry. With mounting gravity he builds up to the final apocalyptic vision in which all the accumulating fears of the last decade concerning culture and intellectual corruption are imaginatively realized as Dulness' dread Empire, 'Chaos is restor'd; And Universal Darkness buries all'. A new fourth book was sufficient reason for revising the first three books for a complete new edition. The major change was the substitution of Colley Cibber for Lewis Theobald as King of the Dunces. Cibber was an old enemy of Pope's and had just published *A Letter from Mr. Cibber to Mr. Pope* (July 1742), perhaps the cruellest attack on him ever made (see chapter 2). Besides, Theobald was a friend of Warburton's. *The Dunciad* in four books with Cibber as hero came out in October 1743. It was Pope's last published work.

During the last two years of his life Pope's illnesses became critical. As early as March 1743 we find him writing to his old friend Bethel, describing alarming symptoms of weakness:

> For I have these three months or more, been advancing to an Asthmatic Complaint, (from one Cold to another, as I believe, for I saw no further cause for it). It is now at such a height that I can scarce walk, or go up a pair of Stairs, or move much in my bed, without quite losing breath; and it is attended with a difficulty of urine, which makes me fear a Dropsy . . . and a pain in the breast is join'd to it.

As the year wore on his health deteriorated more and more until in the last five months of his life nearly every letter talks about his ailments. His sense of his own fragility is poignantly described in a note he sent to Bolingbroke and Marchmont in January 1744:

> Yes, I would like to see you as long as I can see you, and then shut my eyes upon the world, as a thing worth seeing no longer. If your charity would take up a small Bird that is half dead of the frost, and set it a-chirping for half an hour, I'll jump into your hands tomorrow, at any hour you send. Two horses would be enough to draw me (and so would two dogs if you had them) but even the fly upon the chariot wheel required some bigger animal than itself to set it a-going.

In his last illness he was watched over by many friends, but especially by those most devoted to him, Bolingbroke, Marchmont, Martha Blount and Spence. He died on 30 May 1744. The next morning his friend David Mallet wrote to the Earl of Orrery describing his death:

> On Monday last I took my Everlasting Farewell of him. He was enough himself to know me, to enquire after Mrs Mallet's Health, and anxiously to hasten his Servant in getting ready my Dinner, because I came late. The same social kindness, the same friendly concern for those he loved, even in the minutest instances, that had distinguished his heart through Life, were uppermost in his Thoughts to the last.

We cannot close this account of Pope's life on a finer note than by quoting Spence's record of Bolingbroke's emotional profession of love for his dying friend. 'I never knew in my life a man that had so tender a heart for his particular friends, or a more general friendship for mankind. I have known him these thirty years; and value myself more for that man's love than . . .' sinking his head and losing his voice in tears.

Epitaph

And so at the age of fifty-six Alexander Pope, the greatest poet of his day, and one of the greatest of any day, had died. The obloquy that had pursued him through life continued to pursue him in death. Until comparatively recent times — that is until Edith Sitwell's *Alexander Pope*, 1930, and George Sherburn's *Early Career of Alexander Pope*, 1934, — Pope has been harshly treated by biographers and critics alike. He has had his defenders, many of them distinguished and eloquent persons such as Samuel Johnson and Lord Byron, but his general lot has been to be cast in the role of the villain, a reputation which his physical infirmity did much to increase. I have tried to show that he did not deserve such a reputation. His behaviour was certainly not flawless, but neither was it vile, and when his character and life are impartially examined there is much to admire.

The best record of his mature physical appearance is that left by Sir Joshua Reynolds:

> He was about four feet six inches high, very humpbacked and deformed. He wore a black coat, and, according to the fashion of the time, had on a little sword. He had a large and very fine eye, and a long handsome nose; his mouth had those peculiar marks of crooked persons; and the muscles which ran across the cheek were so strongly marked that they seemed like little chords.

Dr Johnson says in his *Life of Pope* that 'His stature was so low that, to bring him to a level with common tables, it was necessary to raise his seat. But his face was not displeasing, and his eyes were animated and vivid'. It is noticeable that both Reynolds and Johnson focus on his eyes. A glance at the many portraits of Pope (see W. K. Wimsatt, *The Portraits of Alexander Pope*, 1965) confirms the lively intelligence of his look.

One of his most attractive qualities as a person was his loyalty to his friends. I have already described his unswerving devotion to his parents and the care he took in developing and keeping a wide circle of friends. Indeed he made something of a cult of friendship. 'I have all my life from the first years of my reasoning had a disposition to a friendship with some person or other . . . ' he wrote to Caryll in 1711. He said much the same thing to Gay in October 1730:

> Nature, temper, and habit from my youth made me have but one strong desire. All other ambitions, my person, education, constitution, religion etc. conspired to remove far from me. That desire was to fix and preserve a few lasting dependable friendships.

We can trace this worship of the ideal of friendship in his correspondence with Swift. 'Farewell my dearest friend! ever, and upon every account that can create friendship and esteem', he wrote on 7 February 1735. A month later he wrote saying: 'I am a man of desperate fortunes, that is a man whose friends are dead: for I never aimed at any other fortune than in friends'. Swift, knowing what his correspondent most wanted to hear wrote back to Pope in the same vein a year later saying: 'I cannot properly call you my best friend, because I have not another left who deserves the name, such a havoc have Time, Death, Exile, and Oblivion made'. Such examples of the emphasis Pope attached to the value of friendship could be multiplied many times from his letters to Caryll, Gay and Martha Blount. But if, as Johnson tells us, he was 'zealous and constant in the duties of friendship', it must also be recognized that he did not forget those who offended him. He did not easily forgive an insult and he often returned attacks on his enemies years after they were first made.

His least attractive quality was his almost instinctive equivocation and deviousness. We see it in his public declarations concerning the part Broome and Fenton played in helping him to translate the *Odyssey*, and we see it again in his manipulations concerning the publication of his *Letters*. 'In all his intercourse with mankind', says Johnson, 'he had great delight in artifice, and endeavoured to attain all his purposes by indirect and unsuspected methods. He hardly drank tea without a stratagem'. In extenuation it can be argued that such equivocation was a defence mechanism developed in the face of repeated slander and attack. If he equivocated over matters of authorship, that was no more than anyone else did in the eighteenth century, and he never equivocated over matters of principle.

As numerous accounts indicate, he was most generous with his money. He gave a tenth of his yearly income to charity, and Johnson reports that 'Lord Oxford's Servant declared that in a house where her business was to answer his call, she would not ask for wages'. He was the leading spirit amongst those who tried to help the destitute poet Richard Savage, donating half of the subscription himself. Martha Blount told Spence in 1749 that Mr Pope's not being richer may be easily accounted for:

> He never had any love for money, and though he was not extravagant in anything, he always delighted when he had any sum to spare to make use of it in giving, lending, building, and gardening — for those were the ways in which he disposed of all the overplus of his income.

As he grew older he placed increasing emphasis on the moral responsibility of the artist. 'It is not the worst I have written', he wrote to Caryll in January 1733 with regard to his *Epistle to Bathurst*, 'and abounds in moral example, for which reason it must be obnoxious in this age. God send it does any good! I really mean nothing else by writing at this time of my life'. He told Spence shortly before he died that: ' 'He has writ in the cause of virtue, and done something to mend people's morals' is the only commendation I long for'.

The strong moral seriousness that imbues his later poetry, even when it is most satirically playful, is directly linked to his awareness of the artist's role in eighteenth-century society. Pope wrote at a time when the artist still belonged in the centre of society. He prized his financial and political independence but he felt no need to isolate himself from the main stream of life. He could appeal to a commonly accepted set of inherited, and largely Christian, values that would act as a norm against which to measure the moral and social aberrations he attacked. Such moral touchstones are not available to the artist today, when a belief in absolute values has frequently given way to a philosophy of relativism.

Literature, both documentary and imaginative, was the main means of communication in the eighteenth century, and as such it received an attention it no longer commands. If Pope seems to us over–conscious of his public reputation this is largely because he was so aware of the artist's public role. As a member of a Catholic minority during a period of bare toleration he was only too aware of the danger of his position. Indeed what is remarkable is not that he was so anxious to appear to the best advantage, but that he dared to speak out as boldly as he did.

2 The Urban and Rural Setting

> Know, all the distant Din that World can keep
> Rolls o'er my *Grotto*, and but sooths my Sleep.
> There, my Retreat the best Companions grace,
> Chiefs, out of War, and Statesmen, out of Place.
> There *St. John* mingles with my friendly Bowl,
> The Feast of Reason and the Flow of Soul.
>
> *The First Satire of the Second Book of Horace*
> *Imitated*, 1733 (123-8)

Although Pope lived in the country for most of his life he was not what we would call a nature poet. He predominantly chose the society of man for his subject matter, and as a result London, in all its different aspects, played a central part in shaping the attitudes and beliefs towards society expressed in his poetry. Pope would have strongly disagreed with Dr Johnson that 'when a man is tired of London, he is tired of life; for there is in London all that life can afford'. Indeed Pope believed that life afforded very much more in the retirement of the country. His attitude towards London is succinctly expressed in the opening lines of his versification of the second satire of Dr John Donne:

> Yes; thank my stars! as early as I knew
> This Town, I had the sense to hate it too.

But Pope would at least have agreed with Dr Johnson in recognizing the importance of London as the centre of political, social and cultural life in eighteenth-century England. No author who saw himself as the spokesman for his age could think otherwise, even if he chose to live elsewhere.

One should beware, however, of talking about London as if it were a self-contained entity. As Sir John Fielding, the half-brother of the novelist, says in his *Brief Description of the cities of London and Westminster*, 1776: 'But the name of London we use with latitude, comprehending under that denomination all Westminster and the Suburbs, with the whole range of buildings on the South side of the river from Lambeth palace to the parish of Deptford.' London probably changed more during the seventeenth and early eighteenth centuries than during any other time in its long history. At the time of the accession of James I London was largely contained within its city walls, and yet by the death of Queen Anne, just over a hundred years later, London was composed of two separate cities, one borough, and numerous suburbs (see map of 1707 on pp. 30-31).

A New Map of the Cityes of LONDON, WEST

TOGETHER WITH THE SUBURBS A

1	Bedlam	**6**	Grub Street
2	Billingsgate	**7**	Hungerford
3	Bridewell	**8**	Lombard Street
4	Drury Lane	**9**	Ludgate
5	Fleet Ditch	**10**	Monument, The
		11	Newgate

Map of London and Westminster, 1707

12	St. James' Palace	18	Westminster Hall
13	St. James' Square	19	Westminster School
14	St. Paul's Cathedral	20	Whitehall Palace
15	Smithfield	21	White's **Chocolate House**
16	Strand, The	22	Will's Coffee House
17	Temple Bar		

The medieval walled City of London remained the business and financial centre of English life, as it does today (although the walls and gates have long since been removed), but the social centre had moved to the west end and to the fashionable City of Westminster. Between these two cities, and all around them, the great sprawl of suburban London was already springing up.

Nevertheless London was still small enough for an individual to be familiar with most of its various parts and to attach significance to them. This was certainly so with Pope. When he mentions the name of a parish, or a street, or a building, he nearly always does so because it has a particular set of associations for his audience. A few of these associations are inevitably lost to the modern reader, but the great majority can easily be retrieved with a little help. The reader who needs such help is referred to the gazetter of place names on p. 163. In this chapter I distinguish between three main areas of London and show how these different areas call forth different imaginative responses from Pope, and how they are used by him to establish different patterns of actual and metaphorical significance. I conclude the chapter with a section that contrasts these responses to various aspects of the city with his response to rural retirement.

The City of London and the moneyed men

The ancient City of London was built on the northern shore of the river Thames. Its walled perimeter, which enclosed just under 380 acres, ran in something approaching the 'form of a bow' in the phrase of John Stow's celebrated Elizabethan *Survey of London*, 1598, from the Fleet Ditch in the east to the Tower in the west. This stone wall, which had first been erected in the time of Roman government and had been continuously repaired since then (it is still clearly marked on the map of 1707 reproduced on pp. 30-31), was gradually dismantled during the eighteenth century. Apart from the quays and wharfs on the river front there were eight main entrances and exits to the City through Ludgate, Newgate, Aldersgate, Cripplegate, Moorgate, Bishopsgate, Aldgate and over London Bridge. The main east to west thoroughfare was Cheapside, which joined St Paul's Cathedral in the west to the busy commercial centre around Cornhill in the east. On the southern boundary of the City a series of stairs led down to the river.

Just over twenty years before Pope was born, however, this City was ravaged by one of the worst fires of all time. The Fire of London raged for four days from 2 to 5 September 1666 and consumed all save the north-eastern and extreme western parts of the City. The Royal Exchange, the Custom House, the Guildhall, the halls of forty-four of the Livery companies, St. Paul's itself, and eighty-seven of the parish churches, besides about 13,200 houses, were burned down. Barely one fifth of the City was left standing. Thus the medieval City, which had changed so very little over several hundred years, had to be almost completely rebuilt.

The work of rebuilding began almost immediately, and one of the great glories of this reconstruction was the skyline that Christopher Wren created with the dome of St. Paul's Cathedral and the steeples of his churches. Otherwise the main difference between the old and the new City was that, by Act of Parliament, the houses had now to be built either of brick or stone. The old timber-framed houses of Tudor times had proved hideously combustible in such a dense setting. Apart from this change in building materials, the alterations to the City were not as great as might be expected. The street pattern of the medieval City was hardly obscured, and, most important of all as far as the citizens were concerned, the new buildings in the City increased its status as a focus of commercial life in the nation.

It was this aspect of the City that most concerned Pope. The City had always been a thriving mercantile centre, proud of its guilds and livery companies. Its leading inhabitants, in contrast to those of the City of Westminster, were traditionally men who had made their wealth in business rather than men who had inherited it from landed families. Its citizens were, by and large, industrious and successful tradesmen, as Pope was only too aware, having been born the son of a linen merchant in the very heart of the business district. But towards the close of the seventeenth century a new development in mercantile growth occurred with the extraordinary increase in capitalist activity that took place. As a result the City of London became not only a trading centre but a financial stronghold. The connotation of the word 'City', to imply mysterious dealings in the world of high finance, that we intend today when we use phrases like 'City gent', or 'he does something in the City', originated in Pope's lifetime.

The Bank of England was established by Act of Parliament in 1693. Its imposing building at the end of Threadneedle Street was not built until 1734, but long before then the Bank had introduced paper money:

> Blest paper-credit! last and best supply!
> That lends Corruption lighter wings to fly!
>
> *Epistle to Bathurst* (1733), 69–70.

It was the Bank's funding of the National Debt, however, that most spectacularly dramatized the new concept of living on borrowed credit. In 1688 the Debt was a mere £300,000; by 1720 it was £54 million, and by 1749 it was £80 million.

The other great factor in the capitalist expansion of the early eighteenth century was the proliferation of joint stock companies.

In 1695 the amount of capital invested in joint stock companies was £4 million, by 1717 it had risen to £20 million, and by 1720 to about £50 million. The two largest and most sensational were the East India and South Sea Companies, but the rush of support to buy stock in smaller and totally unproven enterprises is perhaps a better indication of the capitalist fever that seized the country in these years. According to Isaac Kramnick's *Bolingbroke and His Circle* (pp. 66–7):

> A list of the new companies founded in 1720 must also include the Bleaching of Hair Company, Insurance on Horses Company, a company for the Transmutation of Quicksilver, a company to insure Marriages from Divorce, and another to design an air pump for the brain. Subscriptions were opened and filled immediately for a company to plant mulberry trees and breed silkworms in Chelsea Park. Another company would produce a cannon with the capability to discharge round and square cannon balls and bullets. The mania possessing the English that summer is best illustrated by the subscription of three thousand pounds in one day for 'a company to carry on an undertaking of great advantage but nobody to know what it is'.

In such a world the financial rewards went to those most practised in devious forms of wheeling and dealing. It was the attendant parasites of the joint stock companies, the stock-jobbers, projectors, usurers, attorneys and scriveners, rather than the merchants and traders, who most profited from all this investment and who began to derive considerable influence from it. Pope and his Tory friends saw power shifting from the landed interest to the moneyed interest, from the country aristocracy to the City financiers, and they did not like it. As a recent historian has put it, the counting house had begun to replace the country house. Writing to Pope on 10 January 1721 Swift says:

> I ever abominated that scheme of politics (now about thirty years old) of setting up a money'd Interest in opposition to the landed. For, I conceived, there could not be a truer maxim in our government than this, that the possessors of the soil are the best judges of what is for the advantage of the kingdom: If others had thought the same way, Funds of Credit and South-Sea Projects would neither have been felt nor heard of.

It is this moneyed interest, Whig in its politics, and Dissenting in its religion, that Pope attacks so consistently in his poems of the 1730s. Sir Charles Duncombe, a London banker who bought the Duke of Buckingham's Yorkshire estate of Helmsley for £90,000 in 1695, is a typical example. Pope describes the transaction in his *Imitation of Horace, Satire II, ii*, addressed to Hugh Bethel (177–8):

> And Helmsley once proud Buckingham's delight,
> Slides to a Scriv'ner or a City Knight.

Here the terms 'scrivener' (a money-lender) and 'City Knight' have become almost synonymous as the moneyed interest buys what had previously been inherited, while Pope's scorn for both is compressed in the downward motion of the word 'slides'.

We must beware, however, of oversimplification. Pope hated avarice wherever it was found. 'In Soldier, Churchman, Patriot, Man in Pow'r, / 'Tis Avarice all, Ambition is no more!' he says in Dialogue One of *Epilogue to the Satires*. Pope was far too intelligent to suggest that only inhabitants of the City worshipped Mammon. What we find in his poetry is a burning denunciation of the 'One Lust for Gold' that rages throughout the land. In his *Imitation of Horace, Epistle I, i*, addressed to Lord Bolingbroke, it is London's collective voice, from St James's in Westminster to St Paul's in the City, that is imagined creating a new town cry. Rich and poor, old and young, are consumed by the same itch, so that all seem to cry out, 'Get Mony, Mony still'.

Nevertheless the eager desire for monetary gain does seem to be especially associated with the City in Pope's poetry. Nowhere is this more powerfully expressed than in the conclusion to the *Epistle to Lord Bathurst*. The poem is a scathing attack on avarice generally in a country 'sunk in lucre's sordid charms' (145), but it is the superbly sustained closing story about Sir Balaam that is most apposite here.

Sir Balaam originally came from the heart of the City's business district. 'A Citizen of Sober fame' (341), he dwelt near the Monument, erected on Fish Hill in memory of the fire of London, just a stone's throw from the Royal Exchange in Threadneedle Street. Indeed his worship at this temple to Mammon is equated with his worship at the temple to God: 'Constant at Church and Change; his gains were sure . . . ' The telling juxtaposition of 'Church and Change' is skilfully reinforced in the pun on his spiritual and financial 'gains'. Such a portrait seems almost to be written with Max Weber's thesis on the protestant roots of capitalism in mind. The next development is for Balaam to be made a City Knight when Satan tempts him with riches rather than poverty. The plain good man of the opening has become a typical moneyed man dealing in stocks and shares:

> The Tempter saw his time; the work he ply'd;
> Stocks and Subscriptions pour on ev'ry side,
> 'Till all the Daemon makes his full descent,
> In one abundant show'r of Cent. per Cent.,
> Sinks deep within him, and possesses whole,
> Then dubs Director, and secures his soul.
>
> (370–5)

Sir Balaam does not now even make the pretence of attending church as well as Change. 'His Compting-house employ'd the Sunday-morn' (380), and his wife and family represent him at church.

The conclusion to the story leads directly into the next section of this chapter. Having acquired financial status Sir Balaam now sets out to acquire social status. When his first wife dies he marries a nymph of quality, 'bows at Court, and grows polite'. He rejects the City of London for the City of Westminster:

> Leaves the dull Cits, and joins (to please the fair)
> The well-bred Cuckolds in St James's air.

Pope is scarcely less scathing in dealing with the Court than with the City. Sir Balaam's family are individually ruined by their social aspirations. His son 'drinks, whores, fights and in a duel dies'; his daughter marries a Viscount and 'bears a Coronet and Pox for life'; and his Lady gets him into such deep debt through her gambling that Sir Balaam takes a bribe from France and is impeached by the House of Commons. Finally the Court forsakes him, and 'sad Sir Balaam curses God and dies'. The move from the City to the Court has been a move out of the frying pan into the fire.

The City of Westminster and the Court

The City of Westminster takes its name from its abbey, or minster, situated to the west of the City of London. For centuries it was entirely separate from the City of London. A road, running along the edge of the Thames and therefore appropriately called the Strand, connected the two cities, but there were large open spaces between them. According to John Noorthouck's *New History of London* (1773), 'it long continued an insignificant, mean, unhealthy place, remarkable for nothing but the abbey which was very unfavourably placed in a marshy spot' (p. 695). It was during the reign of Henry VIII that the City of Westminster first began to acquire the courtly and fashionable associations that it had for Pope. In 1530 Henry VIII bought York House, as it then was, from Cardinal Wolsey and converted it into his principal residence, the palace of Whitehall. He also acquired and rebuilt St James's Palace, which had formerly been a hospital for leprous maidens, and converted the ground between the two palaces into St James's Park.

From this time forward the City of Westminster continued to gain in social importance and during the early seventeenth century wealthy persons began to move their residences there from the City of London. One of the most important persons to make such a move was the Earl of Bedford who in 1631, with Inigo Jones as his architect, built the square at Covent Garden that later became the model for the development of the West End. But it was not until after the Restoration of Charles II in 1660 that a mass exodus of wealthy persons brought about a complete separation between the fashionable life in the City of Westminster and the mercantile life in the City of London.

During the reign of Charles II, the 'merry monarch', the City of Westminster became the centre of courtly and fashionable entertainment, and, although both William III and Anne led far quieter lives, the city never really lost this reputation. When the theatres reopened in 1660 the two acting companies performed at theatres situated in areas more closely associated with Westminster than London. The Duke's company produced their plays at the Duke's Theatre in Lincoln's Inn Fields, while the King's company produced theirs at the Theatre Royal in Drury Lane. Both companies moved to new theatres before the century ended, but the theatrical world remained essentially connected with the West End. Thus when an opera house was built in 1705 it was erected in the Haymarket in the heart of Westminster. These theatres catered to a small coterie audience dominated by fashion-conscious ladies and gentlemen from the town and Court who came there to meet one another as much as they did to see the play or listen to the opera. Another favourite meeting-place at this time was the coffee-house. Different coffee, or chocolate, houses appealed to different social, professional and political sections of society, so that the *beau monde*, for example, met at White's in St James's Street, while poets and critics got together at Will's near Covent Garden. A further consideration in the development of Westminster as a social centre was the building of great town houses, such as those of Lord Burlington and the Duke of Devonshire in Piccadilly, which brought with them glittering assemblies, levées and balls. Soon Westminster, like London, began to spread its influence further west so that by the beginning of the eighteenth century the adjoining villages of Kensington with its royal palace, and Chelsea with its Ranelagh pleasure gardens, were included in its social, if not in its geographical, milieu.

This is the world that Pope lightly conjures up in his *Epistle to Miss Blount* written on her leaving the Town for her country house at Mapledurham in 1714:

> She went from Op'ra, park, assembly, play
> To morning walks, and pray'rs three hours a day.

There is a smiling ambivalence in Pope's attitude to the fashionable life of Westminster in his earlier poems. He knows that the town is traditionally to be rejected as a place of hypocrisy and affectation, and yet one cannot help sensing the young man's attraction towards its social gaiety. A distinct affection for the glitter of society lies beneath the gently satirical surface of *The Rape of the Lock*. Pope seems ready to forgive the town its vices for the same reason that he forgives Belinda her errors:

> If to her share some Female Errors fall
> Look on her Face, and you'll forget 'em all.

This ambivalent attitude to the City of Westminster and all it represents is most clearly found in the opening line of his poem, *A Farewell to London*: 'Dear, damn'd, distracting Town, farewell!' Pope left the town in 1715, the year this poem was written, to complete his translation of *The Iliad* in the peace of the country. He was never again to write of the fashionable world as vaguely enticing: henceforth its capacity to be damned takes over from its capacity to distract.

But it is the City of Westminster's associations with the Court that most concern Pope. The word 'Court', in this context, describes the place where the sovereign resides and holds state, attended by his retinue. It is worth briefly considering the word's etymology here, for originally it denoted a small enclosed place (cf. courtyard, or tennis court), and this root meaning helps to fix the particular sense of a narrow coterie that pertains to the word as it refers to the king and his household. This household moved around somewhat is Pope's lifetime. Until the time of William III the main royal residence had been at Whitehall, but William found that the London fog aggravated his asthma and he therefore moved his household, first to Hampton Court, and then to Kensington Palace. Queen Anne continued to reside at Kensington, but with the arrival of George I the Court returned to Westminster. The palace of Whitehall, with the fortunate exception of the magnificent banqueting hall designed by Inigo Jones had been burned down by a fire in 1697. Therefore, St James's, which Noorthouck describes as 'an irregular brick building, without one single beauty on the outside to recommend it, being at once the contempt of foreign nations, and the disgrace of our own', became the principal royal palace in England until the death of George II in 1760.

Despite the great constitutional changes that had taken place in the second half of the seventeenth century, the Court still maintained great influence in eighteenth-century England. The sovereign controlled the appointment of all ambassadors and envoys abroad, and of all dignitaries and deputies at home, quite apart from the vast number of pensions and places, for example appointments connected with the revenue, throughout the country. The Court was therefore a great focus for patronage and not only for those in search of social improvement. As Derek Jarrett says in *Britain 1688–1815* (p. 28):

There was no question of a clear-cut division between men who ministered to the King's personal needs and men who helped him rule the country. For most of the eighteenth century the Lord Chamberlain, a Household officer, could attend the Cabinet Council while his counterpart among the Officers of State, the Lord Great Chamberlain, could not; and during Anne's reign it was not unusual for the Groom of the Stole (the particular title given to the first Gentleman of the Bedchamber) and even the Master of the Horse to attend Cabinet meetings. Thus courtiers were frequently councillors and councillors had often to practise the arts of the courtiers. Wherever the King was, there power and influence were to be won.

No one realized this better than Sir Robert Walpole, and his long 'reign' as First Minister was to a great extent dependent on his influence at Court and particularly on his influence with George II's Queen, Caroline of Anspach.

Pope showed two distinct attitudes to the Court at different periods in his life. During the reign of Queen Anne, when his Tory friends Robert Harley and Henry St John had controlling influence there, Pope was full of praise for it, seeing Stuart rule, in *Windsor-Forest*, 1713, as a latterday equivalent to the age of Augustus. But once the House of Hanover came to the throne and the Whigs under Robert Walpole gained control at Court, Pope became increasingly disillusioned, until, in the poems of the 1730s, and especially in the *Imitation of Horace, Epistle II, i*: To Augustus, 1737, and the *Epilogue to the Satires*, 1738, he delivered a sombre protest against what he considered to be the 'insuperable corruption and depravity of manners' brought about by the Hanoverian Court.

There are few more magnificent courtly panegyrics in the language than *Windsor-Forest*. The poem is partly glorifying myth, with Queen Anne seen as Diana, 'The Earth's fair light, and Empress of the Main', and partly a merging of dream and fact as Pope celebrates the Peace of Utrecht:

At length great ANNA said — Let Discord cease!
She said, the World obey'd and all was *Peace*! (327–8)

Given such a conception it is hardly surprising that the image of London and Westminster that emerges bears little resemblance to the description of those two cities drawn in this chapter:

Behold! *Augusta's* glittering Spires increase,
And Temples rise, the beauteous Works of Peace.
I see, I see where two fair Cities bend
Their ample Bow, a new *White-Hall* ascend!
There mighty Nations shall inquire their Doom,
The World's great Oracle in Times to come;
There Kings shall sue, and Suppliant States be seen
Once more to bend before a *British* QUEEN.   (377–84)

This is splendid visionary poetry, but put it beside the fourth book of *The Dunciad*, published exactly twenty years later, and it will prove as insubstantial as Prospero's pageant in *The Tempest*.

Pope's disillusion with the Court begins with the death of Queen Anne. This event scattered the members of the Scriblerus Club, who had gathered round Harley to support the Tory Ministry, into various parts of England and Ireland. With the accession of George I and the return of Whig power, Pope retired from London life to devote himself mainly to the duties of editing and translating. By the time he came to write of the Court again, in the Satires that followed the first *Dunciad* over a dozen years later, his attitude was radically different. A cultural decay, which he blamed on the House of Hanover, seemed to him to have replaced the dream of a second Augustan age that he had associated with the House of Stuart under Queen Anne.

Pope's most sustained denunciation of the Court is to be found in his *Versification of the Fourth Satire of Dr John Donne* published in 1733. The poem is a good example of what it means to be a neoclassical writer. Poets had satirized the Court long before Pope did so, perhaps the most famous English examples being Skelton's *Why Come Ye Not to Court?*, Spenser's *Colin Clout's Come Home Again*, and John Donne's *Satires*. What Pope does in his *Versification of the Fourth Satire of Dr John Donne* is to transmit this tradition and show how it is just as relevant to his own day. He assimilates the past into the present.

The figure of the satirist who speaks in the poem (one should beware of confusing the figure with Pope himself) describes, with a solemn sense of pain, how he was heavily punished for going once to Court. No sooner had he entered than he was intercepted by a courtier, 'a Rogue so civil, whose Tongue can complement you to the Devil'. The courtier having spied him out, engages him in obliging talk, extols the virtues of travel, gossips about Court news, and so totally provokes the satirist's patience that he 'pukes' and 'nauseates'. The satirist only escapes when the courtier flies to the Minister as he comes by. When the satirist contemplates the scene afterwards he falls into a dream in which he realizes that the Court is worse than hell:

Not Dante dreaming all th' Infernal State,
Beheld such Scenes of Envy, Sin and Hate.   (192–3)

The Court is a 'Bladder' (205) and courtiers are 'painted puppets' (208), a 'varnished race of hollow gewgaws' (209). They have no minds of their own and are mere lifeless effigies, 'stately, staring things' (210), like waxworks. Pope's main criticism of the Court is that it produces such artificial veneers. Courtiers act every part but that of themselves. They have no individuality and no self-respect. In despair the satirist concludes that '*Courts* are too much for Wits so weak as mine' (280).

Pope's poem is mainly a general attack on the courtier as a type. It would be a mistake, however, to think that Pope does not condemn individual courtiers and even the sovereign himself in his poetry. Indeed this is where he most differs from earlier English satirists. Skelton and Spenser had both been careful to praise Henry VIII and Elizabeth respectively at the same time as they attacked their Courts. Pope, on the other hand, includes numerous onslaughts on named individuals, not least George II and Queen Caroline. Perhaps the best known, and most typical, courtier of George II's reign was Lord John Hervey, whose *Memoirs of the Reign of George II* are now considered one of the most valuable historical records of the time. Pope's hostility to Hervey is too complex to trace in all its ramifications here, but his portrait of him as Sporus in *An Epistle to Dr Arbuthnot* is clearly relevant as being also the portrait of a typical courtier.

The portrait picks up many of the images of the Court that we have seen in the *Versification of the Fourth Satire of Dr John Donne*. Sporus, like the impertinent courtier in the *Versification*, is full of extravagant show, but at the same time this artificial exterior is linked to a sordid inner reality. Thus he has 'gilded' wings, but he is a 'bug'; he is 'painted', but he is a 'child of dirt that stinks and stings'; he is 'well-bred', but he is also a 'spaniel'; and he has a 'cherub's face', but is a 'Reptile all the rest'. The courtier has been transformed into an image of Satan: the link between the Court and Vice could not be more direct.

Pope's comments on the Court expand to reveal far wider decay. This is most clearly conveyed in the *Imitation of Horace, Epistle II, i,* 1737, where what begins as a satire on George II develops into an attack on the degeneration of culture in Hanoverian England. The poem as a whole is no more solely about George II than the *Dunciad* is solely about Lewis Theobald or Colley Cibber. George II, as King of England, is merely the figurehead for a greater corruption, the decay of poetry and drama generally in his time.

The presentation of George in this poem is one of the most finely controlled pieces of irony in all of Pope's poetry. Horace's respectful tribute to the Emperor Augustus is converted into a mock tribute to George Augustus Hanover:

> While You, great Patron of Mankind, sustain
> The balanc'd World, and open all the Main;
> Your Country, chief, in Arms abroad defend,
> At home, with Morals, Arts and Laws amend;
> How shall the Muse, from such a Monarch, steal
> An hour, and not defraud the Publick Weal?   (1–6)

George is ironically praised for being precisely what he is not – a 'great Patron' – and for doing what he does not do, 'sustain the balanced world'. He is described opening 'all the Main', as if that were praiseworthy, when he should be protecting English shipping. He defends his country abroad in the arms of Mme Walmoden (later the Countess of Yarmouth) instead of in the arms of battle, while at home he 'amends' his country with 'Morals, Arts, and Laws', with the clear implication that the amendment is for the worse rather than the better. The ironic tone ('*such* a Monarch': the italics are mine) is clearly established so that by the time we come to the climax of this opening eulogy, the ambiguity is unmistakable to all except the most obtuse (i.e. George himself):

> Wonder of Kings! like whom, to mortal eyes
> None e'er has risen, and none e'er shall rise.   (29–30)

I do not intend to discuss all the references to the Court in Pope's later poetry, for, as must be clear by now, there are far too many. The interested reader who wants to follow this up should look especially at lines 101–19 of the *Imitation of Horace, Epistle I, i*, addressed to Lord Bolingbroke. I want instead to conclude this section by commenting on a poem in which the allusions to the fashionable world of Westminster are not simply contained in a certain block of lines that attack the Court but are woven into the whole texture of the poem.

The Epilogue to the Satires has already been mentioned as one of Pope's most powerful satires on Hanoverian corruption. One of the chief sources of its power is the dramatic tension set up in the dialogue between its two speakers, referred to in the text as *P*. (Pope) and *Fr*. (Friend). Only when we realize that the Friend is a typical courtier can we appreciate fully the various points of view put into his mouth, and the way Pope, as author, manipulates the 'Friend' as adversary. The 'Friend' (he is of course anything but a friend) approves of Horace because 'his sly, polite, insinuating stile could please at Court' (I, 19–20); he approves of Pope attacking 'some odd Old Whig' (I, 39), so long as he doesn't include the modern Whigs who support the Court; he defends 'Immortal Selkirk' (I, 92), who was a gentleman to the Bedchamber to William III, George

I, and George II; he equates the Court of Hanover with the Court of Heaven (I, 97–104); he is horrified when Pope mentions the King directly (II, 51–2); and he constantly falls back on Court jargon (e.g. II, 123). These are some of the ways in which Pope realizes the courtly character of the adversary so that the reader feels the full validity of the onslaught. Thus when the courtier protests that Pope's filthy simile quite turns his stomach, the reader shares the righteous indignation of Pope's reply:

> So does Flatt'ry mine;
> And all your Courtly Civet-Cats can Vent,
> Perfume to you, to me is Excrement.   (182–84)

This excremental image aptly summarizes Pope's disgust for the Court and all it stands for. It is a disgust that seems to grow stronger throughout the satires of the 1730s. Pope's response to the Court in the *Epilogue to the Satires*, 1738, is that much more indignant than his response to the Court in the *Versification of the Fourth Satire of Dr John Donne*, 1733, and of course put beside his response to the Court in *Windsor-Forest*, 1713, it represents a complete volte-face. In the *Epilogue to the Satires* flattery, affectation, the adoption of airs and graces, false breeding and florid eloquence are merely disguised forms of obscenity. Seen from one point of view, that of the Court, such manners smell sweet, like 'perfume', but seen from another point of view, that of Pope and, hopefully, the reader, such dressings-up smell foul, like 'excrement'.

Grub Street and the war with the Dunces

Grub Street is a term that has been used over the years to cover a multitude of different meanings. It originates from the name of an actual street, in the parish of Cripplegate just outside the City walls but within the 'liberties' of the City jurisdiction, that was largely inhabited by hack writers willing to use their pens for money, whatever the assignment. Grub Street lay in the heart of one of the most depressed areas of eighteenth-century London suburbia. To the east was the notoriously dissolute area of Moorfields, bounded to the south by Bedlam, the asylum for the mad, while to the west was the polluted area of West Smithfield with its meat market. But if Grub Street was originally the name of an actual street it rapidly acquired a metaphorical meaning. The term was used, from the early eighteenth century onwards, to describe any hack writing and not just the street itself. As Dr Johnson says in his *Dictionary*, 1755, Grub Street was 'originally the name of a street in Moorfields in London, much inhabited by writers of small histories, dictionaries, and temporary poems; whence any mean production is called *grubstreet*'. It was the meanness of the production that counted: for

such persons literature was a commodity to be peddled to the highest bidder.

If the City of London was inevitably associated in Pope's poetry with the moneyed interest, and the City of Westminster with the fashionable interest, the Grub Street locale brings with it a third set of associations. Grub Street, Moorfields, Smithfield, Bedlam, Newgate, the Fleet Ditch, St Giles–in–the–Fields and St Giles Cripplegate are all places that fall between the cities of London and Westminster. They are part of a great depressed region lying between and around these two symbolic centres of money and fashion. In placing the Dunces so firmly in such a setting, as he does in *The Dunciad*, Pope was again using real description as a basis for his imaginative transformation. The filth, stench and violence associated with actual slum regions in London become an objective correlative for bad writing. In the Augustan world of absolute moral standards bad art is considered to be as immoral as bad conduct. The prostitute author is an object of contempt, not pity. It was part of the change to a Romantic sensibility at the end of the century that converted the image of the Grub Street writer from an object of scorn to an object of pathos. The nineteenth-century image of the hack writer in his garret as an alienated genius in seclusion is a gross sentimentalizing of the facts of the eighteenth-century literary environment. It was these hack writers, or scribblers, as Pope most frequently called them, who, fiercely envious of his success as a poet and of his financial independence as an author, struck at him with such fury.

I have already described (p. 9) the campaign of careful neglect that greeted the publication of Pope's *Pastorals* in 1709, and have shown Pope's ability to deal with his literary detractors quite as effectively as they had dealt with him. But such opposition appears in a kindly light when compared to the long history of obscene and personal vituperation that followed on John Dennis's *Reflections Critical and Satyrical Upon a Late Rhapsody Call'd An Essay Upon Criticism*, published in 1711. This gross personal comment on Pope's disfigurement opened the floodgates to a torrent of abuse that was to be kept up with little check until his death. It is undoubtedly true to say that no poet in our literature has been vilified so persistently and so virulently as Pope. A recent bibliography of attacks on Pope by J.V. Guerinot lists no fewer than 158 separate pamphlets between the time of Dennis's opening blast in 1711 and the poet's death thirty-three years later. Furthermore, this list deliberately excludes the multitude of passing comments to be found in the newspapers of the day.

Two particular aspects of Pope's character come in for repeated abuse. Both are linked to laboured puns on his name: his simian-like deformity is pointed up by leaving out the middle letters of his name (A.P **E), and his despised religion is attacked through the even more obvious pun on his full name. The violent scurrility of the majority of these pamphlets can be briefly indicated through a sample list of the epithets attached to him: at various times he is called an adder, a baboon, a wasp, a whore, a pimp, an insect, a croaking toad, a portentous cub, the purest Wag-prick, a specious knave, the monkey's paw of a low faction, a true son of an impudent whore of Babylon . . . etc. Clearly such pamphlets have no literary value, but they are helpful, nevertheless, in giving us a better understanding of the conditions that at first surrounded the reception of Pope's work, and later became part of the motive behind the writing of such poems as *The Dunciad* and *An Epistle to Dr Arbuthnot*.

Since it was the conflict with Dennis that began this long warfare it is worth pausing to examine its tenor and motive more closely. Pope had been the first to strike when in six lines of *An Essay on Criticism*, published in May 1711, he wrote:

> Fear not the Anger of the Wise to raise;
> Those best can bear Reproof who merit Praise.
> 'Twere well, might Criticks still this Freedom take;
> But Appius reddens at each Word you speak,
> And stares, Tremendous! with a threatening Eye,
> Like some fierce Tyrant in Old Tapestry!

(582–7)

Pope refers to Dennis by the name of one of the characters in his tragedy *Appius and Virginia*, and makes light fun of his well known 'stare' and favourite adjective, 'tremendous'. From a young man of twenty-three there was some mild disrespect in this description of the older critic, but nothing that could be considered to justify Dennis's furious response published next month:

> As there is no Creature in Nature so venomous, there is nothing so stupid and so impotent as a hunch-back'd Toad; and a man must be very quiet and very passive, and stand still to let him fasten his Teeth and his Claws, or be surpriz'd sleeping by him, before that Animal can have any power to hurt him.
>
> *Reflections . . . Upon . . . An Essay Upon Criticism*
> (1711), p. 26

This, and much more in the same vein, established the predominant tone of the writing on Pope in his lifetime. Pope was startled and hurt by the attack, but he did not reply until two years later when he published *The Narrative of Dr Robert Norris* (see p. 13).

This pamphlet makes open fun of Dennis, but it never descends to the vitriolic insult that is Dennis's stock in trade. In *A True Character of Mr Pope, And His Writings*, May 1716, published by Edmund Curll, Dennis writes:

The Deformity of this Libeller, is Visible, Present, Unalterable, and Peculiar to himself. 'Tis the mark of God and Nature upon him, to give us warning that we should hold no Society with him, as a Creature not of our Original, nor of our Species. . . . They tell me, he has been lately pleas'd to say, That 'tis Doubtful if the Race of Men are the Offspring of Adam or of the Devil. But if 'tis doubtful as to the Race of Men, 'tis certain at least, that his Original is not from Adam, but from the Devil. By his constant and malicious Lying, and by that Angel Face and Form of his, 'tis plain that he wants nothing but Horns and Tayl, to be the exact Resemblance, both in Shape and Mind, of his Infernal Father.

But if the conflict with Dennis, a recognized literary critic, began the long series of insults on Pope, it was the conflict with Grub Street scribblers, who frequently remained anonymous, that continued and sustained it. Edmund Curll, a bookseller who specialized in unauthorized publication and literary scandal, was the most powerful representative of these writers, and directly commissioned a great number of the attacks. Pope's conflict with Curll came to a head in 1716 after Curll had piratically published some poems, written by Lady Mary Wortley Montagu, satirizing the Court. At this stage in his life Pope was anxious to impress Lady Mary and, since he had already suffered from Curll, he took revenge by first dropping an emetic in Curll's drink and then publishing a prose account of his ensuing sickness. This was descending to a level at which Curll was a past master and was to backfire on Pope for the rest of his life. Curll never left him alone after this and when he was not publishing some scurrilous comments on him, for example Dennis's *A True Character of Mr. Pope*, 1716, or Curll's own *The Curliad*, 1729, he was busily dredging up some youthful indiscretion of Pope's never intended for publication, such as *A Roman Catholick Version of the First Psalm*, 1716.

From the time of Dennis's first engagement with Pope in June 1711 to the end of 1718 there were thirty-four pamphlet attacks on Pope. After this things quieted down a bit as Pope retired from the centre of literary attention to work on his translation of Homer and edition of Shakespeare. In the eight years from 1719 to the end of 1727 there were only nineteen onslaughts, and there were never more than three in any one year. Then in May 1728 came the publication of *The Dunciad* in three books with Theobald as hero, and the War with the Dunces was on. In the next three years alone forty-two separate pamphlets against Pope were published.

The Dunciad was Pope's first poetical reply to his enemies since they had begun their campaign in 1711. This is not to say that he had suffered silently for seventeen years; as we have already seen, he had made several prose retaliations, but he had certainly received far more abuse than he had given. He was not unmoved by these feuds, however, and two years earlier on 14 December 1725 had written to Swift saying that although he did not have much anger against the great ones of the world his spleen was raised by the little rogues of it:

> It would vex one more to be knock't o' the head by a pisspot, than by a thunderbolt. As to great oppressors (as you say) they are like kites or eagles, one expects mischief from them: but to be squirted to death (as poor Wycherley said to me on his deathbed) by potecaries prentices, by the under strappers of under secretaries, to secretaries, who were no secretaries — this would provoke as dull a dog as Philips himself.

However, if Pope now thought he could demolish 'the little rogues' of the world by ridiculing them, he was as mistaken as when he tried to demolish Curll by playing a practical joke on him. The main outward effect of *The Dunciad* was to multiply, not decrease, the plague of insect scribblers who pestered him. As he wrote in *An Epistle to Dr. Arbuthnot* a few years later:

> Who shames a Scribler? break one cobweb thro',
> He spins the slight, self-pleasing thread anew;
> Destroy his Fib, or Sophistry; in vain,
> The Creature's at his dirty work again;
> Thron'd in the Centre of his thin designs;
> Proud of a vast Extent of flimzy lines.

(89–94)

Pope had stunned the Scribblers, not shamed them. 'No creature smarts so little as a fool', and these creatures, like Swift's famous spider, had 'a good plentiful store of dirt and poison' in their breasts. They would recover and be themselves.

The abuse poured on Pope as a result of *The Dunciad* plumbed new depths in character assassination. *Farmer Pope and his Son*, for example, published by Curll in September 1728, and probably written by him too, describes Pope, in a fable, as:

> A little scurvy, purblind-Elf;
> Scarce like a Toad, much less himself.
> Deform'd in Shape, of Pigmy Stature:
> A proud, conceited, peevish Creature.

48

A year later, in August 1729, Ned Ward described Pope in the dedication to *Apollo's Maggots in his Cups* as:

> A frightful indigested Lump,
> With here a Hollow, there a Hump;
> A true Epitome of *Wales*,
> Made up of ugly Hills and Dales.

These lines, disgusting enough in themselves, are a mere prelude to the poem which tells, according to J.V. Guerinot, of:

> a drunken feast of the gods in which Apollo visits Parnassus and proposes to the Muses that they form a satirist, a something between a monkey and a man. Having formed a body with muck, they urinate and defecate upon it. Apollo adds the brains and animates it with a bellows, . . . , and drops him down between Thames and Isis (i.e. Twickenham), where he reigns as King of modern wits (pp. 178–9).

These examples are quite sufficient to indicate the 'literary' climate of the war with the Dunces. Before we accuse Pope of sinking to unnecessary depths of indecency in *The Dunciad* we should bear in mind the standard level of pamphlet abuse in the early eighteenth century.

In 1733 his feud with Lady Mary Wortley Montagu and Lord John Hervey came to a head. It is difficult, if not impossible, to determine which party was the aggressor in this particular battle, for relations between Pope and Lady Mary and between Pope and Lord Hervey are clouded with unknown factors. Pope's attitude to Lady Mary had dramatically soured during the 1720s after his early infatuation for her. In January 1733 he produced a devastating allusion to her as Sappho in his *Imitation of Horace, Satire II, i*:

> From furious *Sappho* scarce a milder Fate
> P-x'd by her Love, or libell'd by her Hate.

It was in reply to this that Lady Mary and Lord Hervey collaborated to write the most skilful of all the satires on Pope, *Verses Address'd to the Imitator of the First Satire of the Second Book of Horace*, published in *The Grub-Street Journal* of 29 March 1733. The verses culminate in a vicious curse on Pope full of personal hatred and lacking any redeeming wit:

> Like the first bold Assassin's be thy Lot
> Ne'er be thy Guilt forgiven, or forgot;
> But as thou hate'st, be hated by Mankind,
> And with the Emblem of thy crooked Mind,
> Mark'd on thy Back, like *Cain*, by God's own Hand,
> Wander like him, accursed through the Land.

The controversy stirred up by these verses raged on in the pages of *The Grub-Street Journal* for the rest of the year. It undoubtedly had much to do with Pope's magnificently damning portrait of Lord Hervey as Sporus in *An Epistle to Dr Arbuthnot* published two years later in 1735. As Pope says in the Advertisement to this poem:

> This Paper is a Sort of Bill of Complaint, begun many years since, and drawn up by snatches, as the several Occasions offer'd. I had no thoughts of publishing it, till it pleas'd some Persons of Rank and Fortune [Lord John Hervey and Lady Mary Wortley Montagu] to attack in a very extraordinary manner, not only my writings (of which being publick the Publick judge) but my Person, Morals and Family, whereof to those who know me not, a truer Information may be requisite.

Pope's poem is a defence of his life and writings, but it is, of course, never purely defensive. He pummels his various enemies with far more wit than they ever displayed, metaphorically converting them into grotesque forms of comical amusement. Thus the minor poets who pester him for favour become at one time madmen who 'rave, recite, and madden round the land', and at another a plague of insects who pierce his thickets and glide through his grotto. The pedantic scholars are transformed into some sort of rare ornithological specimen, 'each Word-catcher that lives on syllables', while he playfully imagines that the dunces might be whistled off his hands like trained hawks. The archetypal scribbler becomes a spider:

> Thron'd in the Centre of his thin designs;
> Proud of a vast Extent of flimzy lines.   (93-4)

An Epistle to Dr Arbuthnot and the various imitations of Horace that followed it were more than sufficient provocation to keep the war with the Dunces going throughout the 1730s. It is only necessary to refer individually to one more of the many attacks that continued to be made on Pope right up to his death, and that is Colley Cibber's *A Letter from Mr Cibber to Mr Pope*, published in July 1742. According to Warburton's 'Advertisement to the Reader', printed with *The Dunciad in Four Books* in October 1743, the publication of Cibber's 'ridiculous book ... furnished him [Pope] with a lucky opportunity of improving this Poem, by giving it the only thing it wanted, a more considerable Hero'. Whether Cibber's *Letter* did in fact provoke Pope into elevating Cibber to Theobald's former eminence, or merely confirmed him in making changes he had

The Tom-Tit episode. Frontispiece to A Letter from Mr Cibber to Mr Pope already contemplated, is something that one cannot be sure about, but there can be no doubt that it constituted yet another vicious personal attack on Pope that cried out for some sort of reply. In his *Letter* Cibber includes the notorious 'Tom-tit' episode (see p. 50) in which he tells how he and two other wits had lured Pope to a brothel but that he, Cibber, had saved Pope from the danger of venereal infection:

> But I (forgive me all ye mortified Mortals whom his fell Satyr has since fallen upon) observing he had staid as long as without hazard of his Health he might, I,
> Prick'd to it by foolish Honesty and Love, as *Shakespear* says, without Ceremony threw open the Door upon him, where I found this little hasty Hero, like a terrible *Tom Tit*, pertly perched upon the Mount of Love! But such was my Surprize that I fairly laid hold of his Heels, and actually drew him down safe and sound from his Danger.

As Guerinot points out, it is extremely unlikely that Cibber's story is true, for surely Pope would not have dared to belabour him over the years if he knew Cibber had such a weapon in store.

Finally, let us ask what effect all these attacks had on Pope and how they influenced his life and writing. The most obvious effect on his work is that they turned him towards writing satire. Before *The Dunciad* of 1728 Pope had only written one major poem, *The Rape of the Lock*, that was primarily a satiric poem: after 1728 nearly everything he wrote was strongly imbued with the satiric vein. It can of course be argued that his strength and success as a satirist would have emerged even if he had not been so frequently savaged, but it is far more likely that his turning towards satire as his main mode of expression in the latter half of his life was directly influenced by the many attacks on him. So far as the effect of these feuds on his personal life is concerned we can hardly do better than to conclude this section by quoting from Guerinot, who has made the most thorough study of them: 'To anyone who tries to read through Popiana year by year, it is Pope's forbearance and restraint that come to seem remarkable; the image of a poet eager to make every one of his detractors writhe needs serious revision' (p. 1).

The country and retirement

Pope's rejection of the financial, fashionable and literary abuses of London, described in the preceding sections of this chapter, are drawn into one composite rejection of urban life in his *Imitation of Horace, Epistle II, ii*, 1737, better known as *To a Colonel*. Near the beginning of this poem Pope rhetorically asks the colonel whether anyone can seriously regard London as a fit home for a poet:

Who there his Muse, or Self, or Soul attends?
In Crouds and Courts, Law, Business, Feasts and Friends?

(90–1)

Pope, as correspondent, goes on to describe in detail the press, anxiety and noise of London where he is besieged by lawyers, courtiers and Grub Street writers, 'this jealous, waspish, wrong-head, rhyming Race'. He only finds relief from the 'eternal roar' of urban life when he retires to the country:

> Soon as I enter at my Country door,
> My Mind resumes the thread it dropt before;
> Thoughts, which at Hyde-Park-Corner I forgot,
> Meet and rejoin me, in the pensive Grott.
> There all alone, and Compliments apart,
> I ask these sober questions of my Heart. (206–11)

The country has profound cultural and spiritual significance in Pope's poetry. There the poet can attend 'his Muse, or Self, or Soul', and ask sober questions of his Heart. The country symbolizes, in a variety of ways all the positive values that lie behind Pope's rejection of the city. He puts the life of rural retirement forward as the ideal against which to measure the moral limitations and aberrations of urban life.

The country was never very far away from Pope's London. As Sir Walter Besant puts it in *London in the Eighteenth Century* (1902):

> From any part of London it was possible to get into the country in a quarter of an hour. One realizes the rural surroundings of the City by considering that north of Gray's Inn was open country with fields; that Queen Square Bloomsbury, had its north side left purposely open in order that the residents might enjoy the views of the Highgate and Hampstead Hills. Within the reach of a 'short stage' the country was not only open and rural, but it was extremely beautiful (p. 78).

The village of Twickenham, where Pope lived for the last twenty-five years of his life, is situated on the north (Middlesex) bank of the Thames about fifteen miles upstream from London. Even in Pope's day it was not what one might call a rustic village, for it included many wealthy and noble inhabitants who lived in graceful villas on the river bank. But it was sufficiently separate from London, and surrounded by open fields and meadows, to be clearly considered part of the country in a way it certainly could not be today, it having long since been swallowed up by the endless surburbia of Greater London.

It was in this gentle landscape that Pope settled down to lead a life of rural retirement. It is important to realize that such a life was, for Pope, an extension of his basically neoclassical frame of mind not a first dawning of nineteenth-century Romanticism. Its model lay clearly in the classical motif of the *beatus vir*, or happy man, found in the writings of Virgil and Horace. The retirement theme, considered as a literary tradition, is related to the pastoral tradition in seeing the country as representative of the good values in life. Both traditions give us the other side of the coin to satire, which, from Juvenal on Rome to T.S. Eliot on London, sees the city as representative of corrupt values. But there are also crucial differences between the pastoral and retirement traditions, the most important being that where the pastoral poet deliberately idealizes rural life, so that his shepherds and shepherdesses become consciously artificial figures, the retirement poet offers a realistic appreciation of country life according to stoic principles.

It is well known that Pope's earliest published poems were his *Pastorals*, but it is perhaps less well known that his earliest poem 'written at about twelve years old', as he himself said, was the *Ode to Solitude*. The poem relies heavily on Horace's second epode, which is the basis of the whole retirement tradition. Pope's opening phrase, 'Happy the man', would immediately remind readers of Horace's opening words, *'Beatus ille'*. Pope's ode is a paean to the life of the rural husbandman, and ends with a plea that the poet himself might be allowed to live such a life. Thus early did the retirement ideal enter into the consciousness of the young poet.

The theme of the happy man underwent many changes in emphasis from the time of Horace to the time of Pope, but a certain core of ideals remained essentially unchanged for both poets. The happy man retired to the country first, because it offered a physical quietness that led to peace of mind, in total contrast to the anxiety and strife of the town. Second, he could achieve in the country a degree of self-reliance, by growing his own food and supplying his own attire, that again was altogether unattainable in the town. Third, he could participate in the general harmony of nature and thereby enjoy the greater harmony of God's creation. And finally, the happy husbandman had no ambitious desires. He rejected extravagant taste in favour of a simple but healthy sufficiency; 'Content with little', says Pope in *Sat. II, ii*, 'I can piddle here/On Broccoli and mutton round the year' (137–8). At the core of the retirement tradition then, lay the key values of peace, self-reliance, a harmonious relationship with nature and a healthy sufficiency. Above all, such a life offered the conditions for contemplation. 'Oft in the clear, still Mirrour of Retreat', Pope writes in the *Epilogue to the Satires*: Dialogue II (78), 'I studied Shrewsbury, the wise and great'. Retirement is 'clear' and 'still'. It offers the chance for 'study' in a way that the active life in the city does not, which is not to say, of course, that the husbandman's life is inactive. 'Contemplative life', wrote Pope to Atterbury when the bishop urged him in 1717 to join the Anglican faith and become more active, 'is not only my scene, but it is my habit too.'

The clearest examples of the happy man in Pope's poetry are the portraits of Trumbull in *Windsor-Forest* (235–58), and of the Man of Ross in the *Epistle to Bathurst* (249–90). Sir William Trumbull is praised as an example of those values noted in the previous paragraph. He is content with peace, the 'humbler joys of home-felt Quiet' (239); he is self-reliant, gathering 'Health from Herbs the Forest yields' (241); he lives in accord with Nature, 'to follow Nature' (252); and he lives a life of contemplation, 'wandering thoughtful in the silent wood' (249). The praise for John Kyrle, the Man of Ross, relies on the same set of values with added stress being given to his generosity and good works. It is significant that he too is addressed as a 'happy man' (275).

However, if the portraits of Trumbull and John Kyrle are the clearest individual examples of the 'happy man' motif in Pope's poetry, his composite portrait of himself as speaker, especially as it emerges in the satires of the 1730s, is the most sustained example of the motif. What Pope gives us in these poems is a series of compressed allusions to such an ideal. He nowhere presents such a self-portrait in its entirety, but the overall impression in reading these poems is to feel the cumulative effect of the references to the life of the 'happy man'. The ideal of the *beatus vir* emerges as a mosaic portrait that gives positive substance to the charges made against a corrupt and vicious world.

Horace's *Second Epode* was by no means the only place in which he developed the retirement theme. Equally important, and perhaps even more influential in seventeenth- and eighteenth-century England, was his *Satire II, vi*, containing the celebrated fable of the town and country mouse. Horace's poem includes a wonderful evocation of the retired life–based on the best authors, good food and wine, cheerful company and serious conversation–that he led at his Sabine farm outside Rome. Horace emerges from the poem as a sophisticated person taking comfort in sophisticated moderation. Pope's imitation of the second half of Horace's poem begins by serenely re-enacting the poise and tranquillity of Horace's retirement:

> O charming Noons! and Nights divine!
> Or when I sup, or when I dine,
> My Friends above, my Folks below,
> Chatting and laughing all-a-row,
> The Beans and Bacon set before 'em,
> The Grace-cup serv'd with all decorum:
> Each willing to be pleas'd, and please,
> And even the very Dogs at ease! (133–40)

Pope then goes on to retell the fable of the town and country mouse. In doing so he captures, with urbanity and wit, the essence of Horace's fable defending the life of moderation free from anxieties. The closing speech of the country mouse, as he does his best to remain polite while the cat interrupts his courtly banquet, will have to suffice here to indicate Pope's control of ironic understatement and compression as he moves to a final emphasis on the retirement ideals of frugality and freedom:

> 'An't please your Honour, quoth the Peasant,
> This same Dessert is not so pleasant:
> Give me again my hollow Tree!
> A Crust of Bread, and Liberty.

(220–3)

Allusions to the classical tradition of retirement are merged in Pope's later poetry with allusions to another literary tradition. This second tradition, which has been admirably traced by G.R. Hibbard in an essay which has been reprinted in *Essential Articles for the study of Alexander Pope*, concerns the praise of certain seventeenth-century English poets for the country house. Ben Jonson's *To Penshurst* and Marvell's *Upon Appleton House* are the outstanding achievements of this tradition. Both poets praise their respective houses because they are designed for dwelling in and not for display, and their estates because they yield a generous plenty but not a surfeit. The country house and its estate become symbolic in these poems of a social organism in which man and nature lead an interdependent existence. Man orders and cultivates nature: he does not ransack or despoil it. Above all the country house represents an acceptance, on the part of the owner, of the moral responsibilities falling on him to act as a generous host to the rural community. Such a way of life essentially belonged to the feudal past even in the seventeenth century, and it certainly did by the time Pope came to write about it. This, of course, makes it none the less real for Pope, but it is another reminder that he was, philosophically speaking, a conservative intent on preserving what he considered to be the best of the past.

What Pope did with his small villa and garden of five acres at Twickenham was to act out in miniature a fusion of these two literary traditions. The moderation of the happy man and the hospitality of the country house are merged in both the actual and the fictional life of Pope the husbandman-cum-host:

Content with little, I can piddle here
On Broccoli and mutton round the year;
But ancient friends, (tho' poor, or out of play)
That touch my Bell, I cannot turn away.
'Tis true, no Turbots dignify my boards,
But gudgeons, flounders, what my Thames affords.
To Hounslow-heath I point, and Bansted-down,
Thence comes your mutton, and these chicks my own:
From yon old wallnut-tree a show'r shall fall;
And grapes, long-lingring on my only wall,
And figs, from standard and Espalier join:
The dev'l is in you if you cannot dine.
Then chearful healths (your Mistress shall have place)
And, what's more rare, a Poet shall say *Grace*.
Imitation of Horace, Satire II, ii, (137–50)

A detailed discussion of Pope's views on landscape gardening, and of his cultivation of his own and his friends' gardens, will be found in the next chapter, but one aspect of his garden calls for comment here. This is the famous grotto, which connected his house and garden by providing a passageway underneath the main London to Hampton Court road that separated them. If the need for a grotto can be explained in utilitarian terms, its decoration with shells, stones, pieces of tile, glass and rock, soon outstripped bare necessity. 'He extracted an ornament from an inconvenience', says Dr Johnson in his *Life of Pope*, 'and vanity produced a grotto where necessity enforced a passage'. Pope's grotto came to sum up, more than any other part of his estate, the deep significance, both for him and his poetry, of the retirement theme. As a series of decorated caverns or underground rooms opening up on one another, it suggested associations with worship (the temple of Zeus), with inspired pronouncement (the oracle at Delphi), with contemplation (the retreat of hermits and saints) and with refuge (David's Cave at En-gedi when pursued by Saul, in 1 Samuel, 24):

Know, all the distant Din that World can keep
Rolls o'er my *Grotto*, and but sooths my Sleep.
There, my Retreat the best Companions grace,
Chiefs, out of War, and Statesmen, out of Place,
There *St John* mingles with my friendly Bowl,
The Feast of Reason and the Flow of Soul:
Imitation of Horace, Sat. II, i, (123–8)

I have suggested in the foregoing paragraphs some of the connotations and allusions that the country held for Pope, especially in his later poetry. One last account of the retirement ideal, found in his *Imitation of Horace, Epistle 1, vii*, written in the octosyllabic manner of Dr Swift, will bring this chapter to an appropriate close since it relates the ideal to the poet's own life at Twickenham:

> Give me, I cry'd (enough for me)
> My Bread, and Independency!
> So bought an Annual Rent or two.
> And liv'd — just as you see I do;
> Near fifty, and without a Wife,
> I trust that sinking Fund, my Life.
> Can I retrench? Yes, mighty well,
> Shrink back to my Paternal Cell,
> A little House, with Trees a-row,
> And like its Master, very low,
> There dy'd my Father, no man's Debtor,
> And there I'll die nor worse nor better.
>
> (69–80)

We have here the familiar stress on self-sufficiency ('My Bread'), and self-reliance ('Independency'), coupled with an acceptance that further retrenchment is possible if necessary. The poet rejects the hectic life of the town (see lines 7–14) in favour of the tranquil life of the country. The ideal of the 'little house with trees a-row', which takes over from the 'dust' (11), 'fevers' (13) and 'pox' (14) of the town, is saved from becoming sentimental by the poet's ironic treatment of himself — the joking comparison of his old age to Walpole's Sinking Fund, which likewise had done nothing to hinder inexorable accumulation, and the pun on his own stature, 'And like its master very low'.

Pope's affirmation of the life of rural retirement is not to be confused with a life of rural solitude, or with a life of rural ease. His retirement is not a hermitlike retreat undertaken for the sake of meditation, as in the poetry of Vaughan, where the poet uses his natural surroundings in order to achieve a mystical union with God, nor is it an indolent withdrawal to pleasure and plenty, such as we find in Pomfret's extraordinarily popular poem, *The Choice*, first published in 1700. Pope's retirement is an alternative to the ambitious bustle of the city. His commitment is to society, and his retirement is offered as a better model for society to form itself on, not as personal seclusion or comfortable escape.

A view of Pope's house in 1735

An Exact DRAUGHT and VIEW of M.r POPE'S HOUSE at TWICKENHAM.

59

3. The Kindred Arts

First follow NATURE, and your Judgement frame
By her just Standard, which is still the same:
Unerring Nature, still divinely bright
One *clear, unchang'd*, and *Universal* Light,
Life, Force, and Beauty, must to all impart,
At once the *Source*, and *End*, and *Test* of *Art*.
                    An Essay on Criticism, 1711, (68–73)

How oft' our slowly-growing works impart,
While images reflect from art to art?
                    Epistle to Mr Jervas, 1716, (19–20)

Different kinds of artists express the consciousness of their age through different media and in different ways. But to the extent that any creative artifact is the product of the civilization in which it is born, so the different art forms of any period are bound to bear a certain analogous relationship to one another. Pope's poetry, however, bears very much more than this inevitable relationship to the other art forms of his time. Pope was himself an enthusiastic amateur painter and an ardent landscape gardener. In addition he was knowledgeable about architecture, interested in sculpture and appreciative of music. As a result we find in his work not just a general relationship between poetry and the other arts, but a detailed set of correspondences in which the technical terms of other art forms are frequently used as images and allusions in his own.

Without falling into the trap of drawing simple parallels between different art forms, Pope managed to use his awareness of the different potential of contrasting media to extend the expressiveness and complexity of his poetry. As he says in his *Epistle to Mr Jervas* while talking about the relationship between poetry and painting:

How oft' our slowly-growing works impart,
While images reflect from art to art?

(19–20)

The idea of images reflecting, rather than repeating, from art to art is crucial, for it enables the viewer to see the same object in a varying light, and in different degrees of distortion from reality, depending on the reflecting surface. Pope is fully aware of the autonomous nature of the kindred arts, but he is also aware of the rich response available to the person who is sensitive to a variety of art forms. In his poetry we find a mutual commerce, rather than a strict barter, between the arts. In this chapter I discuss Pope's knowledge of, and delight in, the other fine arts of his time, and show how an understanding of these relationships enriches an appreciation of his poetry.

Architecture

Pope's interest in architecture is closely related to his friendship with Lord Burlington. Richard Boyle, the Third Earl of Burlington, was a young man of twenty when Pope, six years his senior, first met him in 1715. The two men seem to have taken an immediate liking to one another, and, as Pope's correspondence bears witness, struck up an affectionate friendship that lasted throughout Pope's life. Lord Burlington was immensely wealthy, owning extensive properties in Yorkshire and Ireland. He used his wealth to support most of the fine arts, but especially that of architecture. He became patron to a group of persons, including William Kent and Colen Campbell, who were instrumental in changing the direction of English architecture away from the baroque style that had been made so popular by Wren, towards the Palladian style that was to become the leading fashion in the eighteenth century.

Burlington and his circle popularized the simple and classical lines of the Italian architect, Andrea Palladio (1508–80), and his English successor, Inigo Jones (1573–1652). They were especially influential in establishing Palladianism with respect to the gentleman's country house, which they saw as a villa that was a dwelling place related to its rural surroundings rather than a palace full of magnificence, such as Vanbrugh had designed for Marlborough at Blenheim. The Palladian villa should be formal enough to be elevated and elegant, but it must avoid becoming massive and extravagant. The most notable Palladian villa in the eighteenth century was Burlington's own temple of the arts at Chiswick (see p. 62), built between 1725 and 1729, and modelled on Palladio's Rotonda in the suburbs of Vicenza (see p. 62). Pope's own house at Twickenham (see p. 59), only five miles upstream from Chiswick House, was another example of the Palladian villa, but this time on a more modest scale. It is revealing that Pope kept busts of both Palladio and Inigo Jones in his library, as did Burlington at the entrance to his villa.

The essential principle of Palladio's architecture was that it should imitate nature. 'Since architecture, like all the other arts, imitates nature, nothing in it can satisfy that is foreign from what is found in nature', he wrote in his architectural treatise, *I Quattro Libri dell' Architettura*, published in 1570 but not translated into

Palladio's Rotunda at Vicenza (above) and Burlington's Villa at Chiswick (below.)

English until 1715. Such a definition depends, of course, on what one understands by nature. Palladio did not mean that architecture had to copy visible reality, but that it should base itself on the principles of hierarchy, proportion and harmony that he considered to permeate God's creation at large. For Palladio and his admirers, the best architecture must have a direct, albeit stylised, relationship to nature. This involved accepting certain rules inherent in nature — especially those of mathematical proportion — and working as harmoniously as possible within them. It is not difficult to see a similar principle of artistic creation underlying Pope's handling of his couplet art.

Pope's views on architecture are most clearly set out in his *Epistle to Burlington*, first published in 1731. In this poem he insists that Taste is not something that can be bought. Lord Burlington shows us, he says, that Rome was 'glorious not profuse', and that in the best architecture the design is directly related to the use. In architecture, as in poetry, mere outward show does not fool the connoisseur:

> Oft have you hinted to your brother Peer,
> A certain truth, which many buy too dear:
> Something there is more needful than Expence,
> And something previous ev'n to Taste — 'tis Sense:
> Good Sense, which only is the gift of Heav'n,
> And tho' no science, fairly worth the sev'n:
> A Light, which in yourself you must perceive;
> Jones and Le Nôtre have it not to give.
>
> (39–46)

True taste is shaped by 'Sense'. The word suggests various levels of meaning. It involves a proper use of judgment, a kind of common-sense; it involves an ability to respond with feeling, a use of the physical senses; and it involves a certain intuitive grasp, or sixth sense. Finally, it is a quality that one can only discover for oneself; it cannot be acquired secondhand. Thus those who build according to Burlington's rules without understanding them, like those who try to write couplets by rote, merely make blunders out of beauty and fill half the land with imitating fools.

Pope's second great architectural principle in this poem involves a restatement of that emphasis on imitating nature seen in the quotation from Palladio. Again, the principle underlies Pope's conception of his own poetry as well as of Burlington's architecture. The following passage, which binds the two arts of architecture and landscape gardening together should be compared with the famous passage from *An Essay on Criticism* (68–79), beginning 'First follow NATURE, . . .'

To build, to plant, whatever you intend,
To rear the Column, or the Arch to bend,
To swell the Terras, or to sink the Grot;
In all, let Nature never be forgot.

(47–50).

Landscape gardening

After the Restoration of the English monarchy and the return of
Charles II's court from Paris, the prevailing taste in English
gardening became clearly based on the formal gardens of Holland
and France. The most influential gardener in Europe was the
Frenchman, André Le Nôtre (1613–1700), who was responsible
for Louis XIV's elaborate display at Versailles, where the gardens
covered more than 15,000 acres. In gardens of this style everything was laid out according to a strict geometric pattern, divided
into symmetrical units composed of parterres embroidered in floral
scrollwork, terraces, rectangular pools and fountains, and intersect-
ing avenues of trees. Each section of the garden would be marked
off with straight boundaries of clipped hedges, canals or walls so
that the total effect was that of a vast ornamental quilt. The
perspective view of the Duke of Devonshire's gardens at Chatsworth
(see p. 65) shows a garden laid out according to this style at the
end of the seventeenth century.

At the beginning of the eighteenth century a few English professional gardeners, notably Charles Bridgeman (d. 1738) who
created the famous gardens at Stowe; Stephen Switzer (c. 1682–
1745) the royal gardener; and William Kent (1684–1748) Lord
Burlington's protégé, began to break away from such artificial
and restricted designs. While not departing completely from the
formal garden, they strove for something less regular and more
natural. Switzer says in his *Ichnographia Rustica*, 1718, that a little
regularity may be permitted near the house, but beyond that the
designer should pursue nature. Charles Bridgeman is perhaps best
known for his introduction of the sunken fence or *ha-ha,* which was
borrowed from the art of fortification and enabled the gardener
to open up vistas previously shut off by fences and walls. Thus
the gentleman's park could be 'called in' to the view of his
garden.

Later in the century the movement against regularity and
symmetry became more pronounced until, by the time of Lancelot
('Capability') Brown (1716–83), gardens were created that were
meant to look as much like nature as possible, although the prospect
was, of course, very carefully shaped by man. All boundaries and
sharp edges were softened; trees were placed in belts or clumps
rather than avenues or quincunxes; rivers and lakes were used

Chatsworth House being ye Seat of his Grace ye Duke and of Her Maty household (Chief Justice in Eyre of all her Majties Forrests Chaces Parks

Earl of Devonshire, Marquis of Hartington, Baron of Hardwick, Lᵈ Steward &c. Trent North and Kᵗ of the Most Noble Order of the Garter —

View of Chatsworth

65

wherever possible to give gentle serenity to the middle distance; and everything was done to bring out undulating contours that would provide a natural equivalent to Hogarth's serpentine line of grace, and 'lead the eye a wanton kind of chase'.

Pope's place within this tradition is contemporaneous with that of Bridgeman, Switzer and Kent. Traditionally Pope has been regarded as a pioneer in landscape gardening, but more recent scholarship (see James Sambrook, 'Pope and the Visual Arts', in *Alexander Pope*, ed. P. Dixon, 1972) has emphasized his role as a publicist of the professional gardeners' views rather than as a practical pioneer. Pope had far too independent a mind and imagination, however, to be content with merely publicizing other people's views. The important point, whether we see him as a pioneer or publicist, is that he belongs in the forefront of those who were striving to create gardens of greater irregularity. As early as 1713 we find him attacking the artificiality of formal gardens, and especially the modern practice of topiary, in *Guardian* No. 173. The main principle on which his views of gardening are founded in this essay is similar to that underlying his views on architecture and poetry: 'There is certainly something in the amiable Simplicity of unadorned Nature that spreads over the Mind a more noble sort of Tranquillity, and a loftier Sensation of Pleasure than can be raised from the nicer Scenes of Art'. His preference for nature over art in gardening leads on to his view, expressed later in the essay, that 'all Art consists in the Imitation and Study of Nature'.

Pope's own practice as a gardener dates from 1719, when he rented his villa at Twickenham together with five acres of ground on the other side of the London to Hampton Court road. During the remaining twenty-five years of his life, this garden and the grotto that joined it to his house became the cherished pastime of his recreation. We know a great deal about it because of the plan made by his gardener and trusted servant, John Searle, in 1745 (see p. 68). Fifteen years after this, Horace Walpole described it in a letter to Horace Mann, written on 20 June 1760:

> In short, it was a little bit of ground of five acres, enclosed with three lanes, and seeing nothing. Pope had twisted and twirled; and rhymed and harmonised this, till it appeared two or three sweet little lawns opening and opening beyond one another, and the whole surrounded by thick inpenetrable woods.

The guiding principle in its layout seems to have been to surprise the viewer pleasantly with changing perspectives and moving patterns of light and shade. Around the boundary of the garden there was the darkness of the woods, or 'wilderness', and the shade of the serpentine paths that meandered through them. At the centre lay a light and open lawn used as a bowling green. From this point

Kent's drawing of the Shell Temple in Pope's garden

one had views of the garden's two main features which lay at opposite ends of a central axis. At the western end stood an obelisk in memory of his mother, and at the eastern end the Shell Temple that marked the entrance to the grotto. 'From the River Thames', wrote Pope in a letter to Martha Blount's father in June 1725,

> you see thro' my arch up a walk of the wilderness to a kind of open temple, wholly composed of shells in the rustic manner; and from that distance under the temple you look down thro' a sloping arcade of trees, and see the sails on the river passing suddenly and vanishing, as thro' a perspective glass.

Such surprising images and luminous glimpses were an indispensable part of the overall effect in Pope's garden.

It was, of course, a garden designed on a miniature scale compared with the great landscape estates of Pope's wealthy and noble friends—such as Lord Bathurst's at Cirencester, or Lord Burlington's at Chiswick, or Ralph Allen's at Prior Park—but this does not mean that it was either trivial or inconsequential. Pope's friends took his gardening as seriously as he did and frequently sent him presents

67

1 Grass plot between the house and the River Thames 2 The house 3 Grotto and underground passage
4 Road from Hampton Court to London 5 Shell temple 6 Large mount 7 Stoves (i.e. hothouses)
8 Vineyard 9 Obelisk in memory of Pope's mother 10 Small mounts 11 Bowling green
12 Grove 13 Orangery 14 Garden house 15 Kitchen garden 16 Amphitheatre (?)
▫ Square marks indicate urns and statues

of plants or statues for the garden and a wide variety of stones, fossils, bits of marble, flints, pebbles, fragments of crystal, shells and pieces of rock for his grotto. Pope's garden was as carefully wrought as his poetry. Like his poetry it was full of allusions to the past, such as the busts of classical figures and the memorial to his mother, and like the poetry it was imbued with a basic moral significance that stood as a natural expression of the peaceful life of rural retirement he so valued.

His views on gardening are developed most fully in the same poem as are his views on architecture: *The Epistle to Burlington*. The two arts have much in common. Whether one intends to build or plant, nature must 'never be forgot'. This is the great principle that Burlington exemplifies at Chiswick and that Cobham demonstrates so triumphantly at Stowe:

> Nature shall join you, Time shall make it grow
> A Work to wonder at — perhaps a STOW.
>
> (69–70)

Conversely, this is what Timon singularly fails to do in the rigid formal gardens that surround his villa:

> The suff'ring eye inverted Nature sees,
> Trees cut to Statues, Statues thick as trees,
>
> (119–120)

Nature then is the most important guiding principle, but in treating nature the artist, whether architect or gardener, must use an urbane tact. He must neither over- nor under-dress her. The key thing is to suggest as well as to show:

> Let not each beauty ev'ry where be spy'd,
> Where half the skill is decently to hide.
> He gains all points, who pleasingly confounds,
> Surprizes, varies, and conceals the Bounds.
>
> (53–6)

The last couplet here is as appropriate to Pope's own poetry as it is to gardening. He 'pleasingly confounds' the reader by concealing, through a great variety of ways fully discussed in Part Two, the regular bounds of the closed couplet form.

Pope next goes on to argue that the gardener must 'consult the genius of the place'; that is, he must consider the inherent quality or prevailing character, of the place and bring it out in its best colours rather than force a preconceived pattern on the area.

Plan of Pope's garden, re-drawn from Serle's plan, 1745

View of such parts as are seen from the Building at the Head of the Lake.

Vüe de ce qui se voit du Batiment a la Tête du Lac.

The gardens at Stowe as they were re-worked by Kent, showing a softening of the Bridgeman outline.

The gardens at Stowe as they were designed by Bridgeman.

Consult the genius of the Place in all;
That tells the Waters or to rise, or fall,
Or helps th' ambitious Hill the heav'n to scale,
Or scoops in circling theatres the Vale,
Calls in the Country, catches opening glades,
Joins willing woods, and varies shades from shades,
Now breaks or now directs th' intending Lines;
Paints as you plant, and, as you work, designs.

(57–64)

Pope describes the gardener's method here in terms of a landscape painter's. Indeed the landscape paintings of Claude Lorrain and the Poussins were an important influence on the development of gardening in eighteenth-century England. Spence records Pope as saying, in 1734, that 'all gardening is landscape painting. Just like a landscape hung up' (Anecdote no. 606). In the lines from the *Epistle to Burlington* just quoted, the gardener, by consulting the genius of the place, 'catches' opening glades as a landscape painter catches a special mood, or he 'varies shades from shades' as a landscape painter plays with effects of light and colour on his canvas. In the last line of the paragraph the analogy becomes explicit, 'paints as you plant', and then moves on to incorporate an image from architecture as well, 'and, as you work, designs'. This is a good example of the reflection of images from art to art that we find in Pope's poetry. Technical terms from landscape painting and architecture are used to describe the guiding principles of gardening, and the better one understands the background of the terms the more one appreciates the allusiveness of Pope's poetry.

Painting

Poetry and painting have traditionally had very close links with one another. Of all the visual arts these two have been referred to most frequently as the 'sister arts', while the correspondences between them have been commented on by literary critics, art historians and aestheticians alike. One of the earliest of such comments is Horace's celebrated phrase *ut pictura poesis* (*Ars Poetica*, 361), 'as a painting, so a poem'. Unfortunately Horace's phrase has too frequently been taken out of context to assert a parallel relationship between the two arts rather than to suggest, as Horace does, a comparison between them. What Horace actually says is that some poems please only once whereas others bear continual rereading, just as some paintings only please when placed in a dark corner of a gallery while others continue to please after constant viewing in full light. He is not saying that poetry must always be like painting, although many later critics have tended to take his phrase this way.

The Frenchman, Charles Alphonse Du Fresnoy, in his influential Latin poem *De Arte Graphica*, originally published in 1667 but first translated into English as *The Art of Painting*, by John Dryden in 1695, takes up such a position. He quotes Horace's phrase, *ut pictura poesis*, in the opening lines of the poem and then goes on to argue that not only should poetry be like painting, but painting should be like poetry. Du Fresnoy's poem is expanded by a set of remarks, written by Roger de Piles and also translated by Dryden, who argues that poetry and painting are so nearly related that whoever thoroughly examines them will find them so much resembling one another that he cannot take them for less than sisters:

> They both of them aim at the same end, which is Imitation. Both of them excite our passions, and we suffer ourselves willingly to be deceiv'd, both by the one, and by the other; our eyes and souls are so fixt to them, that we are ready to persuade ourselves that the painted bodies breath and that the fictions are truth.

Dryden, in his preface to the translation, entitled 'Preface of the Translator, With a Parallel of Poetry and Painting', lists three main ways in which the two arts are parallel — the Invention, the Design, and the Colouring — and then goes on to elaborate on these general areas of parallelism in considerable detail.

We know that Pope was familiar with Du Fresnoy's treatise and Dryden's translation because he wrote his *Epistle to Mr Jervas* to accompany a revised version of it. In this poem, written about 1715, Pope expresses the hope that his poetry and Jervas's paintings may share a similarly successful partnership:

> Read these instructive leaves, in which conspire
> *Fresnoy*'s close art, and *Dryden*'s native fire:
> And reading wish, like theirs, our fate and fame,
> So mix'd our studies, and so join'd our name,
> Like them to shine thro' long succeeding age,
> So just thy skill, so regular my rage.
>
> (7–12)

It is noticeable that Pope does not say in these lines, as Dryden does in his Preface, that painting and poetry should have a 'parallel' relationship, but that they should share a partnership. The painter and the poet should mix, not repeat or copy, their studies. They should draw inspiration from each other, but remain autonomous. Pope continues:

73

Smit with the love of Sister-arts we came,
And met congenial, mingling flame with flame;
Like friendly colours found them both unite,
And each from each contract new strength and light.

(13-16)

The image Pope presents is that of two artists sharing ideas for the sake of mutual, but independent, re-creation.

Pope was interested in painting throughout his life. 'Which, Sir, gives you the most pleasure, poetry or painting?' asked Spence in May 1730. 'I really can't well say,' Pope replied, 'both of them are so extremely pleasing'. This interest in painting reached its greatest intensity in 1713 when he took a course of lessons with Charles Jervas, a well-established portrait painter. Pope wrote to Caryll on 30 April 1713 saying: 'I've been almost everyday employed in following your advice in learning to paint in which I am most particularly obliged to Mr Jervas, who gives me daily instructions and examples'. Four months later we find him writing to Gay giving a long and witty account of his progress:

I have been near a week in London, where I am like to remain, till I become by Mr. Jervas's help, *Elegans Formarum Spectator.* I begin to discover beauties that were till now imperceptible to me. Every corner of an eye, or turn of a nose or ear, the smallest degree of light or shade on a cheek, or in a dimple, have charms to distract me. . . . I have thrown away three Dr. Swift's, each of which was once my vanity, two Lady Bridgewaters, a Duchess of Montague, besides half a dozen Earls, and one Knight of the Garter. I have crucify'd Christ over again in effigie, and made a Madonna as old as her mother St. Anne. Nay, what is yet more miraculous, I have rival'd St. Luke himself in Painting, and as 'tis said an Angel came and finished his Piece, so you would swear a Devil put the last hand to mine, 'tis so begrimed and smutted. However I comfort myself with a Christian reflection, that, I have not broken the Commandment, for my pictures are not the likeness of anything in heaven above or in earth below, or in the waters under the earth. Neither will anybody adore or worship them, except the Indians should have a sight of 'em, who they tell us, worship certain Pagods or Idols purely for their ugliness.

This period of total immersion in the sister art of painting seems to have come to an end about the spring of 1714 when he turned back to the serious business of translating the *Iliad*. 'I shall now be very much taken up in this work', he says in a letter to Caryll on 25 February 1714, 'which will keep me a poet (in spite of something

74

I lately thought a resolution to the contrary) for some years longer'. Pope's friendship with Jervas did not end at this point; indeed he continued to use Jervas's house in Cleveland Court as his regular residence when he was in London, but the temptation to give up poetry for painting did.

This great delight in painting influenced Pope's poetry in a number of ways. The most important of these is the highly pictorial quality of much of his best poetry. When he describes the shot pheasant, panting for life on the ground in *Windsor-Forest*, he does so like a painter, concentrating on the brilliance of the pheasant's colours more than any other quality:

> Ah! what avail his glossie, varying Dyes,
> His Purple Crest, and Scarlet-circled Eyes,
> The vivid Green his shining Plumes unfold;
> His painted Wings, and Breast that flames with Gold?
>
> (115–18)

The magnificent splendour of the bird's plumage heightens the pathos of his death. The scene is a verbal equivalent to the sort of visual detail that a painter of a still life, like Jan Weenix, might revel in. We find the same pictorial stylization of nature when we come to the description of the fishes a little later in the same poem:

> Our plenteous Streams a various Race supply;
> The bright-ey'd Perch with Fins of *Tyrian* Dye,
> The Silver Eel, in shining Volumes roll'd,
> The yellow Carp, in Scales bedrop'd with Gold,
> Swift Trouts, diversify'd with Crimson Stains,
> And Pykes, the Tyrants of the watry Plains.
>
> (141–6)

Here the rich variousness of the colours pays tribute to the plenitude of God's creation. Again there is very little motion to the scene. The fish are caught in stasis so that their dazzling colours may be the focus of attention.

This painter's interest in colour is just as strong when Pope is dealing with personified concepts or realms of imaginary being as when he is dealing with actual Nature. His descriptions of 'Black Melancholy' in *Eloisa to Abelard* (163–170), or of 'the gloomy Cave of Spleen' in *The Rape of the Lock* (Canto IV, 17–54) are presented with a painter's sensitivity for the delicate contrasts of light and shade. A further example of the pictorial quality of Pope's poetry occurs in *The Dunciad* (Book IV, 21–30). In these lines Pope uses neither colour nor light and shade. Nevertheless the reader is made to visualize the scene through a series of descriptive details that make the Queen of Dulness's abstract captives vividly real:

Beneath her foot-stool, *Science* groans in Chains,
And *Wit* dreads Exile, Penalties and Pains.
There foam'd rebellious *Logic*, gagg'd and bound,
There, stript, fair *Rhet'ric* languish'd on the ground;
His blunted Arms by *Sophistry* are born,
And shameless *Billingsgate* her Robes adorn.
Morality, by her false Guardians drawn,
Chicane in Furs, and *Casuistry* in Lawn,
Gasps, as they straiten at each end the cord,
And dies, when Dulness gives her Page the word.

The descriptions of the forms of imprisonment and torture and the details of dress are highly pictorial. The scene seems to be based on a satirical inversion of one of those grand allegorical history tableaux, such as Sir James Thornhill's painting of William III trampling over Tyranny on the ceiling of the Great Hall at Greenwich, or Rubens's painting of the apotheosis of James I on the ceiling of the Banqueting Hall at Whitehall, that were so popular during the seventeenth and eighteenth centuries.

Another way in which Pope's interest in art seems to have influenced his poetry concerns his satirical character sketches. Although these partly derive from the literary tradition of the *character* going back to Theophrastus, they also derive from the pictorial tradition of the caricature originating with Annibale Carracci (1560–1609). The literary tradition of the *character* tended to describe types rather than individuals and to do so in a fairly realistic way, while the pictorial tradition of the caricature attacked recognizable persons by exaggerating certain defects at the expense of any attractive qualities. To this extent Pope's lines on Atticus, Bufo and Sporus in *An Epistle to Dr Arbuthnot* owe as much, if not more, to the caricature as to the *character*. The similarities between the artistic re-creation and the actual person are great enough to cause recognition, while at the same time the distortions are strong enough to cause laughter or disgust.

The outstanding example of Pope the caricaturist at work is the *Epistle to a Lady*. Here the reader imagines he is being conducted round an art gallery by the painter-poet:

How many pictures of one Nymph we view,
All how unlike each other, all how true!

(5–6)

We are shown outline portraits of twelve ladies in all, and each one is consistent only in being inconsistent. Pope captures their inconsistency in a series of taut and witty couplets, much as a caricaturist would with a few quick strokes of the brush:

Pictures like these, dear Madam, to design,
Asks no firm hand, and no unerring line;
Some wand'ring touch, or some reflected light,
Some flying stroke alone can hit 'em right:
For how should equal Colours do the knack?
Chameleons who can paint in white and black?

(151–6)

The glittering surface attraction of each portrait rapidly gives
way to the inconsistency beneath. The variegated colours of the
artist's palette are necessary, as Pope ironically points out in the last
couplet above, to paint such superficial and changeable personalities.

A further influence of painting on Pope's poetry is suggested by
comparing the narrative technique of his tale of Sir Balaam at the
end of the *Epistle to Bathurst* with that of Hogarth in his comic
history cycles. Pope's lines describe Balaam rising, by various
stages, to a position of great social success, only to conclude with a
crashing fall as Balaam 'curses God and dies'. The narrative structure
of rise and fall and the strong moral disapproval of affectation
are similar to those of Hogarth, but at the same time it needs to
be made clear that Pope draws a somewhat different moral from
that which we might expect Hogarth to draw. Pope sees Sir Balaam's
financial success as a merchant as the inevitable beginning of his
downfall, whereas Hogarth would have seen it as a just reward for
his industry.

Finally it is worth noting that Pope also uses his knowledge of the
technical terms of painting in the traditional Horatian way, that is,
as a form of imagery for writing about poetry. Thus in the *Essay on
Criticism* he uses the analogy with painting to illustrate his belief
that literary reputations will fade away as language changes:

So when the faithful *Pencil* has design'd
Some *bright Idea* of the Master's Mind,
Where a *new World* leaps out at his command,
And ready Nature waits upon his Hand;
When the ripe Colours *soften* and *unite*,
And sweetly *melt* into just Shade and Light,
When mellowing Years their full Perfection give,
And each Bold Figure just begins to *Live*;
The *treach'rous Colours* the fair Art betray,
And all the bright Creation fades away!

(484–93)

Pope was fortunately wrong about true literary merit, which has
always endured despite changes in the language, but the analogy
remains a good one to close this section with, for the traditional
comparison between poetry and painting could hardly be more fully

developed than in this passage. The three main ways in which Dryden claimed in his Preface to Du Fresnoy that the two arts are parallel — through the Design, the Invention and the Colouring — are each elaborated by Pope before he moves to the final comparison between the fading colours of a painting and the fading language of a poem. So far as Pope is concerned the colours of a painting are its least important element. They are potentially 'treach'rous'; the painter who indulges in them for themselves alone is like the poet who has mere verbal ornamentation to offer and no powers of overall design. This is the reason why Pope describes the human and the supernatural beings in *The Rape of the Lock* in such glittering colours. It is his way of establishing their momentary attraction and their long term transience at one and the same time.

Sculpture

Sculpture had been considered one of the sister arts in England since the time of the Restoration when, as Pope says in the *Imitation of Horace, Epistle II, i*, 'Marble soften'd into life grew warm' (147). In the last forty years of the seventeenth century the analogy between sculpture and poetry became almost as common with literary critics as that between painting and poetry. Indeed one might well talk of an *ut sculptura poesis* tradition existing alongside *ut pictura poesis*. Pope more or less does this when, in writing about the art of classical times in his poem *To Mr Addison, Occasioned by his Dialogue on Medals*, 1720, he says:

> The verse and sculpture bore an equal part,
> And Art reflected images to Art.
>
> (51–2)

As in his lines on the relationship of painting and poetry in the *Epistle to Jervas*, the key word in establishing the relationship between sculpture and poetry is 'reflect'. The two arts mutually reinforce one another. At the same time as one remarks on this relationship, however, one should beware of making too much of it. Pope never became as deeply immersed in sculpture as he did in painting, and his verse never took on marked sculptural qualities in the same way that it clearly took on marked pictorial ones.

The growth of interest in sculpture that occurred in England after the Restoration was a revival of earlier sculpture, especially that of Rome, rather than a growth in creative output. As Margaret Whinney says in her definitive study, *Sculpture in Britain, 1530–1830*, 'it is a regrettable fact that the general level of English sculpture of the second half of the seventeenth century is far below the

Figures on Bethlem Gate.

'*Great Cibber's brazen, brainless brothers.*' Dunciad, *II 32,*

Continental average'. The best sculptor of the time was Caius Gabriel Cibber, a native of Holstein who settled in England at the time of the Commonwealth, and who was the father of Pope's great enemy, Colley Cibber. By far the most successful of Cibber's sculptures were the two highly realistic figures of Raving and Melancholy Madness made for the entrance to Bedlam Hospital. These are the statues which Pope somewhat cruelly refers to at the beginning of *The Dunciad* as Cibber's 'brazen, brainless brothers'.

English sculpture of the first half of the eighteenth century was very much more distinguished than that of the preceding period. It was, however, almost entirely dominated by foreign sculptors, especially the Fleming, Michael Rysbrack (1694–1770), who was the leading sculptor of the 1720s and 1730s; and the Frenchman, Louis François Roubiliac (1702/05–62); who succeeded him in eminence from about 1740. These sculptors introduced a strong classical influence, the popularity of which was increased by the fashion for the English gentleman to finish his education by going on the Grand Tour. As a result most sculptors showed their subjects in Roman drapes and in heroic attitudes. The portrait bust grew greatly in popularity and, from the death of Kneller in 1723 to the return of Reynolds from Italy in 1753, it seemed to take over from portrait painting as the most fashionable way of preserving one's image for posterity. According to Margaret Whinney, a gallery of busts became 'the normal decoration of a gentleman's library'. The *Inventory of Pope's Goods Taken after his Death* lists no pictures in his library, which is the more striking when we consider that the inventory lists over fifty portraits on display at other points in the house. In the library the *Inventory* lists marble busts of Homer, Newton, Spenser, Shakespeare, Milton and Dryden, and plaster of paris busts of Shakespeare, Palladio and Inigo Jones. Thus Pope's library, like his garden and his poetry, was packed with literary and classical allusions.

Pope himself sat for both Rysbrack and Roubiliac. Rysbrack's marble bust of him, made about 1725–30, was done in the prevailing Roman style. It shows Pope in a heroic and lofty pose, and as an idealization of him it has great strength. But it apparently bore little likeness to Pope, who wrote to the Earl of Oxford saying that all he could say for it was that 'he neither made the Busto, nor himself'. Roubiliac carved four marble busts of Pope between 1738 and 1741, and these seem to have earned far greater approval from Pope. They are all similar in size and attitude and suggest, with polished simplicity, both the power of the poet's intellectual penetration and the physical suffering he endured.

The poem that most clearly demonstrates Pope's interest in sculpture is *The Temple of Fame*, an allegorical dream vision based on Chaucer's *House of Fame*, first published in 1715. It is a highly pictorial poem, full of visual effects linked to Pope's interest in architecture and painting as well as sculpture. The opening landscape, as the dreamer-poet looks down on the earth, has a Claude-like quality, while the temple of fame itself is a 'glorious pile' designed to excel the architectural beauty of anything in Rome, Greece or Babylon. Statues of heroes in 'animated marble' and legislators who 'seem to think in stone' grace the walls of the temple, which has four fronts, each one standing for a different civilization. Rising from the architrave on the Western Front, which represents Greek civilization, there are statues of Theseus, Perseus, Alcides (i.e., Hercules), Orpheus, Amphion and Cythaeraea. Pope's own footnote tells us that the description of Hercules is 'drawn with an eye to the position [posture] of the famous statue of Farnese'.

In the middle of the temple are six columns on which are placed the statues of the greatest men of learning of all time. The select six are Homer, Virgil, Pindar, Horace, Aristotle and Cicero, and each column is adorned, as Pope's note tells us 'with Sculptures taken from the most striking subjects of their works; which Sculpture bears a Resemblance in its Manner and Character, to the Manner and Character of their Writings'. *Ut sculptura poesis* has become *ut poesis sculptura*. The relationship is a two-way one: images reflect from art to art. The distinguishing quality of the carving that ornaments the column reflects that of the writer's work who stands above it. Thus the carvings around Homer's column suggest the greatly admired 'fire' of his invention:

The Wars of *Troy* were round the Pillar seen:
Here fierce *Tydides* wounds the *Cyprian* Queen;
Here *Hector* glorious from *Patroclus'* Fall,
Here dragg'd in Triumph round the *Trojan* Wall.
Motion and Life did ev'ry Part inspire,
Bold was the Work, and prov'd the Master's Fire;
A strong Expression most he seem'd t'affect,
And here and there disclos'd a brave Neglect.

(188–95)

By contrast, Virgil's column suggests the perfection of his craftman-ship:

A Golden Column next in Rank appear'd,
On which a Shrine of purest Gold was rear'd;
Finish'd the whole, and labour'd ev'ry Part,
With patient Touches of unweary'd Art:
The *Mantuan* there in sober Triumph sate,
Compos'd his Posture, and his Look sedate;
On *Homer* still he fix'd a reverend Eye,
Great without Pride, in modest Majesty.

(196–203)

Pope refers to sculpture in other poems, but nowhere as extensively as in *The Temple of Fame*. Nevertheless it is quite clear that he sees sculpture as an essential member of the sisterhood of the arts in a cultured civilization. He makes this specific point in heralding the arrival of the Renaissance in *An Essay on Criticism*:

Then *Sculpture* and her *Sister-Arts* revive;
Stones leap'd to *Form*, and *Rocks* began to *live*;
With *sweeter Notes* each *rising Temple* rung;
A *Raphael* painted and a *Vida* sung!

(701–4)

One of Pope's most significant allusions to the art of sculpture is found in *The Dunciad*, Book III. At this point in the action Cibber has been transported to the Underworld and is experiencing a vision of what has happened, and what will happen, in the Empire of Dulness. The view of Rome is particularly distressing:

See, the Cirque falls, th' unpillar'd Temple nods,
Streets pav'd with Heroes, Tyber choak'd with Gods:
'Till Peter's keys some christ'ned Jove adorn,
And Pan to Moses lends his pagan horn;
See graceless Venus to a Virgin turn'd,
Or Phidias broken, and Apelles burn'd.

(107–12)

For Pope the great works of sculpture are as important a part of the creative achievements of mankind as the great works of literature, and this vision of their destruction is a significant pointer to the great Anarch's final triumph at the end of the poem.

Music

Of all the arts Music has the most right to be called the sister of poetry. A primitive harmony, symbolized in the mythical figure of Orpheus, had linked the two arts since classical times, although they had separated somewhat with the development of instrumental music in the sixteenth century. There was, however, a renewed impetus in the second half of the seventeenth century towards unifying them again. As Dryden says in his Dedication to *The Vocal and Instrumental Music of the Prophetess*, 1691:

> Music and poetry have ever been acknowledged Sisters, which walking hand in hand, support each other: As poetry is the harmony of words, so music is that of notes: and as poetry is a rise above prose and oratory, so is Music the exaltation of poetry. Both of them may excel apart, but sure they are most excellent when they are joined, because nothing is then wanting to either of their perfections: for thus they appear, like wit and beauty in the same person.

Dryden himself had considerable success in joining the two arts in his two lyrics, *A Song for St Cecilia's Day*, 1687 and *Alexander's Feast; Or the Power of Music, An Ode in Honour of St Cecilia's Day*, 1697, in which he suggests musical effects through a careful manipulation of words and metre. These two poems, and especially *Alexander's Feast*, were greatly admired in the eighteenth century, and we may perhaps take Dr Johnson's comment on this poem as a reasonably typical expression of eighteenth-century acclaim for it: 'The *Ode for St Cecilia's Day* . . . has always been considered as exhibiting the highest flight of fancy, and the exactest nicety of art. This is allowed to stand without a rival'.

Pope too tried his hand at this 'kind' of poem in his *Ode for Music, On St Cecilia's Day*, written about 1708. The poem is one of the young poet's experiments rather than something he felt deeply committed to, and it never reaches the heights of Dryden's two poems in this genre. Pope's account of Orpheus' journey to the Underworld, for example, becomes jangling rather than tragic, and the weight of rhythmical contrivance is far too heavily felt.

On his own admission Pope had no formal training in music. 'Did you ever learn anything of music?' asked Spence in 1744. 'Never,' Pope replied, 'but I had naturally a very good ear, and have often judged right of the best compositions in music by the force of that'. Despite Pope's lack of knowledge concerning the technical aspects of music he seems to have enjoyed it, and especially that of Handel whom he praised handsomely in *The Dunciad*, Book IV:

> Strong in new Arms, lo! Giant Handel stands,
> Like bold Briareus, with a hundred hands;
> To stir, to rouze, to shake the Soul he comes,
> And Jove's own Thunders follow Mars's Drums.
>
> (65–8)

Pope knew Handel through their common friendship with Lord Burlington and is reputed to have written some of the libretto for Handel's masque, *Esther*, first performed in 1720. On the other hand there is no evidence of collaboration between the two men for Handel's famous setting of the aria, 'Where e'er you walk', in his opera, *Semele*, 1744. The words were taken, verbatim, from Pope's second pastoral, *Summer* (73 ff.), written forty years earlier, but the librettist seems to have borrowed them without Pope's knowledge.

Pope's views on the relationship of poetry and music are most clearly set out in the *Essay on Criticism* where he scorns the great number of critics who judge poetry solely by its musical effect:

> But most by *Numbers* judge a Poet's Song,
> And *smooth* or *rough*, with them is *right* or *wrong*;
> In the bright *Muse* tho' thousand *Charms* conspire,
> Her *Voice* is all these tuneful Fools admire,
> Who haunt *Parnassus* but to please their Ear,
> Not mend their Minds; as some to *Church* repair,
> Not for the *Doctrine*, but the *Musick* there.
>
> (337–43)

This scorn for critics who overemphasize an attention to 'numbers' does not mean that he scorns a proper concern for 'numbers'. A concern for the sound of the poetry is an important part of the poet's craft, so long as it is fused with a concern for meaning and is not indulged in for itself. For Pope,

> 'Tis not enough no Harshness gives Offence,
> The *Sound* must seem an *Eccho* to the *Sense*.
>
> (364–5)

Dryden's *Alexander's Feast* is specifically picked out for praise on this account:

> The *Pow'rs of Musick* all our Hearts allow;
> And what *Timotheus* was, is *Dryden* now.
>
> (382–3)

Italian Opera, on the other hand, is attacked in *The Dunciad*, Book IV, as 'a Harlot form soft sliding by, /With mincing step,

83

small voice, and languid eye' (45–6), precisely because Pope felt it offered sound without sense. He sees it as an actual example of Dulness's success in triumphing over the arts of a civilized country. Pope was not alone in attacking Italian opera. It was one of the favourite targets of the Scriblerus Club, and of course John Gay's famous *Beggar's Opera*, 1728, was partly written as a reaction against it. The highly moral and chauvinistic attitude of the Tory satirists towards Italian opera is nowhere more clearly expressed than in the following words of Lord Bolingbroke, writing in *The Craftsman*, 17 March 1727:

> A very little Reflection on History will suggest this Observation; that every Nation has made either a great or inconsiderable Figure in the World, as it has fallen into Luxury or resisted its Temptations. . . . Operas and Masquerades, with all the politer Elegancies of a wanton Age, are much less to be regarded for their Expence (great as it is) than for the Tendency, which they have to deprave our Manners. MUSIC has something so peculiar in it, that it exerts a willing Tyranny, over the Mind, and forms the ductile Soul into whatever shape the Melody directs. Wise Nations have observed its Influence, and have therefore kept it under proper Regulations. . . . A well wrought story, attended with its prevailing Charms, will transport the Soul out of itself; fire it with glorious Emulation; and lift the Man into an Hero; but the soft *Italian* Music relaxes and unnerves the Soul, and sinks it into Weakness; so that while we receive their Music, we at the same time are adopting their Manners.

It is interesting to note that both Pope and Bolingbroke use the same adjective, 'soft', to describe Italian opera .One senses that the Tory satirists objected more to its social and political associations than to its musical quality.

It would be wrong to give the impression that Pope's poetry was deeply influenced by an interest in music, for this was clearly not the case. Of all the sister arts it probably influenced his poetry least. But it would be equally wrong not to challenge the charge, made by Dr Johnson of all people, that Pope was not only ignorant of the principles of music but was also 'insensible of its effects'.

I have tried to show in this chapter that Pope was interested in, and familiar with, the different art forms in the eighteenth century, and how his understanding and appreciation of them affected his poetry. This is not to say that the boundaries between the art forms were blurred in his mind. He was aware of their respective autonomy, but he was also aware of their sisterhood. It does not follow that six sisters have no individuality because they have one mother. Pope accepted the *ut pictura poesis* tradition because he wanted to draw attention to certain similarities between the arts that he believed enriched the artistic experience; Lessing rejected it later in the century because he wanted to draw attention to the differences between the arts that he believed to be more fully experienced in isolation. A Romantic emphasis on the separateness and individuality of the different arts replaced an Augustan emphasis on the coherence and harmony that could exist when 'images reflect from art to art'.

4 Augustan Literary Tenets

A perfect Judge will *read* each Work of Wit
With the same Spirit that its Author *writ*,

An Essay On Criticism, 1711, (233–4)

Any age makes certain intellectual and cultural assumptions about itself which seem dated, and sometimes totally foreign, to succeeding ages, but which come almost unconsciously to the age itself. Any twentieth-century writer, for example, assumes that his audience is familiar with Freudian or Marxist ideas. He refers to the Oedipus complex or to the class struggle without having to explain what he means. Such ideas form an area of allusion from which a modern writer freely draws, and about which he is sure of his reader's familiarity. But in two hundred years time such allusions may well need footnotes to explain them, just as eighteenth-century allusions to the concepts of *concordia discors* and the *scala naturae* need them today. The aim of this chapter is to explain some of the critical assumptions that underlay Augustan expectations about literature, and to show how an understanding of such assumptions helps one to see better what Pope was trying to do in his poetry, and to judge more fairly the degree to which he succeeded in doing it.

One of the most important and helpful documents for an understanding of Augustan literary principles is Pope's *Essay on Criticism*. Although most of this poem was written when he was only twenty or twenty-one, it hardly deserves the scorn poured on it by De Quincey who called it 'the feeblest and least interesting of Pope's writings, being substantially a mere versification, like a metrical multiplication table, of commonplaces the most mouldy with which criticism has baited its rat-traps'. It is true that there is nothing especially new in what Pope says, but that is also its merit. It is an extremely thorough and often memorable account of the Augustan critical position, and, preferring Dr Johnson's words to those of De Quincey, 'exhibits every mode of excellence that can embellish or dignify didactic composition — selection of matter, novelty of arrangement, justness of precepts, splendour of illustration, and propriety of digression'. Part of our difficulty with the poem, if we find one, is due to our lack of familiarity with didactic poetry. In the twentieth century we tend to feel that this is not quite the right subject matter for poetry. But the eighteenth century laid down no such limitations on what was or was not the right subject for poetry. Indeed it is not until one tries to extract a prose meaning from the lines that one realizes how poetically charged they in fact are.

The kinds

When we first read a new poem today we tend to come to it with certain accepted ideas concerning what is and is not good poetry. We expect, for example, that a good poem will be fresh and striking in its imagery, will use everyday colloquial language, and will offer a full expression of the poet's own feelings. But these are peculiarly post-Romantic criteria, and although an eighteenth-century reader also judged poetry according to certain preconceived criteria, he would not have approached a new poem with anything like so narrow a set of preconceptions. He would have a different set of criteria for different *kinds* of poems. He would have read a new poem much as sixteenth- and seventeenth-century readers had done before him, and when they read a new poem the first question they would have asked would have been 'What *kind* of a poem is this?'

So far as the Renaissance was concerned particular kinds of poetry demanded particular kinds of subject matter. The epic, for example, required an elevated subject of a grand scope, while the epistle required a familiar subject of a more parochial scope. There was a wide variety of possible kinds of poetry, just as there was a wide variety of possible kinds of subject matter, but each kind made its own special rules and demands on the poet. What was appropriate for one kind of poetry might be totally inappropriate for another. This is what is meant by the concept of decorum.

The different kinds of poetry had different degrees of importance. Just as the Renaissance world fell into an ordered hierarchy, the Great Chain of Being (see chapter 5) in which all existence from the human to the inanimate had its fit place, so the literary kinds, ideally, fell into an ordered hierarchy in which each kind had its fit place. In practice, however, the order was never as strict or as clearcut as this comparison suggests, and there was considerable difference of opinion about the correct ordering of the kinds. In the sixteenth century we find the kinds ordered, in such works as Julius Caesar Scaliger's *Poetics*, 1561, or George Puttenham's *Art of English Poesie*, 1589, so that hymns and paeans are the highest kind of poetry, because of their divine subject matter, while incantations, epigrams and ditties are the lowest. What matters for us of course is not Scaliger or Puttenham's ordering of the kinds, but that of the eighteenth century. I have begun by mentioning the sixteenth-century belief in the doctrine of the kinds because it shows us that Pope in his acceptance of the doctrine was, as in so many other things, faithful to the past. Furthermore we know that he was familiar with Scaliger's work in particular, for he told Spence in 1739 that 'Scaliger's *Poetics* is an exceeding useful book of its kind, and extremely well collected'.

The main difference between the seventeenth- and eighteenth-century ordering of the kinds and that of the Renaissance concerns the much higher valuation that the seventeenth and eighteenth centuries gave to the epic. The epic was pre-eminently the major literary kind, and any poet aspiring to greatness should have written one. For this reason, if no other, Spenser and Milton were accepted as the great English poets, and although Dryden and Pope, who were accounted the next greatest, failed to write their planned epics (Dryden's was to be on King Arthur, and Pope's on Brutus, the legendary founder of Britain) they did the next best thing by writing translations of the two greatest epics in any language. The more one reads of post-Restoration poetry the more one becomes aware of the very great degree to which the epic shaped and formed it. Without the idea of the epic in the background *MacFlecknoe*, *Absalom and Achitopel*, *The Rape of the Lock* and *The Dunciad* would have been impossible. Each of these poems constantly alludes to, quotes from, imitates, parodies or mocks specific lines and incidents from the great epics of Homer, Virgil and Milton. One can only fully appreciate the satiric wit of the poems when one has a knowledge of the epics on which they are based.

This is no place to discuss the separate traditions lying behind all the different kinds of poetry that Pope attempted, for he tried his hand, not always with equal success, at a great number — the mock epic, the georgic, the pastoral, the dream vision, the didactic, the heroic epistle, the elegy, the familiar epistle, the formal verse satire, the moral epistle, the prologue, the epilogue, the ode, the epigram and the epitaph. What matters is that the reader should be aware that each kind of poem Pope writes has a different tradition behind it, and therefore a different framework in which it needs to be viewed. This is important because Pope expects the reader to recognize the tradition in which he is writing and then to admire the way in which he gives it a new turn. Where the nineteenth- or twentieth-century poet hopes the reader will think his poem original and new, the eighteenth-century poet considers that he has failed if he ignores tradition by being too original.

At the same time as the doctrine of the kinds created certain formal expectations it also allowed an inventive poet to create surprise by breaking those expectations in unusual ways. This, of course, is the basis of the mock epic where the poet uses an elevated form for unsuitable subject matter. In *The Rape of the Lock* a trivial event is treated with a mock seriousness that is totally inappropriate to its importance. The same sort of deliberate unrelatedness between form and subject lies behind many Augustan satiric writings. Gay's 'Newgate Pastoral', *The Beggar's Opera*, and Swift's mock aubade, *A Description of the Morning*, are two cases in point. In both these works the success of the satire depends not only on the reader's recognizing the fact that form and subject are at odds with one another, but also in his implicitly knowing how the literary kinds of the pastoral and the aubade would be correctly handled. The reader's appreciation of the poem is increased through his self-esteem in recognizing the distortion that has taken place.

One other way in which an awareness of the doctrine of the kinds helps in an appreciation of Pope's poetry concerns the reader's being responsive to the possibility of a shift in kinds, even within a single poem. Pope never allows the kinds, to become so mixed that the overall effect is one of confusion, but he does frequently move into a style that is appropriate to a kind other than that in which he is writing. For instance, in his *Imitation of Horace, II, vi*, which tells the famous story of the town and country mice, Pope writes in the familiar and colloquial language appropriate to the formal verse satire. Then, suddenly, in describing the home of the town mouse he shifts into a mock epic language that is strictly inappropriate to the kind of poem he is writing:

> Behold the place, where if a Poet
> Shin'd in Description, he might show it,
> Tell how the Moon-beam trembling falls
> And tips with silver all the walls:
> Palladian walls, Venetian doors,
> Grotesco roofs, and Stucco floors:
> But let it (in a word) be said,
> The Moon was up, and Men a-bed,
> The Napkins white, the Carpet red:
> The Guests withdrawn had left the Treat,
> And down the Mice sate, *tête à tête*.
>
> (189–99)

The transition from the elegant pictorial language of the trembling moonbeams that tip the walls with silver in the first six lines to the curt and clipped telegrammatic language, that so perfectly captures the style of Swift, in the last five lines, shows a wonderfully urbane turn of wit.

Decorum

The Augustan concept of decorum is directly connected with the doctrine of the *kinds* just discussed. In the same way as there is an appropriate kind of poetry for a certain subject matter, so there is an appropriate language for each kind of poetry. Decorum is another word for propriety, and the literary concept of decorum involves proper words in proper places. The language must be suited to the purpose, or as Ian Jack puts it in his book *Augustan Satire*, the idiom must be level with the intention.

Pope expresses the doctrine clearly enough in the *Essay on Criticism*:

> Expression is the *Dress* of *Thought,* and still
> Appears more *decent* as more *suitable*;
> A vile Conceit in pompous Words exprest,
> Is like a Clown in regal Purple drest;
> For diff'rent *Styles* with diff'rent *Subjects* sort,
> As several Garbs with Country, Town, and Court.

> (318–23)

The analogy between literary decorum and civilized behaviour is a crucial one. Just as there is an art in doing certain things well — dressing, eating, courting — so there is an art in expressing them well. One dresses according to the occasion. It would be ridiculous to wear one's best suit and new shoes to go gardening in, and it would be disrespectful to wear one's tattiest clothes to attend a wedding. In the same way, it is ridiculous to use an elevated style to describe a trivial event like the removal of a lock of hair from a young lady's head, just as it is disrespectful to use an earthy style to praise the King. As the above examples imply there are times when Pope deliberately breaks the concept of decorum for satiric effect, but in breaking it he is of course tacitly acknowledging its fundamental importance.

The epic demands a specially well-chosen style. It should be written in a language appropriate to its grand purpose. Indeed, one of Pope's rare criticisms of Dryden concerns the inappropriateness of part of his translation of the *Aeneid*:

> I agree with you [he writes to his friend Henry Cromwell in 1710] in your censure of the use of sea-terms in Mr Dryden's Virgil; not only because Helenus was no great Prophet in those matters, but because no Terms of Art, or Cant-Words, suit with the majesty and dignity of style which epic poetry requires.

An understanding of the literary concept of decorum helps us to appreciate two particular aspects of Pope's vocabulary that have given readers trouble and concern over the years: his use of poetic diction, and his use of scatologic words.

Poetic diction is a term used by Pope in his Preface to the *Iliad* to describe that quality in Homer's expression which is especially alive and glowing and more highly charged than ordinary speech. But the term was taken up by the Romantics and used in a much narrower and more pejorative sense to describe the artificial language that they felt to be the overriding fault of eighteenth-century poetry. The most famous and influential attack on poetic diction comes in Wordsworth's Preface to *Lyrical Ballads*, 1800:

There will be found in these volumes little of what is usually called poetic diction: as much pains has been taken to avoid it as is ordinarily taken to produce it; this has been done for the reason already alleged, to bring my language near to the language of men.

Later on Wordsworth refers to poetic diction as 'adulterated phraseology' and a 'motley masquerade of tricks, quaintness, hieroglyphics and enigmas'.

Wordsworth's attack on poetic diction is particularly a rejection of personification and periphrasis: phrases like the 'scaly breed', used by Pope to describe fish in *Windsor-Forest*, or the 'glitt'ring forfex', to describe a pair of scissors in *The Rape of the Lock*. These are words specially chosen to raise the respective scenes in which they occur, either seriously or ironically, above an ordinary scene. Furthermore, they add a dimension to the meaning that the more ordinary words could not possibly add. In calling the fish the 'scaly breed' in *Windsor-Forest*, for example, Pope shows through the adjective what the individual fish that he is about to describe in great detail have in common that distinguishes them from other creatures in the *scala naturae*; through the noun he points out that they are at the same time a generative part of that *scala naturae*, thus adding to the sense of creative plenitude found in the forest at large. The more ordinary word 'fish' could not have suggested these additional areas of meaning. Similarly detailed reasons can be given for the periphrastic description of the scissors in *The Rape of the Lock* (see under 'Periphrasis' in the Glossary of Technical Terms, p. 162).

Because Pope can be shown to be using poetic diction here for a deliberate purpose, however, it does not follow that there is not a great deal of substance in Wordsworth's attack on it. There certainly was a decaying poetic style among the minor poets of fifty years later, who frequently used the formulaic quality of poetic diction as a way of constructing stock effects, and Wordsworth's rejection of this habit was more than welcome. What needs to be pointed out here is that the best poets, such as Pope, Thomson and Gray, used poetic diction as an integral support to their poetic feeling, not as a substitute for it.

The difficulty with scatologic words is similar. Pope is gratuitously obscene in *The Dunciad*, Book II, critics will say, or his image of excrement being passed on from 'hog to hog in huts on Westphaly', in *Epilogue to the Satires: Dialogue II*, 171–80, is unpardonably filthy. But this is exactly what Pope wants us to say. To an audience that is not shocked by his attack on moral decay, only the analogy with physical decay remains. Again the concept of decorum is at work, for just as the epic requires a suitably elevated style, so satire requires a suitably vigorous and scabrous one. Pope did not hesitate to call a spade a spade if it was appropriate, and he did not shrink from calling it a shovel if it was necessary. When Boswell objected to a certain phrase in Pope as being low, Dr Johnson replied: 'Sir, it is intended to be low: it is satire. The expression is debased to debase the character'.

The rules

Much of the foregoing discussion might suggest that Pope and the Augustans believed poetry should be written according to a set of pre-ordained rules. But there is a great difference between the person who believes that poetry should be written according to a narrow set of sharply defined rules and the person who believes that the poet's imagination works the more freely for operating within a broad set of shared expectations. The theoretical discussion concerning whether a poet is born or made is a simplification of the same issue. A poet, of course, is both born and made: he has both genius and skill. The critical question is where the emphasis should lie, which is the more important? The question was indeed a lively and perennial one in the seventeenth and eighteenth centuries, but only the most stereotyped of neoclassical critics, like Thomas Rymer, believed in a strict and uncompromising adherence to the rules. The great creative writers, especially Dryden and Pope, were far too aware of the complex workings of the imagination to subscribe to limiting formulae without making serious reservations.

The rules received their greatest support and popularity in seventeenth-century France. Boileau's *Art Poétique*, 1674, Rapin's *Réflexions sur la Poétique*, 1674, and Le Bossu's *Traité du Poème Épique*, 1675, belong to a common school of criticism in that they each set out to abstract a set of guidelines for the writing of poetry from the works of the Ancients, and particularly from Aristotle and Horace. Perhaps the most notorious rules abstracted from the Ancients were those concerning drama. The demand that plays be written according to the three unities of time, place and action has long since been shown to be totally irrelevant to the stage, and nowhere more effectively than by Dr Johnson in his *Preface to Shakespeare*, 1765. But for a short period during the last quarter of the seventeenth century this theoretical demand held great sway in both France and England. Thomas Rymer's vituperative attack on Shakespeare in *A Short View of Tragedy*, 1692, shows such a position taken to its logical and absurd conclusion. Rymer's 'commonsense' approach demonstrates an extraordinary aesthetic insensitivity and has earned him the reputation among most latterday students of being, in Macaulay's words, 'the worst critic that ever lived'.

Dryden's attitude to the rules is, like that of Pope, mixed. Both men skilfully pick their way between the strict rigidity of the formalist critics and the boundless freedom of their opponents. Where Rymer sees the rules as ends in themselves, Dryden and Pope see them as means to an end:

> I never heard of any other foundation of Dramatic Poesy than the imitation of nature; neither was there ever pretended any other by the ancients, or moderns, or me, who endeavour to follow them in that rule. This I have plainly said in my definition of a play; that it is a just and lively image of human nature . . . if nature be to be imitated, then there is a rule for imitating nature rightly; otherwise there may be an end, and no means conducing to it.
>
> Dryden, Defence of Dramatic Poesy, 1668.

Pope begins his discussion of the rules in *An Essay On Criticism* in much the same way:

> Those RULES of old *discover'd*, not *devis'd*,
> Are *Nature* still, but *Nature Methodiz'd*;
> *Nature*, like *Liberty*, is but restrain'd
> By the same Laws which first *herself* ordain'd.
>
> (88–91)

The modern reader may feel that Pope is trying to have his cake and eat it, but there is a great deal of validity in what he says. He neatly sidesteps involvement in the debate between the proponents of rules and the proponents of imitating nature by saying that the two are essentially the same. He makes the identical point later in the poem when he says:

> Learn hence for Ancient *Rules* a just Esteem;
> To copy *Nature* is to copy *Them*.
>
> (139–40)

Pope draws, in *An Essay on Criticism*, on many of the same persons who so influenced Rymer — Boileau, Rapin and Le Bossu — but never in so slavish a way. He struggles throughout to effect a reasonable reconciliation between the adherents and the opponents of the rules, a reconciliation that is summed up in the antithetical force of the second line in the following couplet:

> Hear how learn'd *Greece* her useful Rules indites,
> When to repress, and when indulge our Flights.
>
> (92–3)

He defends 'just precepts' drawn from 'great examples', but the emphasis in both phrases is as much on the adjective as the noun. What really counts, however, is the 'Poet's Fire', that is, his imagination (cf. Pope's admiration for Homer's fire which 'burns every-where clearly and everywhere irresistibly', *Preface to the Iliad*), and for as long as critics admired that 'coelestial fire' (195) criticism remained in a healthy state:

> Then Criticism the Muse's Handmaid prov'd,
> To dress her Charms, and make her more belov'd.
>
> (102–3)

But later critics grew jealous of what they could not themselves achieve and, elevating criticism above the art it presumed to study, used 'mistaken rules' to attack the poets they were meant to serve:

> But following Wits from that Intention stray'd;
> Who could not win the Mistress, woo'd the Maid;
> Against the Poets *their own Arms* they turn'd,
> Sure to hate most the Men from whom they *learn'd*.
>
> (104–7)

Critics who slavishly adhere to precept are seen as quack apothe-caries (108–11), insects (112–13) and even as cooks, who 'write dull *Receits* [recipes] how Poems may be made' (115).

For Pope the only true way to sharpen one's critical discrimination is to soak oneself in the classics:

> Be *Homer's* Works your *Study*, and *Delight*,
> Read them by Day, and meditate by Night,
> Thence form your Judgment, thence your Maxims bring,
> And trace the Muses *upward* to their *Spring*.
>
> (124–7)

Pope's strategy in effecting a reconciliation in the debate concerning the rules is to redefine what is meant by them so that following them becomes the same thing as following nature. Yet even when he has thus carefully qualified his approval he still finds it necessary to insist on the escape clause:

> Some Beauties yet, no Precepts can declare,
> For there's a *Happiness* as well as *Care*.
>
> (141–2)

He goes on to stress the mysterious quality that exists in the greatest poetry, the *'nameless Graces* which no methods teach', and which depend on a 'Lucky LICENCE' [Pope's capitals], or a *'brave Disorder'* that will part from *'vulgar Bounds'* and *'snatch a Grace* beyond the Reach of Art' (144–55).

What this account of Pope's discussion of the rules in the *Essay on Criticism* shows us is that, far from being the fervent disciple of the rules that he is sometimes described as being, Pope gives them, at most, a qualified vote of approval. He admits their usefulness when they lead us back to the great works of creative genius, but once they become dogmatic or limiting they must be put aside. On the whole he is a far fiercer defender of the 'Liberties of Wit' than he is of the 'vulgar Bounds' of 'Foreign Laws despis'd'.

Wit

Of all the literary terms current in the Augustan period 'wit' is the most difficult to define. The word is used in the late seventeenth and early eighteenth centuries to cover a variety of widely different meanings, each one of which forces us to see the other in a slightly different light. Pope was concerned with the word's complexity from a very early age. In 1704, for instance, we find him writing to William Wycherley offering the following definition: 'True Wit I believe, may be defin'd as a justness of Thought, and a Facility of Expression; or (in the Midwives phrase) a perfect Conception, with an easy Delivery'. The definition is itself an example of one kind of wit, but the sixteen-year-old Pope was fully aware of the elusive nature of the term, for he continued in the next sentence: 'However this is far from a compleat definition; pray help me to a better, as I doubt not you can'.

In his *Dictionary*, 1755, Dr Johnson lists eight different meanings of the word, while the *OED*, published almost two hundred years later, lists fourteen main meanings and any number of subordinate and compound ones. William Empson has pointed out in *The Structure of Complex Words* that the word appears on an average every sixteen lines in *An Essay on Criticism* and in a somewhat different sense nearly every time, though he adds that 'there is not a single use of the word in the whole poem in which the idea of a joke is quite out of sight'. All this is of little comfort to the new reader, but it is a warning against expecting a clear cut definition of so complex a word.

The basic meaning of the word, from which all others derive, concerns the various powers of the mind. The term could refer either to all the mental faculties working together, or to individual mental faculties, such as the imagination, judgment and memory. It is because the word originally covered each of these very different faculties that its meaning became so complex when writers tried to limit its application to a particular faculty. We still use the term in its overall sense, albeit somewhat unconsciously, when we talk about being at our 'wit's end', but by and large the word has a very much narrower meaning in its most commonly accepted usage today, referring to a person's ability to say clever and 'witty' things.

There are four main ways in which Pope uses the expression in *An Essay on Criticism*. First, he occasionally uses it in its original sense to refer to all the mental faculties considered together:

> Nature to all things fix'd the Limits fit,
> And wisely curb'd proud Man's pretending Wit:
> As on the *Land* while *here* the *Ocean* gains,
> In *other Parts* it leaves wide sandy Plains;
> Thus in the *Soul* while *Memory* prevails,
> The solid Pow'r of *Understanding* fails;
> Where Beams of warm *Imagination* play,
> The *Memory*'s soft Figures melt away.
> One *Science* only will one *Genius* fit;
> So *vast* is Art, so *narrow* Human Wit.

(52–61)

Wit, as it is used in the last line of this passage, refers to each of the cognitive faculties in turn whether one is considering the 'soft figures' of Memory, the 'solid power' of Understanding [i.e. Judgment], or the 'beams of warm' Imagination. No man can excel in all the faculties of the mind, 'so vast is Art [Learning], so narrow Human Wit', and man must therefore fit his genius to one particular branch of knowledge.

The second meaning of the word, and the one with which he begins the poem, is as a synonym for genius, or the indefinable gift of the poet:

> In *Poets* as true *Genius* is but rare,
> True *Taste* as seldom is the *Critick*'s Share;
> Both must alike from Heav'n derive their Light,
> These *born* to Judge, as well as those to Write.
> Let such teach others who themselves excell,
> And *censure freely* who have *written well*.
> *Authors* are partial to their *Wit*, 'tis true,
> But are not *Criticks* to their *Judgment* too?

(11–18)

In the first line here the distinguishing mark of the poet is 'true Genius' which must be derived from Heaven (cf. *poeta nascitur non fit*), but by line 17 the distinguishing mark of the poet is his 'Wit'. The term 'wit' has become interchangeable with 'genius' and distinct from 'judgment'. We shall see when we come to Pope's fourth meaning that, in other places, he stresses the importance of its liaison with judgment. Such paradoxes are an essential part of the word's complexity.

A third way in which Pope uses wit is to refer to the quality of ingenuity in a writer. It is this quality of verbal and intellectual agility that the Restoration Wits strove after. At its best the pursuit of such a quality leads to piercing illumination, but at its worst it leads to a purely superficial glamour, to writing that is all frothy extravagance without any ethical basis, or what Pope so aptly calls, 'One glaring Chaos and wild Heap of Wit' (292). Pope is totally scornful of this kind of wit:

> Some have at first for *Wits*, then *Poets* past,
> Turn'd *Criticks* next, and prov'd plain *Fools* at last;
> Some neither can for *Wits* nor *Criticks* pass,
> As heavy Mules are neither *Horse* nor *Ass*.
> Those half-learn'd Witlings, num'rous in our Isle,
> As half-form'd Insects on the banks of *Nile*;
> Unfinish'd Things, one knows not what to call,
> Their Generation's so *equivocal*:
> To tell 'em, wou'd a *hundred Tongues* require,
> Or one vain Wit's, that might a hundred tire.
>
> (36–45)

The comparison of the 'witlings' to insects (cf. the opening lines of *An Epistle to Dr Arbuthnot*), the pun concerning their proliferation and the final epigrammatic dig at their endless loquacity show the brilliant effectiveness of Pope's own satiric wit being used to annihilate the glittering falsity of the poetasters and pretenders to wit. At its best, wit of such intellectual agility adds a sprightliness to poetry that both charms and surprises the reader. It involves a liveliness of mind that should not be underrated, though, as Pope would be the first to admit, it is only part of the great poet's equipment.

The fourth and by far the most important meaning that Pope attributes to 'wit' concerns the imagination. Towards the end of the poem he describes Horace as:

> He, who supream in Judgment, as in Wit,
> Might boldly censure, as he boldly writ,
> Yet *judg'd* with *Coolness* tho' he sung with *Fire*;
> His *Precepts* teach but what his *Works* inspire.
>
> (657–60)

Here wit involves the 'fire' of the imagination, an image that picks up the earlier reference to the 'Beams of warm *Imagination*' (58). Wit, as it refers to the imagination, is, like the sun, the source of all light. Pope explicitly makes the comparison when he compares 'envy'd Wit' to '*Sol* Eclips'd' (468). When the Sun's beams are too strong they draw up vapours that at first obscure but finally reflect added glory. In the same way Wit's shining light at first attracts dull critics, but finally endures despite them.

Perhaps the most important point Pope makes about wit in this sense, however, is that imagination is not in itself sufficient for the poet:

Some, to whom Heav'n in Wit has been profuse,
Want as much more, to turn it to its use;
For *Wit* and *Judgment* often are at strife,
Tho' meant each other's Aid, like *Man* and *Wife*.

(80–3)

In the best writing the imagination must be at one with the judgment. The two qualities cannot be separated. As 'grave *Quintillian*', whom Pope praises for his clear method (669–74), says in his *Institutio Oratoria*: 'I do not believe that invention can exist apart from judgment, since we do not say that a speaker has invented inconsistent two-edged or foolish arguments, but merely that he has failed to avoid them' (Loeb translation). La Rochefoucauld, whose maxims were translated into English in 1706, just a few years before Pope wrote his poem, says much the same thing:

> The making a Difference between Wit and Judgement, is a Vulgar Error. Judgement is nothing else but the exceeding Brightness of Wit, which, like Light, pierces into the very Bottom of Things, observes all that ought to be observed there, and discovers what seemed to be past anybodies finding out: From when we must conclude, that the Energy and Extension of this Light of the Wit, is the very Thing that produces all those Effects, usually ascribed to the Judgement. (Maxim 98)

It is this idea of wit as the marriage of imagination and judgment that lies behind the best-known couplets in the poem:

> *True Wit* is *Nature* to Advantage drest,
> What oft was *Thought*, but ne'er so well *Exprest*,
> *Something*, whose Truth convinc'd at Sight we find,
> That gives us back the Image of our Mind.

(297–300)

True wit involves both the imagination and the judgment, both nature and art. It involves subject matter and form welded together in the creative mind so that the truth that results convinces us at sight and 'gives us back the Image of our Mind'.

I have suggested four different ways in which wit is used by Pope in *An Essay on Criticism,* and the question that now arises is whether these differences in the meaning of one word are the result of confusion or deliberate strategy. In order to answer this we need to say something about the distrust of the imagination found in the writings of the most influential seventeenth-century philosophers and scientists. Contrary to popular opinion, this is not a distrust that is found among Augustan poets. On the other hand they could not help being aware of it and of the corresponding attempt to downgrade the importance of poetry as a medium for expressing truth about human nature.

Francis Bacon was the chief originator of this distrust of the imagination. For Bacon poetry was almost totally a means of escapism that allowed deception to triumph. In *The Advancement of Learning*, 1605, he admitted the power of poetry and the imagination but he distrusted it as a vehicle for truth because it transformed reality. For Bacon poetry was 'the play of the mind'. This distrust was taken up by Bacon's disciples, the members of the Royal Society, and eloquently expressed by their official historian Thomas Sprat in his *History of the Royal Society*, 1667. Sprat described the wit and imagination of the poet as being inconsistent with a sincere enquiry into the works of Nature.

A further example of the philosopher's distrust of the imagination occurs in Thomas Hobbes's *Leviathan*, 1651. For Hobbes imagination 'is nothing but *decaying sense* and is found in men, and many other living creatures, as well sleeping as waking'. John Locke also considered the imagination a hindrance in arriving at the truth. The emphasis in his *Thoughts Concerning Education*, 1695, falls on the importance of judgment and the frailty of imagination. He defines wit as 'lying most in the assemblage of ideas, and putting those together with quickness and variety, wherein can be found any resemblance or congruity, thereby to make up pleasant pictures in the fancy'. Judgment on the other hand 'lies in separating carefully one from another ideas wherein can be found the least difference, thereby to avoid being misled by Similitude'. In aligning wit with fancy and opposing it to judgment, Locke is managing further to discredit poetry as likely to mislead the mind. If a child has a poetic vein, he argues, the parents 'should labour to have it stifled and suppressed as much as may be'.

It is against this background that we need to consider Pope's definition of 'wit' in *An Essay on Criticism*, in which he defends poetry against these attacks as subtly as he can. He does this by taking the word most frequently associated with poetry — namely wit — and working it over and over in a variety of different ways that stress the complexity of the creative process and, above all, the fusion of those faculties of judgment and imagination that Bacon, Hobbes and Locke had been trying to separate. In redefining 'wit', Pope is attempting to redefine and secure poetry itself. For Pope 'wit' is what E.N. Hooker calls 'the unique mode of the creative artist'. It is the essence of poetry entailing the inspiration of genius, the mental agility of ingenuity, the fire of imagination and the control of judgment. It involves, in direct contrast to Eliot's notorious phrase, an association of sensibility.

Imitation

One thing that should be clear from the foregoing discussion is that Augustan wit, and hence Augustan poetry, has nothing to do with originality. The true poet should say things in a new way, but the idea that he can say things that have never been said before, that he can be totally original, is a post-Romantic one. For the Augustan poet there are only a few irrefutable human truths, and they have been discovered long ago. The idea that anyone can come up with original truths is merely an indication of man's presumption and pride. All the living poet can do is reinterpret the validity of established truths as they apply to the modern world:

> *True Wit* is *Nature* to Advantage drest,
> What oft was *Thought*, but ne'er so well *Exprest*.
>
> (297–8)

A person who claimed to be original was looked on with some suspicion. Indeed the noun, an 'original', was a term of abuse reserved for laughing at eccentric and singular persons like Captain Lismahago in Smollett's novel *Humphry Clinker*, 1771.

Instead of trying to be original, the Augustan poet assimilated his knowledge of the past into his awareness of the present. Dryden praises the young Anne Killigrew's poetry by saying that:

> Such noble vigour did her verse adorn
> That it seem'd borrow'd, where 'twas only born.
>
> (*To the Memory of . . . Mrs Anne Killigrew*, 75–6)

Although her poetry had the limitation of being original, it had such vigour that it at least seemed to have the excellence of imitating the ancients.

The Augustan poet, then, sees imitation as more important than originality. But this does not mean that he feels in duty bound simply to copy earlier writers. 'Those who say our thoughts are not our own because they resemble the Ancients', wrote Pope in the Preface to his *Works*, 1717, 'may as well say our faces are not our own, because they are like our fathers'. True imitation involves both borrowing and recasting. The youthful Pope, writing to his friend William Walsh in 1706, said:

> I wou'd beg your opinion too as to another point: it is how far the liberty of *Borrowing* may extend? I have defended it sometimes by saying, that it seems not so much the Perfection of Sense to say things that have *never* been said before, as to express those *best* that have been said *oftenest*; and that Writers in the case of borrowing from others, are like Trees which of themselves wou'd produce only one sort of Fruit, but by being grafted upon others,

may yield variety. A mutual commerce makes Poetry flourish; but then Poets like Merchants, should repay with something of their own what they take from others; not like Pyrates, make prize of all they meet.

The poet both takes from others and repays with something of his own. Like Swift's famous bee in *The Battle of the Books*, he visits 'all the flowers and blossoms of the field and garden', and 'by an universal range, with long search, much study, true judgment, and distinction of things, brings home honey and wax'.

Pope visited the flowers and blossoms of the literary field widely, especially in his youth. He told Spence, shortly before he died, that in his great reading period, (from about thirteen or fourteen to twenty-one), he went through 'all the best critics, almost all the English, French and Latin poets of any name, the minor poets, Homer and some of the greater Greek poets in the original, and Tasso and Ariosto in translations'. He not only read widely in classical and English literature, but he also wrote many imitations of earlier English poets including Chaucer, Spenser, Waller and Cowley, and many translations of earlier classical poets including Homer, Virgil, Ovid and Horace. This was an essential part of his apprenticeship as a poet for, as he put it to Spence, 'my first taking to imitating was not out of vanity, but humility. I saw how defective my own things were, and endeavoured to mend my manner by copying good strokes from others'. Reuben Brower has revealed in his illuminating and subtle book, *Alexander Pope: The Poetry of Allusion*, just how present the classical poets were to Pope and his eighteenth-century readers. Brower shows how, for Dryden and Pope, allusion to the past is 'a resource equivalent to symbolic metaphor and elaborate imagery in other poets'. We find the same thing, in a more strained and self-conscious way, in the poetry of T. S. Eliot.

But imitation was more than just a frame of mind for the Augustan poet. It was also an accepted form, or literary 'kind', that grew out of the great interest and activity in verse translation that took place in the seventeenth century. During the first half of the century most English verse translation tended toward a fairly close adherence to the original, for example Ben Jonson's translation of Horace's *Ars Poetica*, but during the second half of the century verse translators increasingly took more freedom with their models. It became more important for a translator to catch the spirit of a work than to give a word-for-word rendition.

The imitations written in post-Restoration England are a further extension of this concept of free translation. In the 'Advertisement' prefacing his version of Horace's *Ars Poetica* Oldham says that he thought of turning the work to an advantage which had not occurred to those who went before him in the translation (Jonson and Roscommon) by making Horace speak as if he were then living:

> I therefore resolved to alter the scene from Rome to London, and to make use of English names, places, and customs, where the parallel would decently permit, which I conceived would give a kind of new air to the poem, and render it more agreeable to the relish of the present age.

Oldham was not the first to modernize classical poems in this way. Cowley, Sprat and Rochester had each done it before him and would each have agreed with his reasons for taking such liberties. As the imitation developed and became more popular, so it became completely independent of various levels of translation. It made different assumptions of its audience: where translation was primarily intended to help those readers who could not understand the original, imitation assumed that the reader would be sufficiently familiar with the original to appreciate the author's wit in adapting it. For this reason the Latin (and most imitiations were of Roman poetry) was frequently printed on the facing page or at the foot of the poem, while parallel passages were indicated by linking arabic numerals.

Imitation is a way for a poet to give depth and authority to his writing. The poet does not simply rely on his own opinion, he calls on acknowledged classical masters to support his case. He searches for a peculiarly appropriate classical equivalent to the modern subject he wants to write about, or for a peculiarly appropriate modern equivalent to the classical poem he wants to adapt, and then fits his treatment to the overall organization of the classical poem. This relationship between the present and the past can be handled in a variety of ways. It can either be used to add emphasis to the condemnation of the present, as in Oldham's *Satire in Imitation of the Third of Juvenal*, where London is shown as not only bad but as bad as Juvenal's Rome, or it can be used ironically to undercut the present by creating a contrast with the past. The outstanding example of such a usage is Pope's *Imitation of Horace, Epistle II, i* (To Augustus) where the compliments sincerely paid by Horace to Augustus are ironically paid by Pope to George Augustus Hanover.

Satire

It seems appropriate to close this chapter by saying something about the chief mode of Augustan literature. When all is said and done, it is for the brilliance of its satire that the age in general, and Pope's poetry in particular, is most highly valued. But what did the Augustans understand by satire? What were its aims and intentions, and why was it so popular among Augustan writers? What kind of pressures impel someone to write satire in preference to other literary modes? These are some of the questions that a study of Augustan literature forces one to consider.

The word 'satire' as it is used today describes a mode of writing rather than a form. It describes a spirit of conception, or state of mind, that can operate through any number of different forms. Thus an epic poem, such as *The Dunciad*, or a prose account of imaginary travels, such as *Gulliver's Travels*, or an opera, such as *The Beggar's Opera*, are each referred to as satires because they share certain common qualities in terms of their overall conception.

At the most general level one can say that satire attacks human evil and stupidity by making fun of it from a standpoint that at least implies, if it does not state, a consistent moral position. There are three distinct elements of conception involved here — attack, laughter and morality — and a careful fusing of all three elements is necessary for successful satire. If the author concentrates on attack alone then the work of art tends towards mere invective; if he concentrates on laughter alone then he moves into a region of the purely comic; and if he concentrates on morality alone then he moves towards the area of the homily. Clearly satire cannot be completely separated from other allied modes, especially comedy, for, as many critics have pointed out, some of the greatest comic characters also have strong satiric dimensions. Falstaff's gluttony, cowardice and dishonesty, for example, are clearly satirised by Shakespeare, but since his superabundant jollity and massive zest for life so dwarf these vices we see him finally as a comic rather than satiric character.

I have suggested three main qualities that compose the satiric vision overall, but we can also point to certain particular structural elements that are common to most works of satire, whatever their form. Satire frequently involves, for instance, the imaginative creation of absurd, or even grotesque worlds, such as Swift's Yahoos in *Gulliver's Travels* or Pope's Cave of Spleen in *The Rape of the Lock*, that ridicule man by containing both exaggerations and real depictions of his pretensions and frailties. The satirist creates at the same time as he destroys, and this paradox lies at the root of his power to excite our attention. There is a tendency among some readers to dwell on the destructiveness of satire and to see satire as a totally negative mode. It is, of course, a destructive mode, but the best satirists are never purely destructive. They protest against the viciousness and absurdity of the present world, both by creating grotesque transformations of it in a nightmare world and by suggesting alternative and better ways of proceeding. Their destructiveness goes along with equally important elements of creativity and constructiveness.

The satirist sees through man's affectations, and sets out to expose them to laughter and scorn. He does not do this out of meanness or envy but because he feels indignation at the wastage and corruption of human potential. The satirist confronts man with his own nakedness and with his own tenuous grasp on existence. He uses his pen partly as a weapon to attack people with and partly as a scalpel with which to lay them open. Consider the defence put forward by Pope's irate satirist in his *Imitation of Horace, Satire II, i*:

> What? arm'd for *Virtue* when I point the Pen,
> Brand the bold Front of shameless, guilty Men,
> Dash the proud Gamester in his gilded Car,
> Bare the mean Heart that lurks beneath a Star;
> Can there be wanting to defend Her Cause,
> Lights of the Church, or Guardians of the Laws?
> Could pension'd Boileau lash in honest Strain
> Flatt'rers and Bigots ev'n in *Louis'* Reign?
> Could Laureate *Dryden* Pimp and Fry'r engage,
> Yet neither *Charles* nor *James* be in a Rage?
> And I not strip the Gilding off a Knave,
> Un-plac'd, un-pension'd, no Man's Heir, or Slave?

> (105–16)

The satirist describes himself in an aggressively militant way. He points, brands, dashes, bares, lashes and strips his enemy. The verbs draw comparisons between the satirist's profession and that of the public prosecutor: both see it as their duty to publish and punish, to strip bare and to whip.

The satirist forces man to come face to face with the most brutal and least attractive part of himself. As a result we often find in satire scenes of crowded humanity portrayed at its most barbaric and uncivilized. The unthinking mob that surges through the stinking streets of London in *The Dunciad* Book II is related in this way to the wretched mass of humanity that accompanies Tom Idle on his way to execution at Tyburn in Hogarth's *Industry and Idleness*, Plate XI. The satirist forces us to watch not only a close clinical analysis of man's anatomy, but very often a dissection, or even a vivisection of it. 'Yesterday', says Swift's scientist persona in his most complex satire *A Tale of a Tub*,

> I ordered the carcass of a beau to be stript in my presence; when we were all amazed to find so many unexpected faults under one suit of clothes. Then I laid open his brain, his heart, and his spleen, but I plainly perceived at every operation, that the further we proceeded we found the defects increase upon us in number and bulk.

The satirist analyses man and his world with brutal and often horrifying frankness. At his most extreme he is not content with confronting man with his own nakedness, but lays open the flesh and exposes the festering innards.

The satirist protests against the state of the world as he finds it, largely because he knows there are other and better states. In looking for examples of better states he frequently looks to the Golden Age of Mythology, or to the security of the past. Sometimes this becomes mere nostalgia for the good old days, but in Pope and Swift it is very much more than this. Both men share a deep-rooted belief in the stability of inherited order. The satirist nearly always finds himself in a minority position, for if his viewpoint was that of the majority he wouldn't feel the need to protest in the first place. Thus in the early part of the eighteenth century, when the government was nearly always Whig, it is hardly surprising that most satire is written by opponents of the Whigs. Pope, Swift, Arbuthnot, Gay, Fielding and Thomson were all, at various times and in various differing degrees of commitment, affiliated to the Tory opposition to Robert Walpole.

The satirist's traditional justification for his art is that he does it for the good of society. He hopes to reform and correct corruption, and for this reason frequently takes on the role of the defender of virtue or spokesman for the public good. Whether or not he really believes in such a role is another question: it is sufficient for him that he has a conventional framework within which to carry out his attack. 'Ask you what Provocation I have had?' says Pope's satirist in the *Epilogue to the Satires*, Dialogue II,

> The strong Antipathy of Good to Bad.
> When Truth or Virtue an Affront endures,
> Th' Affront is mine, my Friend, and should be yours.
>
> (198–200)

Above all else the satirist is committed to the living world. He cares about its decay, and if he does not, if he merely uses his wit in a virtuoso way, then his satire will be shortlived.

So far I have talked about satire as a mode in literature, but the word has not always been used in this all-embracing sense and it is helpful to consider briefly its origins as a particular form of poetry. The English word satire derives from the Latin word *satura* (meaning medley or mixture), which was the name Horace (65–8 B.C.) first gave to a genre of poetry he inherited from Ennius and Pacuvius. This genre, or form, was later taken up by Persius (A.D. 34–62) and Juvenal (A.D. 60–140) and imitated at the same time as it was further developed. Horace and Juvenal wrote poems in which they attacked particular vices and follies of their day. They were so effective that a word which was originally used to designate a particular literary form, with a definable rhetorical structure, has

INDUSTRY AND IDLENESS.

PLATE 11.

THE IDLE PRENTICE EXECUTED AT TYBURN.

Engraved by E. Smith.

From the Original Design by Hogarth

'*Hymning Tyburn's elegiac lines.*' Dunciad, *II, 41*

been extended to cover a whole mode of writing. That literary form does, however, have an independent and continuing tradition in English literature which we usually refer to as formal verse satire. It is a form that reached its peak in England during the eighteenth century, particularly in the poetry of Pope, Swift and Dr Johnson.

Although Horace and Juvenal use the same form, *satura*, there are important differences in the way they use it. Where Horace's satirist sets out to persuade with witty and urbane ridicule, Juvenal's attempts to chastise with fierce and savage denunciation. Horace tries to laugh us into truth, while Juvenal sets out to provoke our indignation and horror. In the First Satire of his First Book Horace asks why one cannot tell the truth with laughter, as a teacher gives children sweets to persuade them to learn to read. Juvenal, in his first satire, tells us that it is indignation and anger that drives him to write satire. As a result of this difference of tone in the satires of Horace and Juvenal we have developed the habit of referring to milder, more gentle satire as Horatian, and of referring to harsh and savage satire as Juvenalian. The dominant influence on English verse satire from Skelton through Donne, Hall and Marston to the great satirists of the Restoration and Augustan periods has been that of Juvenal, and although it was Horace's poems that Pope chose to imitate so widely in the 1730s it makes a great deal of sense to say that in imitating Horace he has 'Juvenalized' him.

We can find useful hints about Pope's concept of satire and his reasons for writing it by consulting his *Correspondence*. He writes to Swift in March 1732 saying, 'I know nothing that moves strongly but Satire, and those who are ashamed of nothing else, are so of being ridiculous'. He clearly feels that the satirist aims at an emotional as well as an intellectual response. Satire 'moves' the reader, and furthermore it moves him 'strongly'. Two years later, on 17 July 1734, Arbuthnot wrote to Pope urging him to 'continue that noble *Disdain* and *Abhorrence* of Vice which he seem'd naturally endued with,' but begging him to show a certain regard for his own safety and to 'study more to reform than chastise'. This distinction that Arbuthnot presses on Pope is similar to that we have already described between Horatian and Juvenalian satire.

Pope's reply to Arbuthnot's letter offers the clearest prose statement we have of his theory of satire. He thanks Arbuthnot for his comments about his disdain of vice and for the concern he expresses for his safety, but with regard to Arbuthnot's request that he study more to reform than chastise he argues that such a separation is impossible:

But General Satire in Times of General Vice has no force, and is no Punishment: People have ceas'd to be ashamed of it when so many are joined with them; and tis only by hunting One or two from the Herd that any Examples can be made. If a man writ all his Life against the Collective Body of the Banditti, or against Lawyers, would it do the least Good, or lessen the Body? But if some are hung up, or pilloried, it may prevent others. And in my low Station, with no other Power than this, I hope to deter, if not to reform.

If the satirist merely tries to reform without using examples to enforce his reform, then his satire will have little effect. As Pope put it when he rewrote this letter for the publication of his *Correspondence* in 1737, 'to attack Vices in the abstract, without touching Persons, may be safe fighting indeed, but it is fighting with Shadows'. Both the references to 'fighting', in this quotation, and to 'hunting', in the previous quotation, indicate that Pope sees the satirist's role in militant terms.

It is this concept of the satirist's role that emerges most strongly from the poetry. Sometimes he appears as a hunter, as in the *Epilogue to the Satires*, Dialogue II where knaves are seen as 'game' (27) to be 'run down' (29) and where the satirist has to 'beat about' to find an honest man:

> To find an honest man, I beat about,
> And love him, court him, praise him, in or out.
>
> (102–3)

The broken movement of the second line here acts out the image of the hunter thrashing about in the undergrowth to raise the game. At other times the satirist is seen as a bird of prey hovering over the world ready to drop on its victim. Thus in the same poem the satirist 'sowzes' (15) and 'stoops' (110) on mankind. Both words are technical terms taken from falconry, where they describe the action of the bird swooping down on its prey. The image is also found in *An Epistle to Dr Arbuthnot* when the speaker tells us,

> That not in Fancy's Maze he wander'd long
> But stoop'd to Truth, and moraliz'd his song.
>
> (340–1)

The concept of the satirist that informs Pope's satirical poetry is one of a militant defender of the public good, determined to continue 'that noble *Disdain* and *Abhorrence* of Vice' that Arbuthnot describes. Contrary to what has all too frequently been said about the wounded and besieged poet who lashes out at his enemies in desperate retaliation, Pope usually directs his wrath from a position of personal detachment. The satirist's attack is not primarily the result of personal hurt or grievance, nor is it primarily a form of self-defence: it springs rather from a profound disgust at his '*Country's* Ruin' and from a correspondingly strong sense of public spiritedness concerning the '*Public* Weal'.

5 Pope's Beliefs

Papist or Protestant, or both between,
Like good *Erasmus* in an honest Mean,
In Moderation placing all my Glory,
While Tories call me Whig, and Whigs a Tory.
Imitation of Horace, Satire II, i, 1733 (65–8)

The separation of Pope's beliefs into the philosophical, religious and political divisions propounded in this chapter is clearly an oversimplication of complex material. Philosophical ideas can never be set apart from religious and political views for the fundamental reason that any enquiry into the meaning of the universe must also be an enquiry into the existence of God and the behaviour of man. Pope's philosophical views are, therefore, both the result of and the basis for his religious beliefs and political commitments. The divisions used here for the sake of convenience are put forward in full awareness of the false separation frequently involved.

For the major part of his life Pope strove to avoid too contentious a position with regard to any one of these areas of thought. In his religion he was a practising member of the Catholic Church. At the same time he was only too aware of the precariousness of his position as a practising Catholic and took care not to make any too obvious demonstration of his faith. In *An Essay on Man* we find him treading a cautious path between respectable defence of established Christian orthodoxy and open interest in new interpretations of it. In his politics he was by temperament and instinct a conservative, but for most of his life took, if anything, even more care not to commit himself to the Tory party than he took not to draw special attention to his Catholicism. It was only during his later years, when his social position was assured and his political disillusion intense, that he openly espoused the cause of the Patriot opposition. And in his philosophical beliefs he was a clear and eclectic thinker, but rarely took either an extreme or an original position. As he says in the introductory note to *An Essay on Man*, 'If I could flatter myself that this Essay has any merit, it is in steering betwixt the extremes of doctrines seemingly opposite . . . '

An Essay on Man is the clearest and most sustained expression Pope made of his philosophical and ethical beliefs. It is also a forceful and concise introduction to ideas widely prevalent in early eighteenth-century England, and this chapter will be as particularly concerned with discussing this poem as the last chapter was with *An Essay on Criticism.*

Philosophy

Pope was not a professionally trained philosopher. He was widely read in philosophy, but he was not formally educated in the logical study of either science, ethics or metaphysics. He had an intellectual interest in the ordering of the universe and a profound concern for the behaviour of man and his pursuit of happiness, but this interest and concern were those of the creative poet rather than the professional philosopher. The reader will be disappointed if he goes to *An Essay on Man* looking for a regular system of philosophical thought.

This is not to say that the poem is valueless as philosophy, but that its primary value is poetic rather than philosophical and that its philosophical content is subservient to its artistic purpose. *An Essay on Man* is a mélange of philosophical ideas, some traditional, some current, that show Pope's powers as an eclectic more than as a speculative thinker. The only idea in the poem that might be called original is that of the *ruling passion,* and even that has distinct origins in the medieval belief concerning the shaping power of the bodily humours. Out of this mixture of ideas Pope precipitates a poetic realization of man and the universe he lives in that is consistent in itself, powerfully felt and keenly visualized. It is a poem of changing moods in which the speaker steers from 'grave to gay' and from 'lively to severe'. Sometimes the tone is sombre and reasoning, at other times it is witty and satiric, but most of the time it is exhortatory and didactic. It is a poem that sets out to 'vindicate the ways of God to man', and though one would not want to call it a religious poem the voice of the Christian advocate is never very far away.

Pope believes in an ordered universe. 'ORDER is Heav'n's first law', he tells us in his fourth epistle (49). It is not an easy order to explain, however, for though the Universal Cause 'acts to one end', it 'acts by various laws' (III, 2). The result is that the scene of man is 'A mighty maze! but not without a plan' (I, 6). The universe has a 'frame', 'bearing' and 'ties' (I, 29) that give it a coherent structure similar to that of a building, but man is not able to see the structure of this building as clearly as he might like because of obstacles he himself has erected. Pope's poem is an attempt, an *essai,* to describe this structure and define the right order as he sees it.

Pope inherited the popular medieval and renaissance idea, familiar in their day to both Chaucer and Shakespeare, of the Great Chain of Being. This was a metaphysical doctrine — based on *a priori* assumptions about God — that explained the existence, plenitude and unity of creation. It did this in accordance with deductive argument, concluding that the world was the best that God could have created, where nothing apart from him could be perfect. The important point for our purpose is that Pope adopted only certain parts of this belief. What he describes in *An Essay on Man* is the ladder of created nature, or *scala naturae*, which is one element in the Great Chain that can nevertheless be separated from it and argued on *a posteriori* grounds. The *scala naturae* describes the world of observable reality, 'Creation's ample range', from the 'green myriads in the peopled grass' to 'Man's imperial race' (I, 207–210). But it does not go any higher, as the Chain of Being does, and it is this limitation that Pope accepts when he says, near the beginning of the poem:

> Say first, of God above, or Man below,
> What can we reason, but from what we know?
> Of Man what see we, but his station here,
> From which to reason, or to which refer?
> Thro' worlds unnumber'd tho' the God be known,
> 'Tis ours to trace him only in our own.
>
> (I, 17–22)

Both Pope's present poem and his habits of mind generally are rootedly empirical. One need only recall the gloomy clerk in *The Dunciad*, Book IV, who 'nobly takes the high Priori Road' and then loses himself in a mist, to indicate Pope's consistent distrust of deductive habits of thought.

Pope certainly refers to the Great Chain of Being in *An Essay on Man*, but when he does so he is using the term to refer to empirically observed Nature. The chain and the ladder or scale become interchangeable terms for him:

>   On superior pow'rs
> Were we to press, inferior might on ours:
> Or in the full creation leave a void,
> Where, one step broken, the great scale's destroy'd:
> From Nature's chain whatever link you strike,
> Tenth or ten thousandth, breaks the chain alike.
>
> (I, 241–6)

If we are to be asked to entertain, as in that closing couplet, the possibility of a breakable chain, then Pope must stand some way outside the strict Great Chain philosophy, as it is called, and be using the terms *chain* and *scale* in his own fashion as interchangeable concepts. However, the underlying philosophy cannot be understood as so readily interchanged as this may sound. In the last analysis Pope remains critical of deductive methods of thought, preferring instead the empirical methods common in the eighteenth century that depend upon personal observation.

The order that Pope espouses in *An Essay on Man* is a paradoxical one based on integrated opposites. It is 'A Wild where weeds and flow'rs promiscuous shoot' (I, 7) and where 'ALL subsists by elemental strife' (I, 169). It is an order and harmony that Pope describes most powerfully in the opening lines of *Windsor-Forest* (see pp. 132–35), where,

> . . . Earth and Water seem to strive again,
> Not *Chaos*-like together crush'd and bruis'd,
> But as the World, harmoniously confus'd:
> Where Order in Variety we see,
> And where, tho' all things differ, all agree.
>
> (12–16)

This harmony of opposites, or *concordia discors* (Horace, *Epistle*, I, xii, 19), comprehends both strife and antagonism, so that 'All Discord, [is but] Harmony, not understood' (*Essay on Man*, I, 291), and 'jarring int'rests of themselves create / Th'according music of a well-mixed State' (III, 293–4). As Pope says at the opening of the third epistle: ' "The Universal Cause / Acts to one end, but acts by various laws" ' (III, 1–2).

These ideas concerning the organization of the universe at large form a backdrop in the poem for a unifying concept of man that develops in complexity. The presumptuous creature, or 'vile worm' as Pope calls him, who dominates the first two epistles becomes through a proper regard for virtue and love of God the regenerate subject of Epistles III and IV. Maynard Mack, in his introduction to the Twickenham edition of *An Essay on Man*, describes this fundamental pattern of development within the poem and its close relationship to Milton's great theme in *Paradise Lost* (see *Essay on Man*, I, 16) as follows: 'Beginning with a reminder of a paradise man has lost, the poem ends with a paradise he can regain'.

Behind every philosophical idea in the first two epistles of *An Essay on Man* there lies the voice of the poet wittily, ironically and scornfully cutting man down to size. Two particular aspects of man come in for repeated attack, his pride and his dullness. The two qualities are inseparable, making him a being both 'darkly wise, and rudely great' (II, 4). They are given metaphorical force through the contrasted but connected motions of ascension and descension that run through both epistles. Thus Pope ironically describes man sightlessly soaring (I, 12), or upward soaring (I, 173), or soaring with Plato (II, 23) in his pride, at the same time as he contemptuously depicts him blindly creeping (I, 12) or dropping into himself to be a fool (II, 30) in his ignorance.

It is the contrast between man's pride in his own potential and his actual dullness that makes him so obvious a target for ridicule. In Pope's view man is so presumptuous that he needs to be forcibly reminded of his own weakness, littleness and blindness (I, 36). He may seem principal on earth, but in fact he is only a minute part of the greater whole. His life fills merely a moment in eternity and a point in infinity (I, 72), but he is so proud that he aspires to the power of an angel, just as Satan aspired to the power of God:

> In Pride, in reas'ning Pride, our error lies;
> All quit their sphere, and rush into the skies.
> Pride still is aiming at the blest abodes,
> Men would be Angels, Angels would be Gods.
>
> (I, 123–6)

Man thinks he is the 'Great Lord of all things' and the 'Sole judge of Truth', but in fact he is a 'prey to all' and is hurled in 'endless Error' (II, 16–17). Even the wisest of men, Newton, is merely an ape when compared to the angels (II, 34). Again and again in these two epistles Pope brings man face to face with his feeble significance within the overall pattern of the universe.

Pope continually confronts the reader with the brevity of human life and the imminence of death. As early as the third line of the poem he says that 'life can little more supply / Than just to look about us and to die'. Further on in the first epistle death is described as 'the great teacher' (I, 92), and man is reminded of the fact that he is helplessly subject to plagues, earthquakes and tempests (I, 142–4). At the beginning of the second epistle man is described as 'born but to die', as if this were the sole reason for life (II, 10). Next we are told that man, at the very moment of his birth, 'receives the lurking principle of death' (II, 134). The theme is continued in the third epistle where the brevity and insignificance of human life is compared to the transience and fragility of a bubble:

> All forms that perish other forms supply,
> (By turns we catch the vital breath, and die)
> Like bubbles on the sea of Matter born,
> They rise, they break, and to that sea return.
>
> (III, 17–20)

Seen from the almost godlike perspective and detachment that the speaker assumes for himself, man's existence is purely momentary.

What Pope urges in the first two epistles is a Christian humility before these facts. Pope's advice is the same as that of Raphael to Adam in *Paradise Lost*, Book VIII:

> Solicit not thy thoughts with matters hid,
> Leave them to God above, him serve and fear;
> Of other Creatures, as him pleases best,
> Wherever plac't, let him dispose: joy thou
> In what he gives to thee, this Paradise
> And thy fair *Eve*: Heav'n is for thee too high
> To know what passes there; be lowly wise:
> Think only what concerns thee and thy being;
> Dream not of other Worlds, what Creatures there
> Live, in what state, condition or degree,
> Contented that thus far hath been reveal'd
> Not of Earth only but of highest Heav'n.
>
> (167–78)

According to Pope too, man must be lowly wise, he must recognize his limitations, know his 'own point' (I, 283), 'hope humbly' (I, 91), and learn to 'welcome Death' (II, 260). 'To reason right', he says, 'is to submit' (I, 164). This central directive comes again at the end of the first epistle:

> Submit — In this, or any other sphere,
> Secure to be as blest as thou canst bear.
>
> (I, 285–6)

'I believe', Pope wrote to Caryll on 3 September 1718, 'that there is not in the whole course of the Scripture any precept so often and so strongly inculcated, as the trust and eternal dependence we ought to repose in that Supreme Being who is our constant preserver and benefactor'. Man must submit to God's disposing power, and so far as Pope is concerned this means accepting traditional Christian explanations of the way the world is ordered.

Pope selects two main principles in human nature for special attention. These are Self-Love, which he sees as the 'urging' principle, and Reason, which he calls the 'restraining' principle. Thus the idea of a tension between opposites producing overall harmony (*concordia discors*), which we saw operating in the macrocosm, or world at large, is also seen operating in the microcosm of man. Shifting his imagery from that of horse-riding to that of watch-making, Pope calls self-love 'the spring of motion' and reason the 'comparing balance' (II, 59–60). Both qualities are necessary if man is to act to the best purpose, but self-love is naturally stronger, whereas reason must be developed through 'attention, habit, and experience' until it is capable of restraining self-love.

Pope then breaks self-love down into its different modes, or passions, which he groups into sets of opposites, such as love and hate, hope and fear, joy and grief, whose 'well accorded strife / Gives all the strength and colour of our life' (II, 121–2). It is at this point in the poem that Pope develops his theory of the ruling passion. This idea, developed further in the *Epistle to Cobham*, is that God gives every man one particular passion which will operate as a 'strong direction', or focal point, that will enable him to cope with the complexity of his other passions. Whether man lets this ruling passion lead him on to vice or virtue is entirely up to him and the way he uses his restraining reason. As a result there are both vicious and virtuous men, and this becomes yet another part of the variety that goes to make the overall order.

Reason is the faculty that separates man from the animals, but this does not mean that man is superior to the animals. In a strict Great Chain of Being philosophy this would be so, but the *scala naturae* doctrine that Pope develops is descriptive rather than hierarchical. It is quite clear in *An Essay on Man* that reason has severe limitations. The point is worth insisting on, for too many readers still come to Pope with unfavourable preconceptions of him as the great poet of 'an age of prose and reason'. But for Pope reason is not as good a guide in man as instinct is in animals. Reason is 'cool at best', and 'cares not for service, or but serves when prest', whereas 'honest instinct', to continue the military metaphor, 'comes a volunteer' (III, 85–8). Where 'heavier reason' labours at happiness in vain, instinct gains it by 'quick Nature'; and where reason is merely a direction imposed by man, instinct is the direct power of God operating in animals. Reason, then, must learn from instinct. The idea is parallel to that expressed in *An Essay on Criticism* where art, which is made by man, must copy nature, which is made byGod.

The fourth epistle deals with the possibility of human happiness. Pope takes the traditional Christian view that happiness has nothing to do with external goods or material wealth. For him the key to human happiness involves conforming to God's order, and the best way to do this is to fulfil the particular gifts that God has given one: 'Act well your part, there all the honour lies' (IV, 194). One acts one's part well when one leads a virtuous life — 'Virtue alone is happiness below' (IV, 310) — and one leads a virtuous life when one pursues humility, honesty, justice, truth, public-spiritedness and benevolence. These values, which emerge so strongly from the fourth epistle, form an important basis for an appreciation of Pope's later satires, for they are the positive criteria that underlie and inform all his attacks on the corruptions of Hanoverian England.

The effect of self-love on the virtuous mind is like that of a pebble thrown into a peaceful lake. Just as the pebble creates perfect circles which grow in size and perfection until they finally merge into the lake itself, so self-love will stir the virtuous mind first into love for its friends, parents and neighbours, next for its country and finally for the whole human race:

Self-love but serves the virtuous mind to wake,
As the small pebble stirs the peaceful lake;
The centre mov'd, a circle strait succeeds,
Another still, and still another spreads,
Friend, parent, neighbour, first it will embrace,
His country next, and next all human race,
Wide and more wide, th'o'erflowings of the mind
Take ev'ry creature in, of ev'ry kind;
Earth smiles around, with boundless bounty blest,
And Heav'n beholds its image in his breast.

(IV, 363–372)

Thus the poem that began with images of man's intellectual pride and physical mortality closes with images of man's spiritual regeneration and earth's boundless bounty. The vile worm has become an image of Heaven, and the threat of damnation that dominated the first two epistles has given way to the possibility of redemption in the last two.

Religion

It would be absurd to call Pope a religious poet in the sense that one calls George Herbert or Gerard Manley Hopkins religious poets. Religion is not the main concern or subject matter of his poetry, but its acceptance is always assumed and in indirect ways shapes much of the structure of his poetry.

Pope inherited his faith from a devoutly Catholic mother and a series of family priests who were appointed to educate him. He was never a fervent Catholic, however, and clearly gave his friends some hope that they might persuade him to join the Anglican Church. When his father died suddenly in 1717, Bishop Atterbury wrote to Pope offering his condolences and suggesting that now was the time for him to make this change of allegiance. Pope's reply is worth quoting at length because it is one of the fullest statements we have of his religious and political position:

> Whether the change would be to my spiritual advantage, God only knows: this I know, that I mean as well in the religion I now profess, as I can possibly ever do in another. Can a man who thinks so, justify a change, even if he thought both equally good? To such an one, the part of *joyning* with any one body of Christians might perhaps be easy, but I think it would not be so to *renounce* the other. . . . I'll tell you my politick and religious sentiments in a few words. In my politicks, I think no further than how to preserve the peace of my life, in any government under which I live; nor in my religion, than to preserve the peace of my conscience in any Church with which I communicate. I hope all

churches and all governments are so far of God, as they are rightly understood, and rightly administered: and where they are, or may be wrong, I leave it to God alone to mend or reform them; which whenever he does, it must be by greater instruments than I am.

It would be misleading to take this statement as a lasting testament of his religious and political beliefs — his political views, especially, became very much more definite as he grew older — but it does help to indicate his distinctly undogmatic feelings about Catholicism. His attitude to the Church he belongs to is similar to his attitude to the universe in *An Essay on Man*: it is not for man to presume to scan God's affairs. If there seems to be a certain lack of commitment to the Roman Catholic Church in this letter, there is at least a firm avowal of Christian faith and not the slightest doubt about his belief in God.

Pope lived at a time of important scientific discoveries concerning the universe. The development of the microscope had led to greatly increased knowledge of natural history in the latter part of the seventeenth century, and, most important of all, Newton had explained the gravitational basis of the universe in his *Principia*, 1687. These discoveries, unlike those of the nineteenth century, were taken as giving mathematical corroboration to God's majestic creation. What had before been a matter of faith was now regarded as a matter of scientific proof. Pope's epitaph intended for Sir Isaac Newton in Westminster Abbey sums up this attitude:

> Nature, and Nature's Laws lay hid in Night.
> God said, *Let Newton be*! and All was Light.

Pope's concept of a God who is both immanent and transcendent (*Essay on Man*, I, 267–80) is very close to Newton's concept in the *Opticks* of a divine spirit who is omnipresent at the same time as he is a uniform Being.

Pope's poetry is rarely either explicitly Catholic, or even explicitly Christian. His *Messiah*, 1712, is something of an exception, although even here one senses that the religious content is subservient to the carefully wrought display of grandeur. Nevertheless, his religious beliefs are deeply rooted in the general pattern of his thought and affect the structure and imagery of many of his poems. His delightful account of Belinda's toilet at the end of *The Rape of the Lock*, Canto I, for example, takes on a greater cogency when one sees it as a vain inversion of the Catholic mass. Similarly, the satiric description of Timon's banquet in *An Epistle to Burlington* gains additional force when one sees it as an Epicurean parody of the communion service. And, to take one more example of implicit structural influence, Earl Wasserman has shown that the portrait of the Man of Ross in

An Epistle to Bathurst is an '*imitatio Christi*', and that 'beneath the surface of the language there is a current of references to Christ's life and miracles'.

Allusion to scripture is another way in which Pope's religious beliefs become a subsumed part of his poetry. Sometimes he uses such allusion to give emphasis to a point he is making, as in the following couplet from *An Epistle to Bathurst*:

> Riches like insects, when conceal'd they lie,
> Wait but for wings, and in their season, fly.
>
> (171–2)

This is a rewriting of Proverbs 23; 5 — 'Wilt thou set thy eyes upon that which is not? for *riches* certainly make themselves wings; they fly away as an eagle toward heaven'. At other times Pope uses allusion to the Bible for ironic purposes in order to create a deliberate contrast between a corrupt present and an ideal past. Nowhere does he do this to more effect than in the magnificent finale to *The Dunciad*, where the catastrophe of the 'Universal Darkness' that 'buries All' is heightened through the ironic allusion to the universal light that began all in Genesis. It is through the use of allusive and associative religious imagery, rather than through formally structured divine poems, that Pope's religion makes itself felt in his poetry.

Politics

Pope is perhaps better known than any other poet in our literature for his close involvement with politics, yet until the last ten years or so of his life he went out of his way to cultivate a neutral position towards political parties. 'The general division of the *British* Nation is into Whigs and Tories', wrote Addison in *The Freeholder* of 25 June 1716, 'there being very few, if any, who stand Neuters in the Dispute, without ranging themselves under one of these denominations'. At the time of Addison's writing Pope was one of these few, and in order to understand both this early neutrality and his later commitment we need to take a brief look at the political scene in England during the early part of the eighteenth century.

The party warfare that so dominated early eighteenth-century English politics had its roots in the Exclusion Bill struggle of 1679–80 over whether the Duke of York, the future James II, should be allowed to succeed to the English throne as a Catholic. The term 'Tory' was used to describe those who supported the royal prerogative with regard to the succession, while the term 'Whig' was applied to those who supported the idea of a constitutional monarchy with government by parliament. The question of succession was crucial in the development of the political parties and came to a head again in the Glorious Revolution of 1688 and the Hanoverian succession of 1714. Broadly speaking the Tories can be identified with the High Church and the landed gentry, while the Whigs can be identified with the Low Church and the commercial interest. The trouble with such a simplification, of course, is that the actual patterns of allegiance were very much more complex than this suggests. There were some Tories, for example, who supported the revolutionary settlement of 1688, and there were some Whigs who later betrayed its principles.

An additional difference between the two parties during the reign of Queen Anne was that the Whigs supported the war with France while the Tories increasingly looked for an end to it. At first Marlborough's victories were more than enough to keep the Whigs in power, but as war-weariness increased so did the pressure for peace, and in 1710 the Whigs were replaced in office by the Tory Ministry of Robert Harley. Harley's administration lasted for four years until the death of Queen Anne in 1714. The resulting establishment of the Hanoverian succession led to the total collapse of the Tory party and the impeachment of its leaders. Harley himself was committed to the Tower, where he remained for two years. With the accession of George I there began a period of Whig supremacy in British politics that was to last for almost fifty years.

The important figures in this scenario as far as Pope is concerned are Henry St John, Viscount Bolingbroke, and Robert Walpole, Earl of Orford. Apart from Harley, Bolingbroke was the most dominant personality in the Tory Ministry of 1710–14. Indeed it was the struggle for power between these two men that finally brought the Ministry down. Rather than face the impeachment proceedings about to be brought against him by the Whigs, Bolingbroke fled in 1715 to France, where he became involved in the Pretender's court. He soon became disenchanted with the inefficiency of Jacobite plans, however, and dissociated himself from them in order to devote his time to the study of history and philosophy. In 1723 he was granted a pardon and returned to England where he eventually settled down at Dawley Farm near Twickenham. From 1725 until 1735, when he again left England for France, Bolingbroke led the Tory opposition to Walpole. Since he had been deprived of the right to hold political office, as a condition of his pardon, he had to do this in an extraparliamentary way through the columns of his newspaper, *The Craftsman*. Two of Bolingbroke's major works, *Remarks on the History of England*, and *A Dissertation on Parties*, first appeared in the weekly pages of this paper. It was during these years of opposition to Walpole that he became such a close friend of Pope's, influencing him deeply in both philosophical and political matters. Pope's admiration for Bolingbroke, or 'all-accomplish'd St JOHN' as he calls him in the *Epilogue to the Satires*, was almost

Sir Robert Walpole, aged about 54

unlimited. In addition to the great tribute to him in *An Essay on Man* there are references to him in the letters as 'a Being paullo minus ab angelis' (Pope to Warburton, 12 January 1744), and as 'the Greatest Man I ever knew' (Pope to Ralph Allen, 17 April 1739).

Sir Robert Walpole first came into prominence during the reign of Queen Anne, but he achieved his real fame under George I. From 1721 onwards he held power as First Lord of the Treasury for an unbroken period of twenty-one years. He was an even more dominant figure in the Whig party than we have just described Bolingbroke as being in the Tory opposition. He was an extremely skilful financier and an adroit manager of men. The main achievements of his long and successful administration were to give the country peace and prosperity. These were no mean achievements, but both were obtained at considerable cost in terms of personal principle. By the end of his period of supremacy he was widely considered to be a totally corrupt politician who had only managed to remain in office for so long because of the confused nature of the opposition.

Pope tried for a long time to keep on good terms with Walpole and in the summer of 1725 received a visit from him at his villa in Twickenham. During this and the next five years there are several references in Pope's correspondence to his having dined at Walpole's 'Sunday-Tables'. About 1730, however, his friendship with Sir

Robert, which had only been diplomatic at the best of times, began to waver, and after 1733 it changed to scarcely veiled personal antipathy and overt political opposition.

But this is to anticipate an account of Pope's earlier position with regard to party politics. He first came to public notice as a promising poet during those years at the end of Queen Anne's reign in which party warfare was reaching its height of contention. In this situation Pope did all he could to maintain a neutral position. Naturally drawn by his religious sympathies and friends in the Scriblerus Club to the Tory party, he nevertheless managed to retain acquaintances and friends among the leading Whigs. Not least of these was Addison who, as Pope later told Spence, advised 'me not to be content with the applause of half the nation. He used to talk much and often to me of moderation in parties, and used to blame his dear friend Steele for being too much of a party-man'. Addison was no doubt trying to win Pope over by stages to the Whig cause, but be that as it may, Pope seems to have accepted the advice. What he set out to do, as he later put it in his *Imitation of Horace, Satire II, i*, was to place all his glory in moderation with the result that 'Tories call me Whig, and Whigs a Tory'. It was a claim for neutrality that he repeated in the *Epilogue to the Satires*, Dialogue I (8), and that has a strong resemblance to his statement to Atterbury in 1717, already quoted in this chapter, that in politics he thought no further than how to preserve the peace of his life in any government under which he lived. This uncommitted position towards both political parties, which he maintained with considerable care over a long period of time, is clearly summed up in a letter he wrote to Swift on 28 November 1729:

> You know my maxim to keep clear of all offence, as I am clear of all interest in either party. . . . I have given some proofs in the course of my whole life (from the time when I was in the friendship of Lord Bolingbroke and Mr. Craggs even to this, when I am civilly treated by Sir R. Walpole) that I never thought myself so warm in any Party's cause as to deserve their money; and therefore would never have accepted it.

Gradually during the 1730s, however, and especially after the defeat of Walpole's Excise Bill in 1733 which so raised Tory hopes for the 'Great Man's' downfall, Pope began to join forces with the Patriot opposition. This was not quite the same thing as joining the Tory opposition, and Pope would no doubt have defended himself by insisting that what he was fighting for was a resurgence of public spirit, not of a political party. Nevertheless we need to ask why he should have chosen at this stage in his career to get embroiled in political warfare after studiously cultivating detachment to it over such a long period? There are perhaps two main reasons: the increasing personal influence over him exerted by Bolingbroke, and his growing dislike for Walpole.

Whatever the reason it is certainly true to say that the *Versifications of Donne* and *Imitations of Horace* written in the five years between 1733 and 1738 are full of pointed attacks on Walpole's administration that show a clear departure from Pope's earlier political impartiality. In the *Versification of Donne's Fourth Satire*, for example, he uses the character of an impertinent courtier to attack Walpole's graft:

> Then as a licens'd Spy, whom nothing can
> Silence, or hurt, he libels the *Great Man*;
> Swears every *Place entail'd* for Years to come,
> In sure Succession to the Day of Doom:
> He names the *Price* for ev'ry *Office* paid,
> And says our *Wars thrive ill*, because *delay'd*;
> Nay hints, 'tis by Connivance of the Court,
> That *Spain* robs on, and *Dunkirk*'s still a Port.

(158–65)

By putting the attack on Walpole into someone else's mouth Pope could always claim to be free of guilt. A few years later in the *Imitation of Horace, Epistle I, i*, addressed to Bolingbroke, he adopts a persona who talks about being a Patriot and battling for the State. In the same poem Walpole is referred to as a 'screen' and a 'wall of brass', and George II's court is seen as a lion's den. Finally, in the *Imitation of Horace, Epistle II, i*, Pope makes merciless fun of Walpole's peace policy while ironically praising George II:

> Oh! could I mount on the Maeonian wing,
> Your Arms, your Actions, your Repose to sing!
> What seas you travers'd! and what fields you fought!
> Your Country's Peace, how oft, how dearly bought!
> How barb'rous rage subsided at your word,
> And Nations wonder'd while they dropp'd the sword!
> How, when you nodded, o'er the land and deep,
> Peace stole her wing, and wrapt the world in sleep;
> Till Earth's extremes your mediation own,
> And Asia's Tyrants tremble at your Throne —

(394–403)

By the time one comes to the two dialogues of the *Epilogue to the Satires*, 1738, there is a new note of disillusion in Pope's attitude to party politics. His country's ruin makes him grave and he seems to be totally disenchanted with both parties. The attack on Walpole and the Court party is as strong as in the preceding five years, but there is a new dissatisfaction with both Tories and Patriots. The apocalyptic image of Vice corrupting the whole country that ends Dialogue I, for example, includes the Patriots:

> In Soldier, Churchman, Patriot, Man in Pow'r,
> 'Tis Av'rice all, Ambition is no more!
>
> (161–2)

When we come to Dialogue II the same sort of attitude is present. It is Vice he attacks, not Whigs, and Virtue he praises, not Tories. His list of worthy men includes Sommers, Halifax and Shrewsbury (77–9), each of whom had been a leading Whig earlier in the century. Pope insists that he follows Virtue and praises her wherever she shines, whether she point to 'Priest or Elder, Whig or Tory' (95–6).

What we find in these later poems is a disillusioned return to his earlier moderation, with a strong suggestion of a plague on both your houses. In the rewritten *Dunciad* of 1743, Cibber asks Dulness in Book I whether she would have him take up party politics:

> Or bidst thou rather Party to embrace?
> A friend to Party thou, and all her race;
> 'Tis the same rope at different ends they twist . . .
>
> (I, 205–7)

Tories and Whigs are merely different sides of the same coin, and it is quite clear that for Pope fervent partisans of either party serve Dulness's cause equally well.

It is perhaps ironic that at the very time when Pope's own attitude to party politics should have become so disenchanted his reputation in the country should have risen to the point at which he was represented by the party hacks as the 'spiritual patron of the poetical opposition to Walpole'. (Mack, *The Garden and the City*, p. 190). This emblematic significance attributed to his life can best be illustrated by the flurry of pamphlets printed at the end of 1740. The first of these, a savage denunciation of Walpole called *Are these things so?*, took the fictional form of an open letter from Alexander Pope, 'An Englishman in His Grotto', to Robert Walpole, 'A Great Man at Court'. In the two months between the 23 October, when *Are these things so?* was first published, and the 20 December, when *A Supplement to Are these things so?* appeared, no fewer than nine separate poems (four attacking Walpole and five defending him) were released, each directly related to one another and each written by an unnamed author. Though Pope had nothing whatever to do with this furious spate of party activity, it vividly illustrates the close relationship between literature and politics in the first half of the eighteenth century. While it is inconceivable that the publication of any poem in our own day, even by a major writer, should arouse such a response, it is reasonably typical of the first half of the eighteenth century that the publication of an occasional poem by a minor, indeed anonymous writer should do so.

I have argued that there was nearly always a certain detachment from party politics in Pope's poetry. This should not however be confused with a lack of involvement in the society around him. Pope was deeply committed to the society of his day, but his commitment is to its state of morality not the state of the parties. What he really attacks in the satires of the 1730s is not party political issues but the deeper corruption, as he saw it, of the new moneyed society. This was a state of affairs that had repelled him since at least as early as 1723 when he wrote to Broome saying that:

> Every valuable, every pleasant thing is sunk in an ocean of avarice and corruption. The son of a first minister is a proper match for a daughter of a late South Sea Director, — so money upon money increases, copulates, and multiplies, and guineas beget guineas in *Saecula saeculorum*.

It is this disgust for the new capitalism that rings most stridently through the poems of his later period. It perhaps gives an added perspective to our own views on the limitations of the capitalist system that Pope should challenge it not from a socialist point of view, but from a profoundly conservative one.

As Pope saw it his poetry was above all else a moral song. In January 1733 we find him writing to Caryll saying that his *Epistle to Bathurst* is,

> not the worst I have written and abounds in moral example, for which reason it must be obnoxious in this age. God send it does any good! I really mean nothing else by writing at this time of my life.

As we read through Pope's correspondence this emphasis on the poet's moral duty strikes us again and again. It is there at the beginning of the 1730s and it is there at the end. He tells Warburton on 12 November 1741, that he 'has no other merit than that of aiming by his moral strokes to merit some regard from such men as advance Truth and Virtue in a more effectual way'.

In the satires of the 1730s we find Pope, driven desperate as he sees the critical condition of his country – the sons of Mammon in charge and public spirit nowhere – responding to that condition by creating the figure of a satirist who protests his outrage and disgust with increasing fervour. The persona Pope creates in the *Imitations of Horace* is not content simply to pass moral comment on his times. He feels he must join the battle and he therefore enters the public arena, but he does so in no narrow party political way. The urbane friend of the great who speaks through Horace's poems takes on an unrelentingly aggressive public-spiritedness that transforms him into something akin to a public prosecutor. Morality becomes militant.

Part Two

Critical Survey

The winged Courser, like a gen'rous Horse,
Shows most true Mettle when you *check* his Course.

An Essay on Criticism, 1711, (86–7)

He gains all points, who pleasingly confounds,
Surprizes, varies, and conceals the Bounds.

Epistle to Burlington, 1731, (55–6)

The closed heroic couplet

All Pope's significant poetry is written in what is generally known as heroic couplets: five foot (pentameter) lines rhyming in pairs and with each foot containing the iambic structure of an unstressed syllable followed by a stressed syllable. There are occasional variations on this pattern, but they are extremely rare and, when they do occur, Pope clearly expects us to measure them against this norm. It is a form of extraordinary compression that stretches a poet's resources with language to the utmost. When used by an unskilled poet it can easily result in a stiff and monotonous effect, but when handled by a poet as skilled as Pope its very limitations provide a challenge that concentrates the poet's mind and imagination, and results in a remarkable variety of effects being achieved. At one point we may find Pope using its terse compactness to give punch to a satirical thrust, while at another we may find him exploiting its fundamental balance to evoke a lyrical scene. The immense variety of movement and tone that Pope achieves in his poetry is nearly always a matter of working within the bounds that the couplet imposes, rather than a matter of breaking away from them. His poetry illustrates the traditional paradox that one moves more easily for being in harness, or, to borrow the lines that Pope himself wrote in *An Essay on Criticism* when describing the strife between wit and judgment:

> The winged Courser, like a gen'rous Horse,
> Shows most true Mettle when you *check* his Course.

The heroic couplet had been used in English poetry long before Pope perfected it. Indeed, since each line is an iambic pentameter, its development is an integral part of the basic metrical tradition in English poetry. Chaucer had used the decasyllabic couplet in *The Canterbury Tales*, and two hundred years or so later John Donne had used it in his *Satires*. When he was still a young poet, Pope wrote 'modernizations' of parts of both these works as an exercise in developing his skill. But there is a crucial difference between Pope's couplets and those of Chaucer and Donne before him. Pope's poems are all written in the closed couplet form. This means that each couplet has a distinct element of self-enclosed completeness to it. This is not to say that each couplet is totally independent of those that surround it, but it does mean that there is a clear pause at the end of each line, and a more emphatic pause at the end of the second line. The open, or enjambed, couplet on the other hand, is one in which the meaning frequently flows across the line-end without any clear pause. It is so different in the expectations it creates in the reader, and in the demands that it makes on the writer, that it is easier to think of it as belonging to a separate tradition, though somewhat confusingly the open and closed couplets are frequently referred to under the same label of the heroic couplet.

It was in the second half of the seventeenth century and first part of the eighteenth that the heroic couplet reached its greatest popularity and, in the poetry of Dryden and Pope, its peak of performance. After Pope's death the heroic couplet continued to flourish in the poetry of Johnson, Goldsmith, Cowper and Churchill in the eighteenth century, and in that of Crabbe and Byron in the early part of the nineteenth. The change to a Romantic sensibility brought an end to its popularity. Wordsworth used it in some of his earlier poems and Keats tried it in both *Endymion* and *Lamia*, but on the whole it is fair to say that the classical astringencies of the couplet form were unsuited to the visionary nature of the Romantic theme which demands not stricture but freedom.

Dr Johnson tells us in his *Life of Dryden* that though 'some advances toward nature and harmony had been already made by Waller and Denham', it was to Dryden that the new versification owed its establishment. Pope makes much the same point in his *Imitation of Horace, Epistle II, i* when, through a rare use of the triplet, he says:

> Waller was smooth; but Dryden taught to join
> The varying verse, the full resounding line,
> The long majestic march, and energy divine.
>
> (267–9)

Throughout his life Pope considered Dryden as his great master in the use of the couplet. His tributes to Dryden are many and unwavering. Consider, for example, what he told Spence just before he died: 'I learned versification wholly from Dryden's works, who had improved it much beyond any of our former poets, and would probably have brought it to its perfection, had not he been unhappily obliged to write so often in haste.' Pope would have fully endorsed Dr Johnson's praise for what Dryden did to English poetry: '*laeteritiam invenit, marmoream reliquit*: he found it brick and he left it marble'.

There is not room here to give details of all the technical skills in the use of the couplet that Pope inherited from Dryden, but one particular development must be mentioned since it is one of the chief things that distinguish the two poets from the mass of journey-men practitioners of the form. This is the quality, referred to by Pope above, as Dryden's 'long majestic march', or his ability to use the couplet cumulatively to gain great oratorical effects that sweep away the limitations of the couplet working by itself. This is not to say that Dryden and Pope do not frequently use individual closed couplets for variety and contrast when they need to, but it is to point out that the basic unit in their poetry is the carefully composed paragraph rather than the two line closed couplet. Traditional accounts, which still recur in literary handbooks where Pope's use of the closed couplet is defined as one in which the two lines form a completely separate and individual unit of meaning, should be treated with considerable scepticism. In very few of Pope's couplets is it possible to appreciate the complex allusiveness of the various parts without considering the couplets that precede and follow. One of the great advances in the development of the form made by Dryden and Pope is this incorporation of the individual closed couplet into the larger organizational unit of the verse paragraph.

Pope's use of the closed couplet form is ideally suited to his concept of a universe in which particular and observable disorder yields, in a larger perspective, to overall harmony. The component parts of Pope's couplets, whether it be the entire first line operating against the second line, or the first half of the line operating against the second half, or the first quarter operating against the second quarter, establish a tension that is heightened for being caught in an overall form of such assured correctness, lucidity, and ease. Thus the final ironic paradox in *The Dunciad* is that, though the whole poem has illustrated in a thousand and one different ways the triumph of dread chaos and eternal night, that triumph is described by the poet in a medium of perfect order and clarity. We are enabled to see Universal Darkness burying all precisely because Pope's verse form creates so brilliant a light. Pope's couplets, like *Windsor-Forest* itself, are:

> Not *Chaos*-like together crush'd and bruis'd,
> But as the World, harmoniously confus'd:
> Where Order in Variety we see
> And where, tho' all things differ, all agree.
>
> (13–16)

The two main principles behind the following selection of Pope's poetry are first, an attempt to indicate how Pope handles the same form in different ways, depending on the 'kind' of poem he is writing; and second, an attempt to show how his handling of the form becomes increasingly accomplished until one arrives at the consummate mastery of *The Epilogue to the Satires* and *The Dunciad*, Book IV. For this reason the passages are arranged in chronological order of composition.

'Paper-sparing Pope.' Pope's handwriting from the manuscript of
An Epistle to Dr Arbuthnot.

(1)

Shut, shut the door, good John! fatigu'd I said,
Tye up the Knocker, say I'm sick, I'm dead.
The Dogstar rages; nay 'tis past a doubt,
All Bedlam, or Parnassus, is let out:
Rags on their back, & Papers in their hand,
They rave, & beg, & madden round the land.

What's _____ who prints before Term

obliged by Hunger, and Request of Friends

& just what you w'd have them make them.

To one, of Business, Sickness, I complain:
He leaves his Papers, comes, & comes again.

Three things another's modest wishes bound,
My Friendship — and a Prologue — & ten pound. 180
one Welsted sends to pre-

And I'm a Stranger — Ask him for a Place.

Sir Robert, & to turn Divine.

Bless me! that Pacquet! Patience —

An orphan Tragedy — a Virgin muse — 190
Enough! if I dislike it, Death & Rage!
If I approve, commend it to the Stage.
There, thanks _____ my whole commission ends,
Cibber & I are (luckily) no friends

print it

_____ think the Price too much —
Not Sir, if you revise it, & retouch.
All my Demurs but double his attacks,
At last he whispers, Do, & you go snacks.
Glad of a Quarrel, strait I clap the door,
Sir, let me see your works or you no more.

with Hymns to _____ & Satires upon _____

Think you, these authors' anger is a curse?
Ah Cleland
Believe me, their Repentance is a worse.

The weary Sun, as Learned Poets write,
Forsook th' *Horizon*, and roll'd down the Light;
While glitt'ring Stars his absent Beams supply,
And Night's dark Mantle overspread the Sky.   370
Then rose the Guests; and as the time requir'd,
Each paid his Thanks, and decently retir'd.
    The Foe once gone, our Knight prepar'd t'undress,
So keen he was, and eager to possess:
But first thought fit th'Assistance to receive,
Which grave Physicians scruple not to give;
Satyrion near, with hot *Eringo*'s stood,
Cantharides, to fire the lazy Blood,
Whose Use old Bards describe in luscious Rhymes,
And Criticks learn'd explain to Modern Times.   380
    By this the Sheets were spread, the Bride undrest,
The Room was sprinkled, and the Bed was blest.
What next ensu'd beseems not me to say;
'Tis sung, he labour'd 'till the dawning Day,
Then briskly sprung from Bed, with Heart so light,
As all were nothing he had done by Night;
And sipt his Cordial as he sate upright:
He kiss'd his balmy Spouse, with wanton Play,
And feebly sung a lusty Roundelay:
Then on the Couch his weary Limbs he cast;   390
For ev'ry Labour must have Rest at last.

CONTEXT. This passage is taken from *January and May*, Pope's youthful translation of Chaucer's *Merchant's Tale*. Although the translation was not published till 1709 it was written about five years earlier when Pope was only sixteen years old. At this point in the tale the merchant, having described the wedding celebrations of January, the old knight, and May, the young bride, and having contrasted his lecherous desires with her fresh beauty, comes to the comic consummation of their hypocritical marriage.

CRITICISM. The passage is included here as an example of the somewhat stiff nature of some of Pope's early couplets, and as something against which to measure the flexibility of his later poetry. Chaucer's handling of this episode has a mock heroic force. The incident begins with an elaborate description of the sunset, as if in preparation for the narration of an epic event, and keeps up the suspense by pausing to describe the parting guests. This is reduced to six rather jangling lines in Pope's translation with the caesura falling unfailingly at the end of the fourth or fifth syllable. Each noun has its regulation adjective and the whole picture is very generalized. The lines are lifeless, as though written for an academic exercise. Pope's second paragraph is even more mechanical in its movement with the caesura falling monotonously at the end of the second foot in seven of the eight lines. In none of these lines is there more than one caesura, and the overall effect is of verses written by rote.

But it is in the third paragraph that the loss in comparison to Chaucer is greatest. There is no parallel in Pope's translation for Chaucer's description of January taking May into his arms:

> And Januarie hath faste in armes take
> His fresshe May, his paradis, his make.
> He lulleth hire, he kisseth hire ful ofte;
> With thikke brustles of his berd unsofte,
> Lyk to the skin of houndfissh, sharp as brere —
> For he was shave al newe in his manere —

The rhythmic variety and colloquial directness of these lines is entirely absent from Pope's modernization. Chaucer then develops the comedy by having January make a hypocritical speech to May in which his bravado struggles to cover up for his failing physical performance. But all this is reduced to one coyly prurient line in Pope's versions: 'What next ensu'd beseems not me to say.' Finally Chaucer's superb description of January's pathetically grotesque dawn chorus next day,

> He was al coltissh, ful of ragerye,
> And ful of jargon as a flekked pye.
> The slakke skin aboute his nekke shaketh.
> Whil that he sang, so chaunteth he and craketh.

has been diminished to 'And feebly sung a lusty Roundelay', by Pope.

It is of course unfair, and to a certain extent misleading, to compare the early verses of an apprentice poet with the poised production of a mature artist. The point of this excerpt is not to attempt any comparative evaluation of two great poets, but first to demonstrate the stiffness and over-balanced rigidity that the couplet form creates when the poet is not fully in control of his material, and second to indicate, through an examination of what Pope leaves out as much as of what he puts in, the somewhat academic quality of the young poet's sensibility. One must beware, however, of attempting to draw any sweeping generalizations about the young Pope from an analysis of one isolated passage. His short

imitation of Chaucer, written sometime before 1709, is a strong
reminder that he had a wonderfully sensitive ear for the rhythms
of Chaucer's poetry when he wanted to preserve them, and to read
the opening lines of *Windsor-Forest* (the next excerpt), written at
approximately the same time as the translation of the *Merchant's
Tale*, is to become immediately aware of a poet in full command of
the couplet form. The chronological closeness of these two passages
illustrates the danger of suggesting neat conclusions about Pope's
development from early experimentation to achieved mastery of
the couplet form. All one can say, perhaps, is that the young poet
probably had to work harder and more carefully at his verse to
attain the desired effects than the mature poet. One senses in
reading the *Imitations of Horace*, for example, that Pope can make the
verse do whatever he wants to without really trying. It is a matter of
practice and experience:

> True Ease in Writing comes from Art, not Chance,
> As those move easiest who have learn'd to dance.

What we can see in *January and May*, and other early pieces, is
Pope learning to dance.

from *Windsor-Forest*

Thy Forests, *Windsor*! and thy green Retreats,
At once the Monarch's and the Muse's Seats,
Invite my Lays. Be present, Sylvan Maids!
Unlock your Springs, and open all your Shades.
Granville commands: Your Aid O Muses bring!
What Muse for *Granville* can refuse to sing?
    The Groves of *Eden*, vanish'd now so long,
Live in Description, and look green in Song:
These, were my Breast inspir'd with equal Flame,
Like them in Beauty, should be like in Fame.   10
Here Hills and Vales, the Woodland and the Plain,
Here Earth and Water seem to strive again,
Not *Chaos*-like together crush'd and bruis'd,
But as the World, harmoniously confus'd:
Where Order in Variety we see,
And where, tho' all things differ, all agree.
Here waving Groves a checquer'd Scene display,
And part admit and part exclude the Day;
As some coy Nymph her Lover's warm Address
Nor quite indulges, nor can quite repress.   20

There, interspers'd in Lawns and opening Glades,
Thin Trees arise that shun each others Shades.
Here in full Light the russet Plains extend;
There wrapt in Clouds the blueish Hills ascend:
Ev'n the wild Heath displays her Purple Dies,
And 'midst the Desert fruitful Fields arise,
That crown'd with tufted Trees and springing Corn,
Like verdant Isles the sable Waste adorn.
Let *India* boast her Plants, nor envy we
The weeping Amber or the balmy Tree,   30
While by our Oaks the precious Loads are born,
And Realms commanded which those Trees adorn.
Not proud *Olympus* yields a nobler Sight,
Tho' Gods assembled grace his tow'ring Height,
Than what more humble Mountains offer here,
Where, in their Blessings, all those Gods appear.
See *Pan* with Flocks, with Fruits *Pomona* crown'd,
Here blushing *Flora* paints th'enamel'd Ground,
Here *Ceres'* Gifts in waving Prospect stand,
And nodding tempt the joyful Reaper's Hand,   40
Rich Industry sits smiling on the Plains,
And Peace and Plenty tell, a STUART reigns.

CONTEXT. These are the opening lines of *Windsor-Forest*, published
in 1713 and written at two different periods. The first part (1–290)
was written in 1704, while the second part (291–434) was written
nine years later to celebrate the Treaty of Utrecht in 1713. The lines
above are therefore almost exactly contemporary with the lines
in the previous passage from *January and May*.

CRITICISM. *Windsor-Forest* stands as a monument to Pope's positive feelings about the Age of Queen Anne at an early period in
his life, just as, in its very different way, *The Dunciad* stands as
a monument to his negative feelings about the Hanoverian Age
at a late period in his life. To place this excerpt alongside the
last in this section of the book, from *The Dunciad*, Book IV, is
to make a dramatic contrast between Pope's early hopes for 'peace
and plenty' and his later fears of 'Universal Darkness'.

Perhaps the most striking thing about the opening paragraph,
especially when compared with the translation of Chaucer, is the
urbane movement of the verse. There is an assurance in the lines
that makes itself felt through the fluctuating ease of the opening
address. This is not simply a matter of a greater variety in the placing
of the caesura, though that is certainly to be found, so much as a
new flexibility that results from a more careful and complex

organization of the syntactical units. In the opening invocation to Windsor Forest there is both sufficient balance in the rhythm (e.g. line 2) to give a sense of harmony, and sufficient check (e.g. the double caesura of line 1) to give a slight contrast and avoid the dangers of mechanical harmony. The elaboration of the subject in the opening sentence that occurs in the first two lines contrasts with the brevity of the main verb and object at the beginning of the third line. The poem then takes a sudden change of direction as the poet moves from the indicative to the imperative mood. The changing pattern in the unfolding syntactical structure of the paragraph forces the reader to pay special attention. At the same time as the mood of the verb changes, however, an element of stability and continuity is retained by keeping the imperative clauses parallel to one another:

> Be present, Sylvan Maids!
> Unlock your Springs, and open all your Shades.

In the fifth and sixth lines Pope moves back to the indicative and emphasizes the compliment to Granville by inverting the verbs so that the couplet has a distinctly heroic quality. The first six lines form a highly conventional opening to the poem, but they do so with an ease and charm that carry the reader into the poem proper in a relaxed and expectant frame of mind.

The description of the forest that forms the subject of the long second paragraph begins with a comparison to Milton's description of Eden in *Paradise Lost*. The actual forest Pope knew so well is transformed through literary allusion into a modern paradise. Windsor Forest becomes a microcosm of the glory of God's creation throughout the world:

> Here Hills and Vales, the Woodland and the Plain,
> Here Earth and Water, seem to strive again,
> Not *Chaos*-like together crush'd and bruis'd,
> But as the World, harmoniously confus'd:
> Where Order in Variety we see,
> And where, tho' all things differ, all agree.

The couplet form, with its inherent structural duality, is ideally suited to the theme of *concordia discors* being expounded here. In the first line and a half, each quarter line is in opposition to the next quarter at the same time as it is bound to it by the parallel structure. In the next couplet each line is opposed to the other through the contrary ideas ('Not . . . , But . . .'), while they are bound together by the repeating rhythm and connecting rhyme.

134

The harmony that results despite the opposition of disparate elements in Pope's poetry is directly related to the harmony that results from the opposition of disparate elements in the physical world. The order in variety that exists in the handling of the couplet form helps to establish the 'Order in Variety' in Windsor Forest.

As Pope develops his description of the forest, so he introduces the technique of antithesis to capture the tension between opposites that is the source of the harmony he celebrates. The daylight in the forest is brighter for being partly excluded by the trees, just as the lover's overtures are heightened for being partly repressed by the coy mistress. Sometimes the antithesis works within the couplet, with one line balanced against the other (23 and 24), and sometimes it works within the individual line, with one half of the line operating against the other (26 and 28). Ideas and images that would move in different directions if developed separately are thus fused together through the verse form to give an overall harmony.

The mood becomes increasingly triumphant as the poem progresses. The rich luxuriance of eastern vegetation, 'the weeping Amber or the balmy Tree', becomes subservient to the sturdy strength of the English oak. Even 'proud Olympus' is seen as no more noble than the humble height of the English hills. The last comparison is clearly farfetched, but it has been so fully prepared for that it is quite acceptable in its context. Thus Windsor Forest, which Pope began by comparing to the Christian Garden of Eden, is now compared to the home of the classical gods. It has become a mythological paradise with Queen Anne transformed, by implication, in the last sentence of the paragraph, into Juno commanding Roman gods on English soil. The opening command to attend ('See . . .), the fullness of the rhythms, the affirmative force of the adjectival participles (blushing, waving, nodding and smiling), the alliteration and personification, and the continuing parallelism of the 'Here' clauses, all serve to reinforce this final panegyric effect.

And now, unveil'd, the *Toilet* stands display'd,
Each Silver Vase in mystic Order laid.
First, rob'd in White, the Nymph intent adores
With Head uncover'd, the *Cosmetic* Pow'rs.
A heav'nly Image in the Glass appears,
To that she bends, to that her Eyes she rears;
Th'inferior Priestess, at her Altar's side,
Trembling, begins the sacred Rites of Pride.
Unnumber'd Treasures ope at once, and here
The various Off'rings of the World appear;   130
From each she nicely culls with curious Toil,
And decks the Goddess with the glitt'ring Spoil.
This Casket *India's* glowing Gems unlocks,
And all *Arabia* breathes from yonder Box.
The Tortoise here, and Elephant unite,
Transform'd to *Combs*, the speckled and the white.
Here Files of Pins extend their shining Rows,
Puffs, Powders, Patches, Bibles, Billet-doux.
Now awful Beauty puts on all its Arms;
The Fair each moment rises in her Charms,   140
Repairs her Smiles, awakens ev'ry Grace,
And calls forth all the Wonders of her Face;
Sees by Degrees a purer Blush arise,
And keener Lightnings quicken in her Eyes.
The busy *Sylphs* surround their darling Care;
These set the Head, and those divide the Hair,
Some fold the Sleeve, whilst others plait the Gown;
And *Betty's* prais'd for Labours not her own.

CONTEXT. This is the closing paragraph of Canto I of *The Rape of the Lock*, in Five Cantos, published in 1714. In the preceding parts of Canto I the poet has announced the theme of the poem (1–12), described Belinda first waking up before falling asleep again (13–26), recounted the warning dream put into her head by Ariel (27–114), and then shown Belinda completely forget the warning when she does finally wake up and her eyes light on a *billet-doux* (115–20). This last paragraph describes, in mock epic terms, her preparation for the day's events as she dresses and puts on her make-up.

CRITICISM. The paragraph is a superb example of Pope's mock epic poetry at its most skilful. Belinda's toilet preparations are invested with all the mock solemnity of the epic hero going to worship before arming for battle. The dressing table is 'unveil'd', like an altar, and all the 'silver vases', containing various kinds of make-up, are transformed into religious chalices laid out 'in mystic order'. Belinda herself is 'rob'd in white' (a petticoat perhaps) like a priest, and she 'adores' (note the careful choice of religious language) the 'Cosmetic Pow'rs', which wittily suggest both cosmic forces and a new class of angels (Powers were an order of angels within the celestial hierarchy).

As Belinda first bows her head to the 'heav'nly Image' she worships (her own reflection), then raises her eyes in adoration, it becomes clear that what Pope is presenting in this passage is an inverted Mass in which all the ritualized ceremony that should be used to worship God is used instead to worship social and personal appearance. Catholic readers especially would be quick to realize the sacrilegious nature of Belinda's toilet. The touch is light enough on the surface, but the full implications of the scene are more farreaching. What we have here is Pope's youthful response to a theme that consistently recurs in his poetry — the theme of man's presumption and pride. Belinda's vanity in worshipping her own image in *The Rape of the Lock* is only a more lighthearted version of man's pride in elevating his own importance in *An Essay on Man*. The difference is that whereas in 1714 Pope can jokingly see Belinda's vanity transforming her into a 'Goddess', in *An Essay on Man*, twenty years later, Pope describes man's pride transforming him into a 'vile worm'.

The parody of religious worship is of course a way of ridiculing feminine vanity not religion itself, just as the use of a mock epic form in the poem as a whole is a way of diminishing trivial events not an attempt to make fun of epic poetry. The parody continues as Betty, 'the inferior Priestess', presents sacrificial oblations, 'the various Off'rings of the World', to the Goddess and decks Belinda with the 'glittering Spoil'. Pope has moved now to the arming of the epic hero for battle. In terms of the toilet the word 'spoil' refers to the various jewels and perfumes used to make up Belinda, but in terms of the mock epic the word describes the arms and armour seized from a defeated enemy. At the same time the word has a further ambiguity, for it also suggests a more general plunder and spoliation. Belinda's beauty depends on imported luxuries pillaged from India and Arabia. The economic criticism that lurks behind the description is an early indication of those concerns that Pope developed with such burning indignation in the satires of the 1730s. The touch here, however, is more jocular, and is perhaps typified by the comic unification of the small and the great as the shell of the tortoise and the ivory of the elephant are converted into combs for a lady's dressing-table. Distortions in scale are intrinsically funny as Swift shows so effectively in the Lilliputian and Brobdingnagian contrasts of *Gulliver's Travels*.

The comparison of Belinda to the epic hero arming for battle continues with the military allusion of the 'files of pins' extending their 'shining Rows' like columns of soldiers lined up in polished armour. Belinda's various items of armour are then listed: 'Puffs, Powders, Patches, Bibles, Billet-doux'. Alliteration gives precision to the catalogue and adds force to the telling juxtaposition of 'Bibles' and 'Billet-doux'. Belinda makes no distinction between spiritual and amatory scripture. As one by one she puts on all her 'arms', so she becomes a more redoubtable protagonist for the epic contest with the Baron. Finally her Beauty is 'awful', and her eyes flash with 'keener Lightnings'.

The whole paragraph has a remarkable deftness of touch. The mock epic allusions are playful without being heavyhanded, and the criticism of Belinda is sufficiently gentle to avoid giving offence. Indeed there is a sense in which Belinda emerges as a figure of praise rather than criticism. She is a heroine whose beauty, charms, smiles, face and eyes are all admired. The final image is one of pleasure in the overall effect she produces.

In terms of the complete poem, what Pope is doing is showing Belinda, who represents the fashionable young eighteenth-century lady, making elaborate preparations to attract the foppish young eighteenth-century man. The scene is an integral part of the analysis of the ritual of courtship that runs through the whole poem. Pope's attitude to such overdisplay is essentially good-natured, even forgiving. If one puts this passage beside his description of Lady Mary Wortley Montagu's toilet preparations in *An Epistle to a Lady*, (25–8), written twenty years later, one is immediately made aware of a very different attitude. Although Belinda's beauty is transient, it is at least delicate and 'glittering' while it lasts. Lady Mary's toilet, on the other hand, is a 'greasy task'. She is compared to an insect rather than an epic hero:

> So morning Insects that in muck begun,
> Shine, buzz, and fly-blow in the setting sun.

Pope's disgust for female vanity has taken on a Swiftian dimension. The interested reader should compare Swift's *The Progress of Beauty*, 1719, or *A Beautiful Young Nymph Going to Bed*, 1731, a kind of anti-toilet poem which describes the process of stripping down rather than making up. Finally the passage should be compared to the opening of 'A Game of Chess' in *The Waste Land*. Eliot too satirizes the fragile world of extravagant luxury, but whereas Belinda is fully at ease in her world, the lady in Eliot's poem is as nervous and unsure of herself as the flickering flames that spring from the sevenbranched candelabra. Augustan confidence has given way to twentieth-century doubt.

How happy is the blameless Vestal's lot!
The world forgetting, by the world forgot.
Eternal sun-shine of the spotless mind!
Each pray'r accepted, and each wish resign'd;   210
Labour and rest, that equal periods keep;
'Obedient slumbers that can wake and weep';
Desires compos'd, affections ever ev'n,
Tears that delight, and sighs that waft to heav'n.
Grace shines around her with serenest beams,
And whisp'ring Angels prompt her golden dreams.
For her th'unfading rose of *Eden* blooms,
And wings of Seraphs shed divine perfumes;
For her the Spouse prepares the bridal ring,
For her white virgins *Hymenaeals* sing;   220
To sounds of heav'nly harps, she dies away,
And melts in visions of eternal day.
    Far other dreams my erring soul employ,
Far other raptures, of unholy joy:
When at the close of each sad, sorrowing day,
Fancy restores what vengeance snatch'd away,
Then conscience sleeps, and leaving nature free,
All my loose soul unbounded springs to thee.
O curst, dear horrors of all-conscious night!
How glowing guilt exalts the keen delight!   230
Provoking Daemons all restraint remove,
And stir within me ev'ry source of love.
I hear thee, view thee, gaze o'er all thy charms,
And round thy phantom glue my clasping arms.
I wake — no more I hear, no more I view,
The phantom flies me, as unkind as you.
I call aloud; it hears not what I say;
I stretch my empty arms; it glides away:
To dream once more I close my willing eyes;
Ye soft illusions, dear deceits, arise!   240
Alas no more! — methinks we wandring go
Thro' dreary wastes, and weep each other's woe;
Where round some mould'ring tow'r pale ivy creeps,
And low-brow'd rocks hang nodding o'er the deeps.
Sudden you mount! you beckon from the skies;
Clouds interpose, waves roar, and winds arise.
I shriek, start up, the same sad prospect find,
And wake to all the griefs I left behind.

CONTEXT. These lines are taken from *Eloisa to Abelard* written during

1716, and first published in Pope's collected *Works*, 1717. Pope's poem is based on the well-known love story of Peter Abelard (1079–1142), one of the most famous theologians and scholars of his day, and Héloïse (1101–64), his almost equally erudite pupil. Their love for each other ended in tragedy when Héloïse's uncle hired ruffians to break into Abelard's chamber by night and castrate him. The two lovers retired to separate convents and only came together again in the grave. The famous love letters were written about twenty years later, after a long series of further calamities. It is worth noting that they are love letters in a rather special sense, being written from the poignancy and pain of accumulated reflection rather than in the heat of passion.

Pope took Eloisa's three letters, which had been translated from Latin to English by John Hughes in 1713, and compressed them into one continuous letter in his poem. Eloisa is imagined speaking throughout the poem, whose main theme is her struggle between love of God and love of man, or, to use Pope's words from *The Argument* to the poem, 'the struggles of grace and nature, virtue and passion'. Passages presenting Eloisa's internal turmoil are mixed with passages describing the sombre romantic setting that Pope gives to the poem in order to heighten the emotion. The poem is loosely constructed around Eloisa's account of the development of their love for one another, but it is not a narrative poem in the usual sense of the word, for Pope assumes the reader's familiarity with the story and sets out to give a particular interpretation of it.

The poem is a heroic epistle in the manner of Ovid's *Heroides*. Eloisa's plight is presented in the grand style, and if we tend to find this somewhat artificial today it is largely because we no longer understand and share in the heroic convention. The purpose of this convention is not so much to make the reader feel with the heroic person as to pinpoint the significant aspects of the heroic situation so that the reader can learn from them. The importance lies, as so often in Augustan literature, on the public rather than the private significance of events. The attempt to get inside a character's feelings is less important than the attempt to present the reader with a clear picture of the moral choices confronted.

CRITICISM. The lines presented here contrast the peace of the true nun, 'the blameless Vestal's lot', with the tumult in Eloisa's 'erring soul', and are chosen partly to show how Pope's poetic range includes the expression of states of feeling not usually associated with him, and partly to show how he can use the heroic couplet to create different effects within the same poem.

In the first paragraph Pope uses all the resources at his command to create a sense of the heavenly tranquillity of the perfect nun's life.

Whereas the natural balance of the couplets' movement is frequently used by Pope to enact a sense of conflict, it is used here to enact an even and serene mood. A single caesura falls in the middle of each line, and the two halves are carefully balanced against one another. The imagery of 'eternal sunshine' and grace that 'shines around her with serenest beams' connects the nun's perfection with the light of God. Indeed the imagery of the paragraph connects her with the perfection of various senses. There is brilliant colour in her 'golden dreams', sweet smell in 'th'unfading rose' and 'divine perfumes', and soft music in the 'sounds of heav'nly harps'. The description of the nun's life mounts to a climax in the last six lines. The rhetorical pattern of this closing sentence, with its parallel introductory 'For her . . . ' clauses leading into the gentle release of the last line, gives a final heroic elevation to the perfect harmony of her life.

By contrast the second paragraph, in which Eloisa describes her own dreams, is broken in movement and menacing in its imagery. The change is immediately apparent from the opening couplet where the repetition of the stress on 'other' prepares the reader for the shift in mood that follows. Once Eloisa's 'conscience' (227) rests 'at the close of each sad sorrowing day', then her 'nature' is free to assert its greater consciousness in her dreams. The inner tumult that disturbs her during her sleep, 'all-conscious night' (229), is established through a poetry of great intensity and drama. Eloisa is telling us what her dreams are like and to this extent the poetry is descriptive, but she makes us feel so much part of her dreams that it is also extremely dramatic. The movement of the verse becomes quite unpredictable as the short phrases act out the struggle between 'grace' and 'nature' going on inside her. The use of a series of oxymorons ('dear horrors', 'glowing guilt', 'keen delight', 'dear deceits', and 'soft illusions') is no mere rhetorical device for heroic embellishment, but a way of compressing the opposite forces that create the turmoil within. The constant reiteration of the first person singular pronoun heightens our sense of the degree to which Eloisa, in recounting her dreams, has become immersed in their actuality.

In the last eight lines she awakes from this dream of guilty pleasure with Abelard, only to find herself plunged into a nightmare of sharper pain in which they wander together through a dreary, almost Gothic, landscape. The gloomy details of the scene are added to heighten the sublimity of Eloisa's grief. She and Abelard traverse a melancholic waste land that contains a 'mouldering tower' covered in 'pale ivory' and 'low-brow'd rocks' that hang threateningly over the ocean. Then, as Abelard leaves her in mystical ascension, images of wild nature further heighten her uncontrollable feelings: 'Clouds interpose, waves roar, and winds arise.'

Finally she wakes to a world that is no less painful even if less frightening:

> I shriek, start up, the same sad prospect find,
> And wake to all the griefs I left behind.

The setting of the nightmare is highly romantic. It both looks back to Miltonic gloom (e.g. *Il Penseroso*) and forward to the ideas and images found in the Gothic novels of Walpole and Mrs Radcliffe, or in the poetry of Keats (e.g. *The Eve of St. Agnes*). It is another reminder of the range of Pope's sensibility and of the dangers of any too rigid conception of what it means to call him a neoclassical writer.

An Epistle to Burlington

My Lord advances with majestic mien,
Smit with the mighty pleasure, to be seen:
But soft — by regular approach — not yet —
First thro' the length of yon hot Terrace sweat,   130
And when up ten steep slopes you've dragg'd your thighs,
Just at his Study-door he'll bless your eyes.
   His Study! with what Authors is it stor'd?
In Books, not Authors, curious is my Lord;
To all their dated Backs he turns you round,
These Aldus printed, those Du Suëil has bound.
Lo some are Vellom, and the rest as good
For all his Lordship knows, but they are Wood.
For Locke or Milton 'tis in vain to look,
These shelves admit not any modern book.   140
   And now the Chapel's silver bell you hear,
That summons you to all the Pride of Pray'r:
Light quirks of Musick, broken and uneven,
Make the soul dance upon a Jig to Heaven.
On painted Cielings you devoutly stare,
Where sprawl the Saints of Verrio or Laguerre,
On gilded clouds in fair expansion lie,
And bring all Paradise before your eye.
To rest, the Cushion and soft Dean invite,
Who never mentions Hell to ears polite.   150
   But hark! the chiming Clocks to dinner call;
A hundred footsteps scrape the marble Hall:
The rich Buffet well-colour'd Serpents grace,
And gaping Tritons spew to wash your face.
Is this a dinner? this a Genial room?
No, 'tis a Temple, and a Hecatomb.

A solemn Sacrifice, perform'd in state,
You drink by measure, and to minutes eat.
So quick retires each flying course, you'd swear
Sancho's dread Doctor and his Wand were there.   160
Between each Act the trembling salvers ring,
From soup to sweet-wine, and God bless the King.
In plenty starving, tantaliz'd in state,
And complaisantly help'd to all I hate,
Treated, caress'd, and tir'd, I take my leave,
Sick of his civil Pride from Morn to Eve;
I curse such lavish cost, and little skill,
And swear no Day was ever past so ill.
   Yet hence the Poor are cloath'd, the Hungry fed;
Health to himself, and to his Infants bread   170
The Lab'rer bears: What his hard Heart denies,
His charitable Vanity supplies.
   Another age shall see the golden Ear
Imbrown the Slope, and nod on the Parterre,
Deep Harvests bury all his pride has plann'd,
And laughing Ceres re-assume the land.

CONTEXT. These lines are taken from *An Epistle to Burlington*, first
published by itself in 1731, but then grouped together by Pope with
three other epistles as part of his great ethical scheme, or 'Opus
Magnum', in his collected *Works*, Vol. II, 1735. Later still, in the
posthumous 1751 edition of Pope's *Works*, Warburton retitled it as
Moral Essay IV, and despite the fact that it was the first of the so-
called *Moral Essays* to be written or published, it is perhaps still
best known by this title. The passage is the first included in this
section that may be said to belong to Pope's later poetry (written
after the collected *Works* of 1717).

Pope's central theme in *An Epistle to Burlington* concerns good
taste in architecture and landscape gardening. The poem's addressee,
Lord Burlington, is an outstanding example of such taste, but, Pope
argues, half the land is filled with 'imitating fools' (26), who think
good taste can be acquired by wealth rather than sense (cf. Lord
Squanderfield in Hogarth's *Mariage à la Mode*). The lines presented
above are taken from the well-known Timon's Villa section of the
poem in which Pope conducts the reader on a guided tour of an imaginary eighteenth-century house and gardens that typify bad taste.
The complete description of Timon's Villa (99–176) is too long to
include here, so the tour of the park and gardens (99–126) has been
omitted in favour of the description of the house (127–68) and Pope's
concluding thoughts on the extravagant expenditure displayed
(169–76).

The identification of Timon calls for a brief note. *An Epistle to Burlington* was Pope's first publication since he had attacked his literary enemies in *The Dunciad* of 1729. There was, therefore, a great number of persons eager for the chance to get even with him. Immediately on the publication of the *Epistle* they fastened on the character of Timon and declared that Pope meant his acquaintance James Brydges, Duke of Chandos, to be portrayed and that this was a typical example of his ingratitude and treachery. Pope was greatly upset by this charge, and first wrote privately, and then publicly, to Burlington denying it: 'For nothing is so evident, . . . as that character of Timon is collected from twenty different absurditys and improprieties, and was never the picture of any one human creature.' Despite this denial the charge stuck and for almost two centuries Timon was popularly supposed to be a character sketch of Chandos. Recent scholarship, however, has confirmed the correctness of Pope's statement to Burlington. Many contemporary examples of conspicuous consumption are clearly satirized in Timon's Villa, and if the portrait is part Cannons (Chandos's house), it is also part Chatsworth (the Duke of Devonshire's house), part Blenheim (the Duke of Marlborough's house), and part Houghton (Robert Walpole's house), to name only three others.

CRITICISM. The excerpt begins with a short transitional paragraph that connects the walk round the garden with the tour through the house. Timon's garden has been notable for its complete absence of proportion. 'Huge heaps of littleness' dwarf the human scale, so that Timon himself appears as no more than a 'puny insect'. And yet this insect is puffed up with pride and pomposity, 'smit with the mighty pleasure, to be seen'. Just as his garden lacks all pleasing intricacy and variety, so the approach to his house is rigid and formal:

> But soft — by regular approach — not yet —
> First thro' the length of yon hot Terrace sweat,
> And when up ten steep slopes you've dragg'd your thighs,
> Just at his Study-door he'll bless your eyes.

The deliberate movement of the couplets and the slow, drawn-out length of the syllables carefully enact the exhausting process of entering the house.

The description of Timon's study is a satire on false learning. Timon is interested in the outside not the inside of books. Old books represent a good financial investment for him (much as paintings by old masters do in the modern market) rather than a source for learning and enjoyment. Pope first lets Timon show the reader round the room, pointing out the books' great age and fine bindings, and then smartly undercuts the display with his own acid comment saved up for the end of the sentence:

> Lo some are Vellom, and the rest as good
> For all his Lordship knows, but they are Wood.

The timing is perfect, and leads quite naturally into the scornful dismissiveness of the last two lines in the paragraph.

When we are led into the chapel and the dining-room we find a total inversion of appropriate values. All the ceremony and ritual that belong in a chapel are found instead in the dining-room, and all the geniality and comfort that belong in a dining-room are found in the chapel. Timon has no sense of propriety or decorum, no idea of what is proper for what purpose. The chapel is an extravagantly ornamented room indicating material rather than spiritual concern. The music that is performed is more suited to a ballroom than a place of worship, and there is something grossly obscene about the paintings on the ceilings. The verb 'sprawl', used to describe the painted saints, picks up the disgust that Pope feels for the Cupids that 'squirt' in the garden, and the Tritons that 'spew' in the dining-room. Pope's scorn for Timon's religious complacency is given a final satiric twist in his equation of the 'soft Dean' with a 'cushion' in the closing couplet of the paragraph.

The guests are then called to the dining-room by 'chiming clocks' that ring out like church bells summoning a congregation. Such a summons directly contrasts to the soft melodious sound that was suggested by the chapel's 'silver bell'. The dining-table itself is ornamented with 'well-coloured serpents' and 'gaping Tritons' that are quite inappropriate to meal-time, while the dinner that the poet receives is a travesty of what dining should be — 'The feast of Reason and the flow of Soul' as Pope describes it in his *Imitation of Horace: Satire II, i,* 128. At Timon's house dining is an occasion for ostentatious show not relaxed conviviality. It is, like Belinda's toilet, a 'sacred rite of pride'. The guests drink and eat in time with the chiming clocks: 'You drink by measure, and to minutes eat'. The silver plates ring out in a grotesque parody of the bells at the communion service:

> Between each Act the trembling salvers ring,
> From soup to sweet-wine, and God bless the King.

The last line is a brilliant example of the deftness and speed of Pope's satiric touch. The whole meal is crammed into one line. The elaborate banquet is reduced to skeletal simplicity, while the toast to the King is presented as an afterthought to be got over and done with as soon as possible.

At this point in the poem the poet brings himself directly into the account of Timon's Villa for the first time. Up to now Pope has kept himself out of things as much as possible. He has conducted the reader round the house, making cruel fun of Timon's bad taste, but he has not allowed the scene to affect him directly. In the last six lines of the paragraph he can no longer control his revulsion and scorn for what he is witnessing:

> In plenty starving, tantaliz'd in state,
> And complaisantly help'd to all I hate,
> Treated, caress'd, and tir'd, I take my leave,
> Sick of his civil Pride from Morn to Eve;
> I curse such lavish cost, and little skill,
> And swear no Day was ever past so ill.

The personal pronouns ring out the more impressively for being introduced for the first time, while the negative force of the verbs — 'hate', 'take my leave', 'curse', and 'swear' — steadily heightens the poet's rejection of such lavish cost and little skill.

In the last two paragraphs of the excerpt there is a crucial change in tone. Pope the irate participant becomes Pope the objective commentator. He has condemned Timon's false taste but he now shows that he is philosophically resigned to it. Borrowing perhaps from Bernard Mandeville's *The Fable of the Bees: or, Private vices, Publick benefits*, he tries to justify Providence by arguing that Timon's charitable vanity at least keeps the labourer employed and his family healthy. The lines ring somewhat hollow to a modern reader. They are full of general benevolence but seem lacking in detailed feeling for the poorer classes. They are also a clear reminder of Pope's philosophical position. What he sees wrong with Timon's prodigality is probably not what most readers today would see wrong with it. Timon is an object of attack not because he has too much money, but because he misuses it. Pope celebrates Christian humility but he is in no way a socialist.

Finally, in four of the finest lines he ever wrote, Pope reminds us of Timon's total insignificance in a larger perspective. In a beautifully modulated sentence, full of rich images of triumphant nature, he calmly enacts the inevitable victory of time. Timon's villa and gardens become a transient plaything that quietly dissolves before a vision of almost paradisal nature.

The Timon's Villa episode gives us Pope at his satirical best. His wit and scorn in dealing with what is rotten, and his lyrical defence of what he believes in, show a mind at full imaginative stretch. He is writing about a subject — the country house and its setting — that has vital implications for the whole structure of his society. For Pope the ideal country house is one in which man and nature exist in mutual harmony. Such a relationship is described by Ben Jonson in his poem *To Penshurst*, written over a hundred years earlier. It is helpful to see Jonson's ideal of the country house, the organic centre of community life, hovering in the background of Pope's poem as an implied ideal against which to measure the aberrations and enormities of the eighteenth-century entrepreneurs he is satirizing.

from *An Essay on Man*

Know then thyself, presume not God to scan;
The proper study of Mankind is Man.
Plac'd on this isthmus of a middle state,
A being darkly wise, and rudely great:
With too much knowledge for the Sceptic side,   5
With too much weakness for the Stoic's pride,
He hangs between; in doubt to act, or rest,
In doubt to deem himself a God, or Beast;
In doubt his Mind or Body to prefer,
Born but to die, and reas'ning but to err;   10
Alike in ignorance, his reason such,
Whether he thinks too little, or too much:
Chaos of Thought and Passion, all confus'd;
Still by himself abus'd, or disabus'd;
Created half to rise, and half to fall;   15
Great lord of all things, yet a prey to all;
Sole judge of Truth, in endless Error hurl'd:
The glory, jest, and riddle of the world!

CONTEXT. This is the opening paragraph of Epistle II of *An Essay on Man*. The second epistle was written in the early part of 1731, but Pope held back its publication until March 1733 because of the fierce reception given to the *Epistle to Burlington*. (For a more detailed account of the poem's publication see p. 19). In the first epistle of *An Essay on Man* Pope deals with the nature of man with respect to the Universe; in this second epistle he turns to the nature of man with respect to himself.

CRITICISM. The paragraph is chosen as an example of Pope's skill at yet another 'kind' of poetry. *An Essay on Man* is a didactic poem and Pope's style here is appropriately instructive, 'Know then thyself, presume not God to scan'. But as one reads on in this paragraph it becomes clear that it is impossible to make a complete distinction between Pope's didactic and satiric styles. Although Pope hoped that *An Essay on Man* would 'put morality in good humour', it is at the same time full of acerbic and withering references to man's presumption and pride that have much in common with poems written directly in the satiric tradition. The subject matter of the *Essay* is more obviously philosophical than the satires, and the tone is more frequently expository, but the overall effect is similar to that of the *Moral Essays* and *Imitations of Horace*. All these poems are essentially poems of what Maynard Mack calls the 'middle

flight': they are poems in which wit, precision and ease are fused to create an urbane and relaxed surface.

This passage is a fine example of the way a poet who is in control of his material establishes his meaning through his style. Each element of expression here, and especially the couplet form itself, reinforces Pope's central concept of the dual nature of man. After the curt imperative force of the self-contained opening couplet we have the extended definition of man, spanning sixteen lines, and yet never for one moment losing direction as the clauses gather toward the clipped and epigrammatic conclusiveness of the last line.

The opening injunction not to 'scan' God is carefully stated. Pope does not say that man should not worship God, but that he should not presume to measure him in a mathematical way. Scientific enquiry is only justified if carried out with modesty (see line 43). So far as Pope is concerned the foundation of all knowledge is self-knowledge, and it is towards this that the rest of the passage is directed.

At the very beginning man is placed on an 'isthmus of a middle state'. The geographical image carries a wealth of associations. It suggests man's temporal position, with the present seen as a narrow strip of land connecting the vast continents of the past and the future; it suggests his spatial position, with this world seen as a narrow passage joining Heaven and Hell; and it suggests his social position in God's hierarchy of creation, with the higher life of the angels above him and the lower life of the animals beneath him. The essential point is the ambiguity of man's position, an ambiguity that is given further force by the oxymorons of the next line. Man is wise and great compared to the brutes beneath, but dark and rude compared to the angels above.

Man is suspended like a pendulum and pulled in alternate directions, 'he hangs between'; he is torn with doubt by a series of philosophical dilemmas; and his whole life is merely an expanded paradox summed up by the fact that he is 'born but to die'. The confusion and opposition of the choices confronting man are embodied in the constant seesaw motion of the verse. Sometimes this movement operates within the couplet (as in lines 5 and 6), sometimes within the line (as in 4), and sometimes within the half line (as in the second half of 7).

The duality of man's nature is constantly established through the duality of the syntactical organization. Nouns, phrases and clauses

The frontispiece to the 1744 edition of An Essay on Man *designed and drawn by Pope himself.*

are repeatedly coupled together to enact the duality of the choices that face man. The syntactical elements I have italicized in the following six lines amply illustrate this:

> Chaos of *Thought* and *Passion*, all confus'd;
> Still by himself *abus'd* or *disabus'd*;
> Created *half to rise*, and *half to fall*
> Great *lord of all things*, yet *a prey to all*;
> *Sole judge of Truth, in endless Error hurl'd*:
> The glory, jest, and riddle of the world!

The last line is a taut summary of the whole passage: the 'glory' summarises man's potential nobility, the 'jest' his potential absurdity, and the 'riddle' his actual confusion.

There is nothing especially new in what Pope is saying about man. The ideas expressed here were embedded in Renaissance thought. This becomes quite clear if we put Pope's lines beside Hamlet's famous soliloquy in Act II, ii:

> What a piece of work is a man, how noble in reason, how infinite in faculties, in form and moving how express and admirable, in action how like an angel, in apprehension how like a god: the beauty of the world, the paragon of animals; and yet to me, what is this quintessence of dust? Man delights not me; nor woman neither, though by your smiling you seem to say so.

The view of man developed in Pope's passage closely resembles that in Shakespeare's play. The originality of Pope's lines does not lie in his ideas but in the way he expresses them. This is a basic Augustan position. Pope believed that there were only a few irrefutable truths in human nature and the duty of the poet was to express those old and permanent truths in a new light:

> True Wit is Nature to Advantage drest,
> What oft was Thought, but ne'er so well Exprest.

from   *Epilogue to the Satires: Dialogue II*

> *Fr.* Tis all a Libel — *Paxton* (Sir) will say.
> *P.* Not yet, my Friend! to-morrow 'faith it may;
> And for that very cause I print to day.
> How shou'd I fret, to mangle ev'ry line,
> In rev'rence to the Sins of *Thirty-nine!*   5
> Vice with such Giant-strides comes on amain,
> Invention strives to be before in vain;
> Feign what I will, and paint it e'er so strong,
> Some rising Genius sins up to my Song.

F. Yet none but you by Name the Guilty lash;　　　　10
Ev'n *Guthry* saves half *Newgate* by a Dash.
Spare then the Person, and expose the Vice.
　　P. How Sir! not damn the Sharper, but the Dice?
Come on then Satire! gen'ral, unconfin'd,
Spread thy broad wing, and sowze on all the Kind.　　15
Ye Statesmen, Priests, of one Religion all!
Ye Tradesmen vile, in Army, Court, or Hall!
Ye Rev'rend Atheists! — *F.* Scandal! name them, Who?
　　P. Why that's the thing you bid me not to do.
Who starv'd a Sister, who forswore a Debt,　　　　20
I never nam'd — The Town's enquiring yet.
The pois'ning Dame — *Fr.* You mean — *P.* I don't. — *Fr.*
　　You do.
　　P. See! now I keep the Secret, and not you.
The bribing Statesman — *Fr.* Hold! too high you go.
　　P. The brib'd Elector — *Fr.* There you stoop too low.　25
　　P. I fain wou'd please you, if I knew with what:
Tell me, which Knave is lawful Game, which not?
Must great Offenders, once escap'd the Crown,
Like Royal Harts, be never more run down?
Admit your Law to spare the Knight requires;　　　30
As Beasts of Nature may we hunt the Squires?
Suppose I censure — you know what I mean —
To save a Bishop, may I name a Dean?
　˙*Fr.* A Dean, Sir? no: his Fortune is not made,
You hurt a man that's rising in the Trade.　　　　35
　　P. If not the Tradesman who set up to day,
Much less the 'Prentice who to morrow may.
Down, down, proud Satire! tho' a Realm be spoil'd,
Arraign no mightier Thief than wretched *Wild*,
Or if a Court or Country's made a Job,
Go drench a Pick-pocket, and join the Mob.

CONTEXT. These are the opening forty-one lines of the *Epilogue to the Satires*, Dialogue II written and published in the early summer of 1738. Throughout the 1730s Pope became increasingly involved in the Patriot opposition to Robert Walpole's Whig Government, and the two dialogues published in May and July of 1738 represent the clearest statement of his political commitment to the opposition. The strength and depth of Pope's indignation at the political state of affairs at this time can be felt by considering the footnote that he appended to the last line of Dialogue II:

This was the last poem of the kind printed by our author, with a resolution to publish no more; but to enter thus, in the most plain and solemn manner he could, a sort of PROTEST against that insuperable corruption and depravity of manners, which he had been so unhappy as to live to see.

CRITICISM. This excerpt has been chosen, not because it represents the most powerful section of Dialogue II, for that distinction belongs to the latter part of the poem, but because it demonstrates the perfect assurance of Pope's handling of the closed couplet in his later poetry. The cut and thrust of the dramatic exchange between the poet and his adversary operates within the boundaries of the closed couplet so naturally that the reader is hardly aware of the slightest formal bondage.

The two poems called the *Epilogue to the Satires* are modelled on the dialogue form that Horace used in Book II of his *Satires*. Indeed the first dialogue was originally titled *One Thousand Seven Hundred and Thirty Eight: A Dialogue Something Like Horace*, but the Horatian model has been assimilated within the Popean creation. Pope's satirist in these two dialogues takes on a far more outspokenly militant position than any that is taken on by Horace's satirist in his *Satires*.

Pope ironically refers to the adversary in the two poems as '*Fr.*' (Friend), but the smooth courtier who assumes such impertinent familiarity with the poet is anything but a true friend. In Dialogue I Pope counters the effrontery of this man with a polite and tolerant irony, but by the time he gets to Dialogue II he seems to have realized that irony is wasted on fools and he quite simply crushes the adversary beneath the force of his indignation.

Dialogue II begins with the Friend making a typically niggling comment. He accuses Pope of writing libel, and yet pretends the accusation is not his but that of the Solicitor to the Treasury, Nicholas Paxton, who was in charge of reporting all libels to the government. Thus he conceals his criticism beneath a pretended objectivity coupled with an obsequious politeness — note the interpolated 'Sir'. But Pope has no intention of letting the Friend develop his position in this poem in the same leisurely way as he did in Dialogue I, and he firmly interrupts him after only one line. When the Friend breaks in again at line 10, and accuses Pope of being too personal in his satire, Pope again replies with great vigour. The shifts in tone, as the argument sways first one way then another, are skilfully handled. The poetry possesses all the intensity of drama as Pope first makes a lively but straight defence of his position, 'How Sir! not damn the Sharper, but the Dice?', and then immediately moves into a heavily ironic invocation to general satire:

> Come on then Satire! gen'ral, unconfin'd,
> Spread thy broad wing, and sowze on all the Kind.

Pope takes one of his favourite images for the satirist, that of the hawk (cf. *Epistle to Dr Arbuthnot*, 340–1), and mockingly pretends that the satirist swoops like a hawk on 'all the kind' rather than on particular victims. The Friend is naturally inquisitive and cannot bear the suspense of not knowing who is being attacked. This, of course, is precisely Pope's point, and from lines 18 to 27 there is a rapid exchange between the two in which Pope manipulates the closed couplet with remarkable flexibility. The chopped movement of line 18, for example, in which there are three distinct caesuras, as the Friend fiercely questions the poet, is followed by the sudden speed of line 19 in which there is no caesura at all between the tripping monosyllables of which the line is composed.

At line 26 Pope drops his ironic stance as a general satirist, and returns in his own voice to a series of questions (26–33) whose urgency is heightened by the dramatic contrast with what has gone before. The image of the satirist as a bird of prey gives way to the image of the satirist as a hunter; both images show Pope's essentially militant concept of his role. After a further temporizing interruption from the Friend (34–5) the excerpt ends with Pope moving into yet another tone, that of indignant sarcasm: 'Down, down, proud Satire! . . . '

I have closed the excerpt from Dialogue II at this point because enough has been done to demonstrate Pope's mastery of the couplet form. In the *Epilogue to the Satires* he manipulates the persona of the public-spirited poet, within the accepted discipline of the couplet form, so as to create a final ringing indictment of a world financially, politically and spiritually rotten. The perfect harmony of the achievement that results from Pope's accepting and working within the laws of poetry contrasts with the manifest discord that results from society's failure to accept and work within the laws of morality.

More she had spoke, but yawn'd — All Nature nods:
What Mortal can resist the Yawn of Gods?
Churches and Chapels instantly it reach'd;
(St James's first, for leaden Gilbert preach'd)
Then catch'd the Schools; the Hall scarce kept awake;
The Convocation gap'd, but could not speak: 610
Lost was the Nation's Sense, nor could be found,
While the long solemn Unison went round:
Wide, and more wide, it spread o'er all the realm;
Ev'n Palinurus nodded at the Helm:
The Vapour mild o'er each Committee crept;
Unfinish'd Treaties in each Office slept;
And Chiefless Armies doz'd out the Campaign;
And Navies yawn'd for Orders on the Main.
    O Muse! relate (for you can tell alone,
Wits have short Memories, and Dunces none)   620
Relate, who first, who last resign'd to rest;
Whose Heads she partly, whose completely blest;
What Charms could Faction, what Ambition lull,
The Venal quiet, and intrance the Dull;
'Till drown'd was Sense, and Shame, and Right, and Wrong —
O sing, and hush the Nations with thy Song!

             .   .   .

    In vain, in vain, — the all-composing Hour
Resistless falls: The Muse obeys the Pow'r.
She comes! she comes! the sable Throne behold
Of *Night* Primaeval, and of *Chaos* old!   630
Before her, *Fancy's* gilded clouds decay,
And all its varying Rain-bows die away.
Wit shoots in vain its momentary fires,
The meteor drops, and in a flash expires.
As one by one, at dread Medea's strain,
The sick'ning stars fade off th'ethereal plain;
As Argus' eyes by Hermes' wand opprest,
Clos'd one by one to everlasting rest;
Thus at her felt approach, and secret might,
Art after *Art* goes out, and all is Night.   640
See skulking *Truth* to her old Cavern fled,
Mountains of Casuistry heap'd o'er her head!
Philosophy, that lean'd on Heav'n before,
Shrinks to her second cause, and is no more.
Physic of *Metaphysic* begs defence,
And *Metaphysic* calls for aid on *Sense*!

See *Mystery* to *Mathematics* fly!
In vain! they gaze, turn giddy, rave, and die.
Religion blushing veils her sacred fires,
And unawares *Morality* expires.   650
Nor *public* Flame, nor *private*, dares to shine;
Nor *human* Spark is left, nor Glimpse *divine*!
Lo! thy dread Empire, CHAOS! is restor'd;
Light dies before thy uncreating word:
Thy hand, great Anarch! lets the curtain fall;
And Universal Darkness buries All.

CONTEXT. These are the last fifty-two lines of *The Dunciad* in four books, first published in October 1743, six months before Pope's death. Although the first part of the passage (605–26) had been written for the close of *The New Dunciad* (i.e. Book IV), published in March 1742, and certain lines from the second part (627–56) had first appeared at the close of *The Dunciad*, Book III, published in 1728, the whole passage has been so carefully reworked as a fit conclusion to the revised *Dunciad* in four books that we can justifiably see it as an expression of Pope's final poetic vision.

At the beginning of Book IV Pope had ironically appealed to Dulness for 'one dim ray of light' so that he might celebrate her restored mysteries. He had described Dulness mounting her throne with all her allegorical captives beneath her. Now, at the end of the book, Dulness, having suspended her 'Force inertly strong' for long enough, gives a last blessing to her children and begins the mighty yawn that envelops the entire civilized world, as all light is finally extinguished.

CRITICISM. The most striking thing to notice about the first paragraph is the way Pope's syntax enacts the extent of Dulness's yawn. The first couplet offers a brief introductory statement of her yawn, followed by a rhetorical question that establishes its epic scale, but the next six couplets are all part of one long sentence that creates the vast scope of the yawn as the sentence itself spreads to its drawn-out close. Just as the clauses pile on top of each other through twelve lines that constitute one meandering sentence, so Dulness's yawn drifts through first London and Westminster, then the whole nation, and finally to armies abroad and navies at sea.

At the same time as Dulness is putting everyone to sleep, however, Pope's wit is keeping his readers awake. Thus the images of 'All Nature' (605), and 'Ev'n Palinurus' (i.e. Walpole, 614) nodding possess a double force since they suggest not only that they are nodding off to sleep, but also nodding in agreement with such a state of affairs. Then again, the image of the yawn as a 'Vapour mild' carries a set of associations with it that are far more ominous. Vapours were directly associated with madness in Pope's day (cf.

155

Swift's 'Digression on Madness' in *A Tale of a Tub*, or even Pope's own description of them as the source of madness in the Cave of Spleen in *The Rape of the Lock*).

The four couplets that constitute the next paragraph are bound together by a basic pattern of structural parallelism ('relate', 619, and 'relate', 621; 'who first' and 'who last', 621; 'whose . . . whose . . . ', 622; 'what . . . what . . . ', 623; and the chiasmus of 624) that sweeps Dulness's various followers (the Wits and the Dunces, 620; the partly and the completely blest, 622; the factious and the ambitious, 623; and the Venal and the Dull, 624) toward the conclusiveness of the last couplet. The paragraph mounts, through the relative pronoun clauses, to the climactic clause introduced by ' 'Till', and clinched with the packing of four nouns of immense moral force into one line. The fundamental moral opposition of Sense and Shame, and Right and Wrong, is subservient to the all conquering force of Dulness. Moral distinction has become as irrelevant as the distinction, in line 621, between those who were first and last to succumb to Dulness. All are included in the one yawn just as all moral standards are crammed together in one line.

In the final paragraph of the poem the Muse herself has yielded to Dulness's power, and the poet alone now stands between the reader and Universal Darkness. The poet's voice assumes an urgency made poignant by the inevitability of the approaching cataclysm:

> In vain, in vain, — the all-composing Hour
> Resistless falls: The Muse obeys the Pow'r
> She comes! she comes! the sable Throne behold
> Of *Night* Primaeval, and of *Chaos* old!

Where the poet had seemed through the preceding part of the poem to speak like an observer describing with minute detail the court of Dulness in eighteenth-century London, he speaks now like an omniscient commentator recording the final work of Dulness in the world. At the same time as the speaker's tone has shifted from that of ironic observer to that of prophetic commentator, so the scene has changed from local to universal. The particularities of the main body of Book IV have given way to the generalities of the close. The Busbys and Bentleys of this world are subsumed within the mountains of casuistry that are heaped over Truth's head, although their example, gives force and validity to that picture.

This last paragraph, which envisages the end of civilization, is built upon a terrible inversion of two of its great beginnings. The account of the Creation at the beginning of the Old Testament, and of the birth of Christ at the beginning of the New, lies just beneath the surface adding a sacrilegious dimension to the restoration of Dulness's empire. In Genesis darkness dies before God's creating command, 'Let there be light', and in the Gospel according to St

John Christ's divinity is similarly described as a light that 'shineth in darkness'. But in *The Dunciad* light dies before Dulness's 'uncreating word', until 'Art after Art goes out, and all is Night'. Dulness's victory has a profoundly evil, even Satanic force. She is the 'great Anarch' just as Satan in *Paradise Lost*, which was never very far from Pope's mind, is the 'great Adversary'.

Dulness has been associated with various images of obscurity — fogs, mists and clouds — throughout *The Dunciad*, but now she is associated with total blackness. Her throne is sable, and the restoration of her reign completely destroys everything connected with the sun. The various rainbow colours of the imagination die away, and the momentary meteoric fires of wit expire. Her destructiveness is heightened through comparison to two great destroyers of classical mythology. Medea, who was celebrated for her sorcery, murdered her own children, and Hermes slaughtered Argus, the hundred-eyed giant. Argus normally slept with only two eyes closed, but Hermes, by playing sweet music on his flute, put them all to sleep and then cut off Argus's head. In such darkness Dulness's approach can only be 'felt' and not seen, while her power, like Medea's possesses a magical and 'secret' might.

The closing couplets are gathered together through the grave imperatives ('See . . .' 641; 'See . . .' 647; and 'Lo! . . .' 653) that command our attention and give an epic strain to the finale. Pope's own moral positives make a last tragic appearance in a scene suggestive of the medieval *danse macabre*. Truth, which should be open, has been forced to sneak off, 'skulking', to her old cavern. Philosophy 'shrinks', like aging flesh, until she 'is no more'. Physic and Metaphysic call out for help. Mystery 'flies' in a frenzy to Mathematics. Religion, 'blushing' at such grotesque happenings, 'veils her sacred fires', and Morality who has been unconscious since the beginning of Book IV (see ll.27–30) and waiting only for Dulness to give her Page the word, finally expires. The whole episode is vividly summed up in the single line: 'In vain! they gaze, turn giddy, rave, and die'. Pope skilfully uses the repeating caesura to create the frantic stepping movement of the Dance of Death. The participants are first dumbfounded as they realize that the Queen of Dulness is Death in disguise, then as the shock of recognition wears off they join dizzily in the dance until, mentally bewildered, they drop dead from madness and exhaustion.

In the last lines the image of the dance merges with that of the theatre. In the same way as all the lights are first dimmed and then extinguished at the end of a play, so the smallest 'Flame', or 'Spark' is snuffed out before Dulness's dread empire is fully restored at the end of the world. The tragedy of the fall of civilization and decay of all moral standards is then brought to its recognized dramatic close:

> Thy hand, great Anarch! lets the curtain fall;
> And Universal Darkness buries All.

And yet the final ironic paradox is that the terrible cataclysm of this darkness is only apparent to us because of the clarity of Pope's poetry. The brilliance of the poetic creation refutes the very darkness it records. Universal Darkness does not, and cannot, bury all when poetry of such intellectual splendour survives.

Part Three

Reference Section

You then whose Judgment the right Course wou'd steer,
Know well each ANCIENT's proper *Character*,
His *Fable, Subject, Scope* in ev'ry Page,
Religion, Country, Genius of his *Age*:
Without all these at once before your Eyes,
Cavil you may, but never *Criticize*.

An Essay on Criticism, 1711, (118–23)

Glossary of Technical Terms

Many of the following terms are used in discussing forms of poetry other than the couplet, and some, for example antithesis and parallelism, are used in discussing prose, especially that of Johnson, Gibbon and Burke.

ALEXANDRINE. A six-foot iambic line, used more often by Dryden than Pope in order to introduce variety of movement. Pope makes his attitude to the Alexandrine clear in *An Essay on Criticism* when he says that for too many poets,

> A needless Alexandrine ends the Song,
> That like / a wound/ed Snake, / drags its /slow length / along.

ANTITHESIS. Two phrases or clauses having an opposite or conflicting meaning brought together in a parallel structure:

> Did some more sober Critic come abroad?
> If wrong, I smil'd; if right, I kiss'd the rod.
> Pains, reading, study, are their just pretence,
> And all they want is spirit, taste, and sense.

Antithesis can work within the individual line, as in line 2 above, or within the couplet, as in lines 3 and 4. It is perhaps the most important single technique for the skilful master of the closed couplet for it enables him to bring together words, phrases and clauses that would otherwise have a diversity of meaning. It therefore functions as a kind of imagery forcing the reader to make connections between surprising or unalike things.

AUBADE. A French term (from *aube*, the dawn) used to describe a piece of music played or sung in the early morning. Originally the dawn song of the Provencal troubadours, an aubade saluted the dawn and announced the sun's imminent arrival. Since the aubade was also associated with the song of lovers parting at dawn, its relationship to the morning can be contrasted with that of the serenade to the evening.

CAESURA. A pause within a line of poetry. In the normal closed couplet this pause usually falls after the second or third foot, but in Pope's poetry, especially the later poetry, it falls in a great variety of places depending on the meaning of the line. Sometimes he will use the caesura three or even four times in one line, and sometimes he will not use it at all. The variation of the place of the caesura is Pope's chief method of varying the movement of the couplet.

Consider, for example, the staccato movement of the first line, and the contrasting release of the second, in the following couplet from *Epilogue to the Satires: Dialogue II*:

> Ye Rev'rent Atheists!//–(*F.*) Scandal!//name them,//Who?
> (*P.*) Why that's the thing you bid me not to do.

CHIASMUS. Two phrases of parallel syntactical structure but reversed word order. Pope's description of old women in *An Epistle to a Lady* reinforces chiasmus with alliteration: 'A Fop their Passion, but their Prize a Sot'. The reversed order of the elements that make up the second phrase awakes the reader from any temptation to gloss over them mechanically, and forces him to re-examine the relation in meaning between them.

ENJAMBEMENT. A run-on line in which the meaning flows directly on to the first word of the next line with no pause at the end of the first line.

> All fly to Twit'nam, and in humble strain
> Apply to me, to keep them mad or vain.

This is much more frequent in Dryden than Pope. It is used as a further way (cf. caesura) of gaining variety of movement.

INVERSION. The changing of the normal English word order. Inversion is a technique that allows the poet to place emphasis on certain key words, particularly those falling at the beginning and end of a line. It undoubtedly owes much to Latin, where the verb comes at the end of the sentence. Two very obvious examples are the opening lines of *The Rape of the Lock* and *The Dunciad*.

ONOMATOPOEIA. The use of words whose sounds suggest their meaning. Pope frequently uses the technique to reinforce his satiric thrusts, but perhaps nowhere so skilfully as in *The Rape of the Lock*. Consider, for example, Ariel's description of the torture awaiting those sylphs who neglect their posts:

> Or Alom-Stypticks with contracting Power
> Shrink his thin Essence like a rivell'd Flower.

OXYMORON. The bringing together of two terms that are usually considered to be contradictory, and whose juxtaposition is therefore especially arresting. In the battle of the sexes at the end of *The Rape of the Lock* Dapperwit cries out: 'O cruel Nymph! a living Death I bear.' It is a highly compressed form of antithesis.

PARALLELISM. The repetition of like elements of syntax. It is a technique that allows the poet to exploit the equal metrical segments of the couplet form, and is far too frequent a technique in Pope's poetry to need illustration.

PASTORAL. A *kind* of literature in which shepherds and shepherdesses speak in an idealized way about life in the country. It originated in the idylls of the Greek poet Theocritus, who described the rustic activities of Sicilian shepherds in the third century B.C. Later poets, especially Virgil, transformed a realistic kind of writing into a convention based on an image of life in the golden age. The convention reached its acme in English literature during the Renaissance particularly in the work of Spenser, Sidney, Shakespeare and Milton.

PERIPHRASIS. A round about way of saying something. Sometimes referred to as circumlocution; in the hands of a good poet, however, periphrasis is never a matter of mere wordiness. When Pope refers to the scissors in *The Rape of the Lock* as 'A two-edged Weapon', or 'The little Engine', or 'the glittering Forfex', he is deliberately investing them with an epic inflation that is ludicrously disproportionate to their trivial significance.

TRIPLET. The use of three, instead of two, rhyming lines. This is another technique, introduced for variation, that is far more frequent in Dryden than Pope (cf. alexandrine and enjambement). Triplets are usually marked off with brackets down the side of the page.

ZEUGMA. The binding together of two terms of totally different meaning through a common verb. Consider Belinda who might 'stain her Honour, or her new Brocade', or Sir Balaam's daughter who 'bears a Coronet and Pox for life'.

Gazetteer of Place Names in Eighteenth-century London relevant to Pope's Poetry

BANK OF ENGLAND. Founded in 1693, the business of the Bank was transacted in the Grocer's Hall until 1732 when it moved into a new building situated at the west end of Threadneedle Street and behind the Royal Exchange. Both buildings were literally and metaphorically in the heart of the City.

BEDLAM, or BETHLEHEM, HOSPITAL. The hospital for lunatics built in 1675 on the south side of the lower quarters of Moorfields, and adjacent to the north wall of the City. The two figures on the grand entrance, one representing raving and the other melancholy madness, were carved by Caius Cibber, the father of Colley (see *Dunciad*, I, 29–32, and illustration on p. 79). The hospital was connected with the house of correction at Bridewell having the same President, Governors, Physician, Surgeon and Apothecary. There were 200 rooms or cells at Bedlam 'furnished with beds when the patient is found capable of using one, or with clean straw every day when the patient is mischievous'. (See *Dunciad*, III, 7, and Hogarth's *The Rake's Progress*, Plate 8, on p. 164).

BILLINGSGATE. The largest watergate on the river Thames in the early eighteenth century, and the site of a great fish market in Thames Street, notorious for the 'shameless' language of its fishwives. (See *Dunciad*, I, 307 and IV, 26). The actual dock was just to the east of London Bridge.

BRIDEWELL. The house of correction, euphemistically called a hospital, situated on the west side of Fleet Ditch and meant for 'all strumpets, nightwalkers, pick-pockets, vagrants, and incorrigible and disobedient servants . . . ' The Inmates were obliged to beat hemp (see Hogarth's *A Harlot's Progress*, Plate 4), and if the nature of their offence required it, to undergo the correction of whipping. (See *Dunciad*, II, 269–70).

COVENT GARDEN. Originally a residential square in Westminster built by the Earl of Bedford in 1631 with Inigo Jones as his architect. The area had become somewhat run down in Pope's time and was best known for its houses of ill fame. The market for fruit, flowers and vegetables was to the south of the square.

CRIPPLEGATE WARD. A large ward lying partly within and partly without the City wall. The gate itself, in the north-west corner of the City between Newgate and Moorgate was named after the cripples who begged there. The ward was a depressed area in the

Bedlam

164

early eighteenth century and was the main residential area for the hack writers, or Dunces, who attacked Pope throughout his life. Grub Street itself (*q.v.*) lay within the ward.

DRURY LANE. A street in the parish of St Giles-in-the-Fields in the suburbs between London and Westminster. It connected High Holborn in the north with the Strand in the south. It was well known for its theatre, but was perhaps even more notorious as a centre for prostitution. (See Pope's *Versification of Donne, Satire 2*, 64).

FLEET DITCH. The town ditch which flowed from Clerkenwell in the north, down along the western limit of the City, and out into the Thames at Blackfriars Stairs. It was a common sewer for human excrement (see *Dunciad*, II, 271–4) and animal offal, especially from the slaughterhouses at Smithfield. (See Swift's *A Description of a City Shower*).

GRUB STREET. A street running north and south in the parish of St Giles, Cripplegate (outside the City walls), and lying just to the west of Moorfields. The street offered cheap lodgings to poor and out of work writers so that the name came to be used figuratively to refer to such a body of persons. (See chapter 2, pp. 43–52 and especially Pope's *An Epistle to Dr Arbuthnot* and *The Dunciad*).

GUILDHALL. The hall for transacting City business, situated at the north end of King Street, Cheapside. It was badly damaged by the Fire of London and rebuilt two years later.

HOCKLEY IN THE HOLE. A bear-garden near Clerkenwell north of Smithfield (see *Dunciad*, I, 222 and 326) where, in 1715, 'the sum of 2s. 6d. gave access to a combined performance of bull and bear-baiting, or to a contest between battling women, or between a dog and a man' (Rudé, *Hanoverian London*, p. 75).

LINCOLN'S INN FIELDS. A large square, partly designed by Inigo Jones, in the ward of Farringdon Without, between London and Westminster. The theatre there was one of the two patent theatres in eighteenth-century London (Drury Lane was the other) until its rights passed to Covent Garden in 1732. (See *Dunciad*, III, 270).

LOMBARD STREET. A street in the centre of the City of London that extended from the Lord Mayor's Mansion House to Gracechurch Street. It was originally inhabited by Italian bankers from Lombardy and was still the home of banking in the eighteenth century. Pope was born and lived the first few years of his life there.

LONDON BRIDGE. The only bridge over the Thames until Westminster Bridge was opened in 1750. Rebuilt after the Great Fire with houses four storeys high and a street twenty feet broad. These houses were removed in the mid-eighteenth century.

LUDGATE. The gate in the west of the City leading from St Paul's to Fleet Street. A gate is supposed to have been first built there by King Lud, who began his reign about 69 B.C., but it is more likely that the name of the gate derives from its situation near the rivulet Flood, Flud, Fleote or Fleet.

MINT, THE. A neighbourhood in Southwark, so called because Henry VIII erected a mint there. For many years it was an asylum for debtors. (See *Epistle to Arbuthnot*, 13 and 156 and *Imitation of Horace, II, i*, 99). Thus *Epistle to Arbuthnot*, 156, means 'I waged no war with the mad or the insolvent'.

MONUMENT, THE. A column erected on the east side of Fish Street hill in commemoration of the Fire of London. The west side of the pedestal was carved by Caius Cibber (cf. Bedlam entrance). The following inscription was carved on the Monument:

> This Pillar was set up in perpetual Remembrance of the most dreadful Burning of this Protestant City, begun and carried on by the Treachery and Malice of the Popish faction, in the beginning of September, 1666, in order to the effecting their horrid Plot for the extirpating the Protestant Religion and English Liberties and to introduce Popery and Slavery.

This inscription was erased on James II's accession, but restored soon after the Revolution. It is not hard to see why Pope, a Catholic, says in the *Epistle to Bathurst* (340) that London's column 'like a tall bully, lifts the head, and lyes'.

NEWGATE. The gate to the south-west part of the City between Ludgate to the south and Aldersgate to the north. It also served as a chief city prison for criminals and debtors, and was notoriously full of infection. There were however commodious and airy apartments for the use of those who were able to pay for them. (See John Gay's 'Newgate Pastoral', *The Beggar's Opera*, where Macheath buys a light set of chains).

ROYAL EXCHANGE. The place for merchants to meet and transact business, situated between Cornhill and Threadneedle Street in the very centre of the City. The original sixteenth-century building was destroyed by the Great Fire but was magnificently rebuilt at a cost of £80,000 and reopened in 1669. In *The Rape of the Lock* (Canto III, 23–4) Pope ironically compares the merchant's return from the Exchange with Belinda's completion of her toilet.

ST GILES-IN-THE-FIELDS. So named to distinguish it from St Giles, Cripplegate. The parish was truly an urban suburb by Pope's time, being contiguous to the two cities of London and Westminster. It was another depressed area 'filled with abundance of Poor' (Strype), particularly in the side streets, alleys and courts around St Giles' church itself and off Drury Lane, the main north south thoroughfare in the parish.

ST JAMES'S PALACE. The chief residence of the Court (particularly that of George I and George II), in London after Whitehall was burned down in 1697. Originally founded in the twelfth century as a hospital for leprous maidens, it was acquired for the Crown by Henry VIII, who also rebuilt it. The palace gave rise to a highly fashionable area around it generally known as St James's. (See *Epistle to Bathurst*, 388; *Epistle to Bolingbroke*, 82 and 110; and *Dunciad*, IV, 280 and 608).

ST PAUL'S CATHEDRAL. The cathedral in the west end of the City of London magnificently rebuilt after the Great Fire according to designs by Sir Christopher Wren.

ST STEPHEN'S CHAPEL. The meeting place for the House of Commons (see *Epistle to Bathurst*, 394). The chapel was situated at the south east corner of Westminster Hall which had been added to Westminster Palace by Edward III in 1347.

SMITHFIELD. The great cattle market just north-west of the City walls. An area of filth and nastiness. It was also, as Martinus Scriblerus reminds us in the notes to the *Dunciad* I, 2,

> the place where Bartholomew Fair was kept, whose Shews, Machines, and Dramatical Entertainment, formerly agreeable only to the Taste of the Rabble, were by the Hero of this Poem and others of equal Genius, brought to the Theatres of Covent-Garden, Lincoln-inn-Fields, and the Hay-market, to be the reigning Pleasures of the Court and Town.

The 'Smithfield Muses' are associated with brutality and vulgarity.

STEWS. A number of brothels situated on the Bank side of Southwark and licensed by Act of Parliament in the reign of Henry II. There were originally eighteen of these houses, which stood in a row and had signs on their fronts towards the Thames, such as the Boar's Head, the Cross Keys, the Cardinal's Hat etc. These houses were subject to strict regulations concerning sanitation, including weekly searches by constables and bailiffs. Henry VIII put them down by public proclamation in 1546, but the allusion remained a common one in the eighteenth century. (See *Epistle to Bolingbroke*, 129, and *Epistle to Murray*, 119).

TEMPLE BAR. A gate, at the point where Fleet Street joined the Strand, marking the end of the 'liberties' of the City of London. The heads of those executed for high treason were placed on the gate. (See *Versification of Donne, Satire 4*, 277).

TOWER OF LONDON. On the eastern boundary of the City, next to the Thames. Tradition claimed that Julius Caesar was the founder. The series of buildings known as Tower of London include the church, the White Tower, the Offices of Ordnance, the Mint, the Jewel House and the Horse Armoury, so that the Tower seemed to the eighteenth century more 'like a town than a fortress'. Prisoners (e.g. Bishop Atterbury) were confined in the dungeons and chambers of the various buildings.

TYBURN. Known in the eighteenth century for the gallows erected where anciently a village used to stand. Tyburn was to the northwest of the city and condemned persons were taken there from Newgate, passing along a route that went through High Holborn and out on the road to Oxford (Oxford Street today). There were eight hanging days in the year and it was considered great sport to toast criminals on their way to execution. (See *Dunciad*, I, 41). Journeymen were given a public holiday on the hanging days. (See Hogarth's *Industry and Idleness*, Plate 11, on p. 106).

WESTMINSTER SCHOOL. A celebrated school lying east of the Abbey. It was famous in the seventeenth century for its headmaster Dr Richard Busby, whose name became proverbial as a type of the severe schoolmaster. Busby was headmaster from 1640 until his death in 1695 and he ruled the school 'with a rod of iron, or rather a birch' *(Dictionary of National Biography)*. Dryden, Locke and Atterbury were among his many distinguished pupils. (See *Dunciad*, IV, 135–74).

WHITE'S. A chocolate-house in St James's Street with a special appeal to fashionable society. It was notorious for the gambling that went on and was converted to a club about 1730 to exclude the professional sharpers. (See *Epistle to Bathurst*, 55–64 and *Dunciad*, I, 203–4, 222, and 321; also Hogarth's parody of the gambling in *The Rake's Progress*, Plate 4).

WHITEHALL PALACE. Purchased by Henry VIII from Cardinal Wolsey in 1530. From this time onwards Whitehall was the chief royal residence of English sovereigns near London until it was destroyed by fire in 1697. There were many plans to rebuild it but they were never carried out. Pope frequently alludes to these plans (see *Windsor-Forest*, 380; *Imitation of Horace, Satire II, ii*, 120; *The Dunciad*, III, 327–8 and Pope's note). It was in the reign of George I that Whitehall became officially connected with the Government when Robert Walpole became the first prime minister to occupy 10, Downing Street. He lived there from 1735 to 1742.

Short Biographies

ADDISON, JOSEPH, 1672–1719. Whig statesman (rising to Secretary of State, 1717–18); poet (*The Campaign* was written for the Whig Government in 1705 to celebrate the victory at Blenheim); playwright (*Cato. A Tragedy* appeared in 1713); and essayist (best known for his contributions to the *Tatler* and *Spectator*). He was the centre of the Whig circle of writers who met at Buttons' coffee-house, and who Pope satirised as 'his little Senate'. Pope fell out with Addison early in his life when Addison praised Philips's *Pastorals* above Pope's (see p. 9). Addison later backed Tickell's translation of the *Iliad* over Pope's, and it was in reply to this affront that Pope wrote his famous character sketch of Addison in the summer of 1715. Pope sent the lines to Addison who, as Pope later told Spence, 'used me very civilly ever after'. The lines were printed piratically in several journals of the time, but were not acknowledged by Pope until 1727. In 1734 they were worked into *An Epistle to Dr. Arbuthnot* with the pseudonym Atticus substituted for Addison who had been dead for fifteen years by then.

ALLEN, RALPH, 1694–1764. As Postmaster at Bath he became famous for devising a system of cross-posts that greatly improved the efficiency of the Post Office. He was a well-known philanthropist whom Pope described in the *Epilogue to the Satires: Dialogue 1* as doing good by stealth and blushing to find it fame. Fielding is reputed to have based Squire Allworthy in *Tom Jones* on Allen. He befriended Pope after the publication of the 'pirated' edition of his letters in 1735, and helped to finance the 'authentic' edition of 1737 (see pp. 23–24). The two men became close friends and Pope spent a considerable amount of time during his later years visiting Allen at his Prior Park estate near Bath.

ANNE, 1665–1714. Queen of Great Britain. Second daughter of James II. Married Prince George of Denmark in 1683. Between 1684 and 1700 she gave birth to seventeen children none of whom survived her. She ascended the throne in 1702 and declaration of war with France soon followed. The Duke of Marlborough prospered enormously under her, especially on account of his wife Sarah Jennings, who was for many years her favourite until Mrs Masham superseded her in 1711. Whig and Tory strife was very strong during her reign with the Whigs holding power for the first eight years, and the Tories for the last four. Pope celebrated her rule in *Windsor-Forest*.

ARBUTHNOT, JOHN, 1667–1735. Physician to Queen Anne. He created the nickname, John Bull, for the patriotic Englishman, and in *The History of John Bull*, 1712, wittily attacked the war policy of the Whigs. He was a member of the Scriblerus Club (see pp. 12–13) and one of the chief contributors to *The Memoirs of Martinus Scriblerus*, first published in 1741. He took part with Pope and Gay in writing *Three Hours after Marriage*, a farce satirizing the antiquarian Woodward, produced in 1717. He also contributed to the notes to *The Dunciad Variorum*. Pope addressed his finest epistle to him and thanked him for preserving his life:

> Friend to my Life, (which did not you prolong,
> The World had wanted many an idle Song)

An Epistle to Dr. Arbuthnot was published on 2 January 1735, two months before Arbuthnot's death on 27 February.

ATTERBURY, FRANCIS, 1662–1732. Bishop of Rochester and one of the leaders of the High Church party. He was involved in the Jacobite cause for which he was tried and exiled in 1723. He was a close friend of Pope's, who gave evidence in his favour at his trial. In the *Epilogue to the Satires*, Dialogue II Pope paid tribute to his courage in adversity:

> How pleasing ATTERBURY's softer hour!
> How shin'd the Soul, unconquer'd in the Tow'r!
>
> (82–3)

BATHURST, ALLEN, EARL BATHURST, 1684–1775. M.P. for Cirencester from 1705 to 1711 when he was made a baron, being one of the twelve men who were raised to the peerage at the same time in order to secure a majority for the Tories. He was a close friend of Pope and Swift, and shared the former's interest in gardening. Pope often visited him at his country seat near Cirencester and addressed his third *Moral Essay, Of the Use of Riches*, 1733, to him.

BENTLEY, RICHARD, 1662–1742. A famous classical scholar who was Master of Trinity College, Cambridge, 1700–42. Throughout this period he constantly feuded with the fellows, treating them with arrogance and disdain. As keeper of the royal libraries at St James's Palace he offended Charles Boyle (later Earl of Orrery) in 1693 and consequently found himself immortalized by Swift in *The Battle of the Books*, 1704, as an arch 'Modern'. He became, for Swift and Pope, the typical modern textual pedant, and his editions of Horace, 1711, and Milton, 1732, which went in heavily for verbal emendations, confirmed this reputation. Pope attacked him in *The Dunciad*, 1728–43, *An Epistle to Dr. Arbuthnot*, 1735, and *Imitation of Horace, Epistle II, i*, 1737.

BETHEL, HUGH, d.1748. M.P. for Pontefract and one of Pope's most intimate and esteemed friends. Pope called him 'blameless Bethel' in *An Essay on Man*, 1734, and cast him as Ofellus, a sturdy peasant farmer, in his *Imitation of Horace, Satire II, ii*, 1734.

BLOUNT, MARTHA, 1690–1763; and TERESA, 1688–? The two sisters came from a family that had long been of the highest position among Roman Catholic gentry. The family seat was at Mapledurham near Reading. Their grandfather, Anthony Englefield, lived near the Pope family at Binfield, and Pope probably first met them at his house. Pope became especially friendly with them from 1711 onwards. Martha, or 'Patty', was his favourite and his friendship with her was perhaps the strongest and most lasting of his life. There was much gossip that she was his mistress, and even that he had secretly married her. But there is nothing to validate such speculation, which is far more likely to be malicious scandal spread by his enemies. Pope addressed his second *Moral Essay, To a Lady*, to Martha Blount, and handsomely complimented her at the end of the poem. His devotion to her remained unbroken throughout his life, and in his will he left her £1,000, all his goods and chattels and a life interest in the rest of his estate.

BOLINGBROKE, VISCOUNT: *see* ST JOHN, HENRY

BOYLE, RICHARD, THIRD EARL OF BURLINGTON, 1695–1753. Celebrated for his architectural interests and his friendship with artists and men of letters. He introduced the ideas of the Italian architect, Andrea Palladio (1508–80) to England, and championed the designs of the English architect, Inigo Jones (1573–1652). He reconstructed Burlington House, Piccadilly, about 1716, acording to Palladian principles, and was the chief patron of a group that included Colen Campbell (architect), William Kent (painter, architect and landscape gardener) and Pope, who was deeply interested in both architecture and landscape gardening. This group wanted to see a return to the simpler, more formal lines of Palladio and Jones. They saw the ideal country house as a villa rather than as a palace. Pope was friendly with Burlington from about 1716 or earlier, and addressed his fourth *Moral Essay, On False Taste*, 1731, to him.

BURLINGTON, EARL OF: *see* BOYLE, RICHARD

CAROLINE, 1683–1737. Queen of Great Britain. In 1705 she married George Augustus, electoral prince of Hanover, who later became George II. In 1719 her husband, then Prince of Wales, bought Richmond Lodge, and it was here that Queen Caroline eventually had the famous Merlin's Cave constructed. Pope satirized this in his *Imitation of Horace, Epistle II, i*, 355. She was a gifted woman who maintained a strong control over her husband. Walpole realized this and one of the secrets of his success was his intimacy with Queen Caroline, to which Pope refers in the *Epistle to Arbuthnot*, 67–81. Her most devoted admirer was Lord Hervey. Pope's image of Sporus as a familiar toad 'at the ear of Eve', in the same poem, alludes to this relationship. She detested both her father-in-law, George I, and her son, Frederick, Prince of Wales, who became the focal point for the Patriot opposition in the 1730s. Pope seems to have especially disliked Queen Caroline and wrote a cruel epigram on her death.

CARYLL, JOHN, 1666–1736. Came from an old Roman Catholic family who lived at Ladyholt House at West Harting in Sussex where Pope paid him frequent visits. Like the Blounts he was related to the Englefields of Whiteknights and first met Pope there. It was Caryll who suggested that Pope write *The Rape of the Lock* about his relative, Lord Petre: 'This Verse to Caryll, Muse! is due'. Caryll was one of Pope's oldest and closest friends and one of his chief correspondents. Pope's letters to him show the poet at his most relaxed. He later published these letters in his 'Authentic' edition, 1737, but frequently changed Caryll's name, which was little known, to that of Addison or Wycherley, which were much better known (see pp. 23–24).

CHARTRES or CHARTERIS, FRANCIS, 1675–1732. A notorious debauchee. Pope's own note to his third *Moral Essay*, *To Lord Bathurst*, 1733, line 20, gives a graphic portrait of this man, who was twice drummed out of the army for cheating. Part of Pope's note reads:

> His house was a perpetual bawdy-house. He was twice condemn'd for rapes, and pardoned: but the last time not without imprisonment in Newgate, and large confiscations. ... The populace at his funeral rais'd a great riot, almost tore the body out of the coffin, and cast dead dogs, etc. into the grave along with it.

Pope then quotes Dr Arbuthnot's Epitaph for Chartres, which begins as follows:

HERE continueth to rot
The Body of FRANCIS CHARTRES,
Who with an INFLEXIBLE CONSTANCY,
and INIMITABLE UNIFORMITY of Life,
PERSISTED,
In spite of AGE and INFIRMITIES
In the Practice of EVERY HUMAN VICE;
Excepting PRODIGALITY and HYPOCRISY:
His insatiable AVARICE exempted him from the
first,
His matchless IMPUDENCE from the second.

Colley Cibber, aged about 80

Chartres, who accumulated a considerable fortune by lending money, was a frequent subject of Pope's satire. He is also satirized in Plate 1 of Hogarth's *The Harlot's Progress*, 1732, where he is the lecher leering from Mother Needham's door.

CIBBER, COLLEY, 1671–1757. A highly successful comic actor, dramatist, theatre manager and autobiographer. A very bad poet, he was rewarded by being made Poet Laureate in 1730. Cibber was a vain man and enjoyed playing the coxcomb, both on and off the stage. His most famous comic role was as Lord Foppington in Vanbrugh's *The Relapse*, 1697. Pope made frequent fun of him in his satires before their feud came to a climax with Cibber's elevation in *The New Dunciad*, 1742. Pope's antagonism to Cibber seems to have sprung from jocular references to Pope and Gay's *Three Hours After Marriage*, which Cibber had made in a revival of Buckingham's *Rehearsal*, 1717.

COBHAM, VISCOUNT: *see* TEMPLE, SIR RICHARD

CURLL, EDMUND, 1675–1747. An infamous bookseller whom George Sherburn describes in *The Early Career of Alexander Pope* as a 'foul bird acting as scavenger for a literary battle-field'. He specialized in scandalous biographies, which according to Arbuthnot, 'added a new terror to death', and in seditious and pornographic pamphlets, which more than once put him in the pillory. He kept a garret full of impoverished authors who wrote to his command. Pope's first major encounter with him came in 1716 when Curll piratically published some poems by Lady Mary Wortley Montagu satirizing the court. Pope avenged Lady Mary by first administering an emetic to Curll and then publishing *A Full and True Account of a Horrid and Barbarous Revenge by Poison on the Body of Mr. Edmund Curll*. This is perhaps the most unsavoury incident in Pope's life and it perpetuated the hostility between the two men. Curll later published numerous attacks on Pope, while Pope satirized Curll in *An Epistle to Dr Arbuthnot* and in *The Dunciad*, Book II. In 1733 Pope manoeuvred Curll into publishing a pirated edition of his *Letters* (eventually published in 1735), so that he, Pope, would have an excuse to publish the 'Authentic' edition of 1737.

DENNIS, JOHN, 1657–1734. Critic and playwright. He was well known for his quick temper and for his constant use of the adjective 'tremendous'. Pope made light fun of both in *An Essay on Criticism* (see pp. 9–10) and Dennis replied with a savage attack on Pope's character. The hostility of the two men lasted, on and off, through both their lifetimes. Pope attacked Dennis in *The Narrative of Dr Robert Norris* (1713), *Three Hours After Marriage* (1717, where Dennis appears as Sir Tremendous), *The Dunciad*, *An Epistle to Dr Arbuthnot* and the *Epilogue to the Satires*.

DRYDEN, JOHN, 1631–1700. Poet, dramatist and critic. He dominated the last quarter of the seventeenth century much as Pope did the second quarter of the eighteenth. Pope saw Dryden at Will's Coffee House in 1700, and retained immense respect for him throughout his life. He told Spence that he 'learned versification wholly from Dryden's works', and praised him in many of his poems.

FORTESCUE, WILLIAM, 1687–1749. A lawyer and judge who rose to be Master of the Rolls. He probably met Pope through Gay with whom he went to school in Barnstaple. Unlike most of Pope's friends he remained a staunch Whig throughout his life and was Robert Walpole's private secretary in 1715. Pope addressed his *Imitation of Horace, Satire II, i*, 1733, to him.

FREDERICK, LOUIS, PRINCE OF WALES, 1705–51. Eldest son of George II and Queen Caroline, and father of George III. He was at loggerheads with his father ever since coming to England in 1728. He became a figurehead for the Patriot Opposition to Walpole after his father had expelled him from St James's Palace in 1737. Pope refers to his friendship with Frederick in the *Epilogue to the Satires*. In 1737 Pope wrote an epigram which he had engraved on the collar of a dog which he gave to his Royal Highness:

> I am his Highness' Dog at *Kew*;
> Pray tell me Sir, whose Dog are you?

GARTH, SIR SAMUEL, 1661–1719. Physician and poet. In 1699 he published *The Dispensary*, a mock epic poem which ridiculed the apothecaries of the day. It was a forerunner of *The Rape of the Lock* n form. Garth was an early friend whom Pope described as 'one of the best-natured men in the world', and dedicated the second of his *Pastorals* to him.

GAY, JOHN, 1685–1732. Poet and dramatist. Pope met him sometime in 1711. His *Rural Sports*, 1713, was dedicated to Pope, and his *Shepherd's Week*, 1714, supported Pope in his battle with Ambrose Philips (see p. 9). He was a member of the Scriblerus Club in 1714, and in 1717 collaborated with Pope and Arbuthnot to write *Three Hours After Marriage*, which ran feebly for seven nights before failing. The Duke and Duchess of Queensberry became his patrons in 1720 and he lived with them for the rest of his life. His most famous work was *The Beggar's Opera*, originally suggested at meetings of the Scriblerus Club and first produced on 29 January 1728. This forerunner of the modern 'musical' had an opening run of sixty-three performances and was produced every year during the eighteenth century. Pope, Swift and Arbuthnot were extremely attached to Gay, and each wrote about him with great affection (see, for example, *An Epistle to Dr Arbuthnot*, 255–6). Pope was deeply moved by Gay's death in 1732 (see pp. 19–20).

GEORGE II, 1683–1760. George II came to the throne in 1727. He was content to let his wife, Queen Caroline, and his First Minister, Robert Walpole, who had a good understanding with one another, decide affairs of state, while he spent much of his time abroad in the arms of his German mistress, Madame Walmoden. After Queen Caroline's death in 1737, George brought Madame Walmoden to England where she was accommodated in the Palace and in 1739 made Countess of Yarmouth. There are numerous satiric allusions to George II's neglect of the arts in Pope's poetry. Nowhere are they more damning than in the *Imitation of Horace Epistle II, i*, To Augustus, 1737, where Pope makes ironic play of the fact that George II was christened George Augustus. George II's opinion of Pope was hardly more flattering: 'Who is this Pope that I hear so much about? I cannot discover what is his merit. Why will not my subjects write in prose?'

GRANVILLE, GEORGE, BARON LANSDOWNE, 1667–1735. Poet, dramatist and statesman, rising to Treasurer of the Household in 1713. One of the twelve gentlemen elevated to the peerage in 1711, in order to create a Tory majority in the Lords (cf. Bathurst). At the accession of George I he fell from favour. Confined to the Tower from 1715 to 1717 under suspicion of helping the Pretender. Spent most of his life abroad after his release. He was an early patron of Pope who dedicated *Windsor-Forest* to him.

HARLEY, ROBERT, FIRST EARL OF OXFORD, 1661–1724. Politician who eventually became Prime Minister, in all but name, of the Tory ministry that held office from 1710 to 1714. He employed both Defoe (in the *Review*), and Swift (in the *Examiner*) to write for him and secure public approval of his peace policy. He could not get on with St John (*q.v.*), and their disagreement finally brought about the collapse of the Tory Ministry. After the death of Anne, he was impeached by the Whigs and put in the Tower from 1715 to 1717. He was a member of the Scriblerus Club and a particular friend of Swift, who described him as 'the most virtuous minister, and the most able, that ever I remember to have read of'. Pope addressed an Epistle to him in 1721 in which he referred to him as 'One truly Great'.

HEATHCOTE, SIR GILBERT, 1652–1733. A founder of the Bank of England, of which he was appointed Governor in 1709. Lord Mayor of London 1710–11. A staunch Whig who was five times elected to Parliament. He was a very wealthy man and was reputed to be the richest commoner in England. He was notorious for his parsimony, which Pope attacks in his *Epistle to Bathurst*, 1733:

> The grave Sir Gilbert holds it for a rule,
> That every man in Want is knave or fool.

HERVEY, JOHN, BARON HERVEY OF ICKWORTH, 1696–1743. The 'Sporus' of Pope's *An Epistle to Dr Arbuthnot* and one of Pope's major enemies in the 1730s. He was a friend of George II when he was Prince of Wales and in 1720 married Mary Lepell, one of his Maids of Honour and a friend of Pope. When George II came to the throne in 1726 Hervey became an important liaison between Walpole's Ministry (he had been elected M.P. for Bury St Edmunds in 1725), and the Court, where he was an intimate friend of Queen Caroline. His *Memoirs of the Reign of King George II*, not published till 1848, are an invaluable historical record of the first ten years of George II's reign. His enmity with Pope did not come into the open till 1732, when Pope attacked him in a short lampoon. The origin of the disagreement is not known. In 1733 Hervey and Lady Mary Wortley Montagu (*q.v.*) collaborated to abuse Pope's shape, amongst other things, in *Verses Addressed to the Imitator of Horace*. Pope's *Epistle to Dr Arbuthnot* was published the following year.

HOGARTH, WILLIAM, 1697–1764. Painter and engraver. After an early apprenticeship as a silversmith he achieved independence in 1720 when he opened his own shop and sold engravings. His great original contribution to art was the narrative cycle. By making engravings of his paintings he was able to reach a wider audience with his satiric portrayal of eighteenth-century society than most artists. He sold over 2,000 sets of the prints of *The Harlot's Progress*, 1732, at a guinea a set. *The Rake's Progress*, 1735, and *Marriage à la Mode*, 1745, continued to boost his reputation and fortune. In order to reach a more popular audience he sold the twelve prints of *Industry and Idleness*, 1747, for a shilling each. His paintings and prints bring eighteenth-century London vividly to life and offer a pictorial complement to much of Pope's satiric poetry.

JERVAS, CHARLES, 1675?–1739. Portrait painter. An Irishman who became a student of Sir Godfrey Kneller when he first came to England. He succeeded Kneller as principal painter to George I and was continued in that post by George II. Pope took lessons from Jervas in 1713, receiving daily instruction for much of the time. The two men became close friends and for a number of years Jervas's house in Cleveland Court became Pope's regular home when he was in town. Pope addressed an epistle to him in 1716, which was prefixed to the publication of Dryden's translation of *Fresnoy's Art of Painting*, and which expands some of Pope's ideas about the sister-arts (see chapter 3). Jervas painted Pope several times. He also painted Swift and Arbuthnot.

JONES, INIGO, 1573–1652. Architect. One of his finest works was the banqueting house at Whitehall, which he designed as part of the plan to rebuild the palace. He also designed Covent Garden and the

JOHN LORD HERVEY *Lord Privy Seal in the Reign of* KING

piazza for the Earl of Bedford. Pope admired his work and praised his taste in the *Epistle to Burlington*.

KYRLE, JOHN, 1637–1724. The Man of Ross (*Epistle to Bathurst*, 1733, 249–90). Lived a life of extreme simplicity at Ross in Herefordshire, devoting the surplus income from his small estate of £600 a year to charity and the improvement of the town and countryside. He was an enthusiastic amateur architect, builder and landscape-gardener. Pope did not know him. The details of the character sketch, which is based on fact, were supplied by Jacob Tonson (*q.v.*).

LINTOT, BARNABY BERNARD, 1675–1736. Publisher of many of Pope's poems including the lucrative *Iliad*, in six volumes, 1715–20, and *Odyssey*, in five volumes, 1725–26. They fell out after this over the number of free subscription copies to be provided, and Pope introduced him into *The Dunciad*, Book II, in which he races against his fellow bookseller, Edmund Curll.

LYTTLETON, GEORGE, FIRST BARON LYTTLETON, 1709–73. Author and politician. Equerry and later Secretary to the Prince of Wales during the 1730s. He was elected M.P. for Okehampton, Devon, in 1735, and soon became one of the leaders of the Whig Opposition to Walpole. He was a patron of Thomson, who described Lyttleton's home in *The Seasons*, and Fielding, who dedicated *Tom Jones* to him. Pope knew him as one of the group of young politicians with whom he became friendly towards the end of his life. He praised him in the *Imitation of Horace, Epistle I, i (To Bolingbroke*, 1737) and in the *Epilogue to the Satires*, Dialogues I and II.

MONTAGU, LADY MARY WORTLEY, 1689–1762. Poet and lady of letters. Married Edward Wortley Montagu in 1712. In the next few years she spent much time at Court where she became well known for her wit. Pope met her in 1715 and formed an infatuation for her that spurred him to revenge Curll's surreptitious publication of her *Court Poems* in 1716 by the infamous administration of an emetic. Later in the same year she accompanied her husband to Constantinople when he was appointed ambassador. While there she wrote the *Letters* (first published 1763) for which she is best known. Pope meanwhile was writing her letters of passionate gallantry. On their return to England in 1718 the Montagus became close neighbours of Pope at Twickenham. Lady Mary's reputation increased during this time when she introduced the practice of inoculation against smallpox. Sometime before 1727 Pope's admiration for her turned sour and for the rest of their lives the two former

Lord John Hervey, 'Sporus'.

friends were ardent enemies. Lady Mary became especially friendly with Lord Hervey (*q.v.*), and collaborated with him in attacking Pope, who, in his turn, frequently attacked her, under the pseudonym of Sappho, in his satires of the 1730s.

MORDAUNT, CHARLES, THIRD EARL OF PETERBOROUGH, 1658–1735. Admiral, general and politician. He had an erratic and wild career, and was already an old man by the time Pope became acquainted with him about 1723. The two men became close friends and Pope frequently visited his home at Bevis Mount, Southampton. They shared an interest in landscape gardening, and it is in this regard that Pope praises him in him *Imitation of Horace, Satire II, i*:

> And He, whose Lightning pierc'd th'*Iberian* Lines,
> Now, forms my Quincunx, and now ranks my Vines.

NEWTON, ISAAC, 1642–1727. Physical scientist and mathematician. Discovered the laws of gravitation and published his account of them in *Principia*, 1687. He also invented the reflecting telescope which enabled him to discover the composition of white light and the nature of colours. He published these theories in *Opticks*, 1704.

OXFORD, EARL OF: *see* HARLEY, ROBERT.

PARNELL, THOMAS, 1679–1718. Poet. Of Irish birth, he was ordained in 1703, and was archdeacon of Clogher, 1706–16. He was a particular friend of Swift's and a member of the Scriblerus Club, for which he wrote the 'Essay concerning the Origin of the Sciences'. He contributed an introductory 'Essay on the life of Homer' to Pope's *Iliad*, Vol. I, 1715. After the death of Queen Anne he returned to Ireland. Pope prepared a posthumous edition of his *Poems* which was published in 1721.

PETERBOROUGH, EARL OF: *see* MORDAUNT, CHARLES.

POPE, ALEXANDER, 1646–1717. The poet's father. A Catholic linen merchant who traded from London. His first wife, Magdalen, died in 1678. He married the poet's mother, Editha, sometime during the next ten years. Their only child, Alexander, was born in the same year that Alexander senior retired from business. He had been a successful merchant, worth at least £10,000 at the time of his early retirement owing to anti-Catholic laws passed on the arrival of William III. For the remaining twenty-nine years of his life he seems to have interested himself mainly in gardening and the upbringing of his son. About 1700 he moved the family to Binfield, in Windsor Forest, where they remained till shortly before his death. For his son's moving remembrance of him see the close of *An Epistle to Dr Arbuthnot*.

POPE, EDITHA, (née Turner), 1642–1733. The poet's mother. Born to a Yorkshire family of some means. Since she was a Catholic no records were kept of her marriage to the poet's father, and hence we do not know the date. Alexander was her only son and she was already forty-six when he was born. He was devoted to her throughout his life, and on her death at the age of ninety-one, he constructed an obelisk to her memory in a prominent position in his garden at Twickenham. His correspondence is full of references to his love for her. Further testimony to it is to be found at the end of *An Epistle to Dr Arbuthnot*.

RYMER, THOMAS, 1641–1713. A literary critic who believed that neglect of the rules had seriously injured English drama. Published *A Short View of Tragedy*, 1692, in which he attacked Shakespeare's *Othello* as 'a bloody farce without salt or savour'. He represents an extreme neoclassical position at the end of the seventeenth century.

ST JOHN, HENRY, VISCOUNT BOLINGBROKE, 1678–1751. Tory statesman, philosopher and man of letters. Held office in Harley's ministry, 1710–14. His disagreement with Harley brought about the fall of the ministry. He then fled to the Pretender's court in France while his lands and titles were seized by Act of Attainder in 1715. He returned to England after a pardon in 1723, and settled near Pope at Dawley Farm, Uxbridge in 1725. He became the leader of the Tory Opposition to Walpole from 1726 to 1735 when he retired to France again. In 1726 he began the Opposition newspaper *The Craftsman*. He was a particularly intimate friend of Pope's, living with him at Twickenham for nine months when he returned to England to sell Dawley in 1738. He was never a member of the Scriblerus Club but was closely associated with it. Pope admired Bolingbroke enormously and told Spence that he was 'something superior to anything I have seen in human nature'. He dedicated *The Essay on Man*, 1733–34, to him and worked some of Bolingbroke's ideas into it. The *Imitations of Horace* were started at Bolingbroke's suggestion, and the *Imitation of Horace, Epistle I, i* was addressed to him. At the close of this poem Pope picks up and restates the tribute he had paid Bolingbroke at the end of *The Essay on Man* (373–98) where he calls him his 'guide, philosopher, and friend'.

'SCRIBLERUS, MARTINUS'. The name of the imaginary hero created by the six members of the Scriblerus Club (Oxford, Swift, Parnell, Arbuthnot, Pope and Gay) which met during 1714. The members of the club set about writing a biography of their hero, in the form of Memoirs, which would ridicule abuses in learning. The club only met for a few months before the death of Queen Anne on 1 August 1714 scattered its members. The true harvest was reaped much later with the publication of Swift's *Gulliver's Travels* in 1726, Gay's

Beggar's Opera and Pope's *Dunciad* in 1728, and finally the belated appearance of the *Memoirs of Martinus Scriblerus* in 1741.

SERLE, JOHN. Pope's gardener at Twickenham. He drew up a plan of the garden at Pope's death which was published in 1745 (see p. 68). Pope addresses him in the opening lines of *An Epistle to Dr Arbuthnot*.

SETTLE, ELKANAH, 1648–1724. Dramatist and poet. He was appointed City poet in 1691, his office being to write pageants for lord-mayor's day. As City poet he celebrated with equal readiness the Tory peace of 1713 (*Irene Triumphans*, 1713) and the Whig triumph two years later (*Rebellion Display'd*, 1715). Pope satirizes him in *The Dunciad*, Book III, where his ghost appears and prophesies the future to Cibber, who is described as his son.

SPENCE, JOSEPH, 1699–1768. Anecdotist and friend of Pope. He first met Pope in 1726, and in 1728 Pope helped to get him elected Professor of Poetry at Oxford. From 1728 onwards Spence recorded Pope's conversations. These anecdotes, which are invaluable for any biographer of Pope, were not published till 1820, although Warburton, Warton and Johnson had each consulted them in manuscript.

SWIFT, JONATHAN, 1667–1745. Tory satirist and Anglican priest. Pope first met Swift in 1712. The two men were both members of the Scriblerus Club in 1714. After the death of Queen Anne Swift returned to the Deanery of St Patrick's, Dublin. He only visited England twice again, first in 1726 to arrange for the publication of *Gulliver's Travels*, and second in 1727. During both visits he spent much of his time with Pope. A moving record of the intimate friendship between the two satirists is to be found in their correspondence, first published in 1737. Pope's most notable public praise of Swift occurs in *The Dunciad*, Book I, 19–28.

TEMPLE, SIR RICHARD, VISCOUNT COBHAM, 1675–1749. Soldier and Whig politician. Supported Walpole until the Excise Bill of 1733, after which he formed an independent Whig section known as the Boy Patriots. He rebuilt the house at Stowe and laid out the famous gardens. Bridgman, Kent and 'Capability' Brown all worked there at some stage. Pope frequently visited Stowe, and addressed his first *Moral Essay, Epistle to Cobham*, 1734, to him.

THEOBALD, LEWIS, 1688–1744. Editor, scholar, dramatist and poet. His *Shakespeare Restored*, 1726, found fault with Pope's edition of Shakespeare which had been published the previous year. Pope revenged himself by making Theobald, whom he considered a verbal pedant, the hero of *The Dunciad*, 1728.

TONSON, JACOB, 1656?–1736. The leading publisher of his day. He was closely associated with Dryden, and was later publisher of the *Tatler* and the *Spectator*. He was Pope's first publisher, printing the *Pastorals* in his *Miscellany* for 1709.

TRUMBULL, SIR WILLIAM, 1639–1716. Statesman who withdrew from active life in 1698. Pope met him about 1705. The two men used to go riding together and talk about poetry. Pope dedicated the 'Spring' pastoral to him and celebrated him as the ideal Happy Man in *Windsor-Forest*, 235–58.

WALPOLE, SIR ROBERT, FIRST EARL OF ORFORD, 1676–1745. Whig First Lord of the Treasury 1715–17 and 1721–42. He was a skilful manager of men, somewhat harshly characterized by the saying attributed to him that 'every man has his price'. He was supported in power by the merchant classes and the new moneyed men. He had a close understanding with Queen Caroline and relied on her influence with the King. He was as unfaithful to Lady Walpole as she was to him, and kept a mistress, Molly Skerrett, from 1728 onwards, marrying her shortly before her death in 1738. He built a palatial mansion on his country estate at Houghton in Norfolk. Pope's portrait of Timon's Villa is to some extent a satire on it. Walpole visited Pope at Twickenham in 1725 but the two men were never close friends and increasingly found themselves representative of opposite ways of life. For a development of this idea see Maynard Mack, *The Garden and the City*. Nicknamed the 'Great Man' (he was extremely corpulent) it is probably true to say that Walpole was more violently attacked by a greater number of literary luminaries than any English politician before or since. Gay, Swift, Pope, Arbuthnot, Thomson, Fielding and Dr Johnson each entered the fray at various stages. Allusions to Walpole and his Ministry are too frequent in Pope's poetry to list here.

WALSH, WILLIAM, 1663–1708. Critic and poet. Lived at Abberley in Worcestershire. Dryden had called him 'the best critic of our nation'. Walsh commended Pope's *Pastorals* before they were published and generally encouraged Pope as a young poet. Pope praised Walsh in *An Essay on Criticism* for having 'the *clearest Head* and the *sincerest Heart*'. He also paid tribute to him in *An Epistle to Dr Arbuthnot*.

WALTER, PETER, 1664?–1746. A moneylender. He made a considerable fortune by lending money to the aristocracy at exorbitant rates of interest, and was said to be worth £300,000 on his death. The original of Peter Pounce in Fielding's *Joseph Andrews*, 1742. Pope attacked him again and again in the 1730s, seeing him as the outstanding representative of the new moneyed interest he so much abhorred.

WARBURTON, WILLIAM, 1698–1779. Bishop of Gloucester. First became associated with Pope late in the poet's life when he defended Pope's *Essay on Man* against the attacks of the Swiss theologian Jean-Pierre de Crousaz, in his *Vindication of the Essay on Man*, 1739. In 1740 he met Pope and during the last four years of his life became his general editor. Pope introduced him to Ralph Allen whose niece Warburton eventually married. In 1741 Pope refused to accept an honorary doctorate from Oxford because they would not give Warburton one too. Warburton brought out a general edition of Pope's *Works* in 1751.

WILD, JONATHAN, 1682–1725. Receiver of stolen goods and informer. He became head of a large corporation of thieves and made money selling 'lost property' back to its original owners. In public he appeared not just as an honest citizen, but as an actual instrument of justice. He was ultimately apprehended, tried and hanged at Tyburn. He was mythologized by political satirists who used him as a pseudonym for attacking Robert Walpole. Gay took him as the model for Peachum in *A Beggar's Opera*, Pope referred to him in the *Epilogue to the Satires*, Dialogue II, and Fielding used the analogy in *The Life of Jonathan Wild, The Great*.

WREN, CHRISTOPHER, 1632–1723. Architect and astronomer who became President of the Royal Society 1680. He is best known for his architecture, especially his rebuilding of St Paul's Cathedral and fifty-two churches in London after the Great Fire of 1666.

WYCHERLEY, WILLIAM, 1640?–1716. Dramatist and poet. A wit at the court of Charles II and a famous writer of Restoration comedies. Pope was a young man of sixteen when he first met Wycherley, aged sixty-four, who introduced him to literary society. When Wycherley asked Pope to correct his poems, Pope suggested that he transpose them into maxims like those of Rochefoucauld. This caused some ill feeling on Wycherley's part but no permanent break in their friendship, which lasted to Wycherley's death. Pope published a posthumous volume of Wycherley's *Poems* in 1729.

Map of Southern England

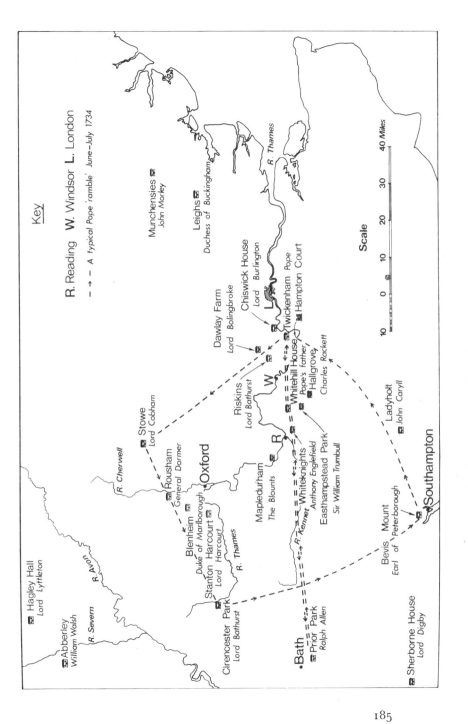

Key

R. Reading W. Windsor L. London

→ → — A typical Pope 'ramble' June–July 1734

Munchensies
John Morley

Leighs
Duchess of Buckingham

R. Thames

Chiswick House
Lord Burlington

Dawlay Farm
Lord Bolingbroke

L

Twickenham   Pope
Hampton Court

Whitehill House
Pope's father

Hallgrove,
Charles Rackett

Stowe
Lord Cobham

Riskins
Lord Bathurst

W

R. Cherwell

Rousham
General Dormer

Oxford

Ladyholt
John Caryll

Mapledurham
The Blounts

R

R. Kennet   Whiteknights
Anthony Englefield

Easthampstead Park
Sir William Trumbull

Southampton

Blenheim
Duke of Marlborough

Stanton Harcourt
Lord Harcourt

R. Thames

Bevis
Mount
Earl of Peterborough

Hagley Hall
Lord Lyttleton

Abberley
William Walsh

R. Severn

R. Avon

Cirencester Park
Lord Bathurst

Bath

Prior Park
Ralph Allen

Sherborne House
Lord Digby

Scale

10   0   10   20   30   40 Miles

Chronological Table

1716	*Iliad*, Books V–VIII. Family move to Chiswick.	Septennial Act.
1717	*Iliad*, Books IX–XII. Pope's *Works* including 'Eloisa to Abelard' and 'Elegy to the Memory of an Unfortunate Lady'. (October) Pope's father dies.	
1718	*Iliad*, Books XIII–XVI.	Death of Parnell.
1719	Pope and his mother move to Twickenham.	Death of Addison. Defoe's *Robinson Crusoe*.
1720	*Iliad,* Books XVII–XXIV.	South Sea Bubble.
1721	Pope's edition of Parnell's *Poems* with 'Epistle to Oxford' as preface. Begins work on edition of Shakespeare.	Robert Walpole becomes Lord Treasurer.
1722	Begins work on translation of the *Odyssey* with Fenton and Broome.	Atterbury charged with complicity in a plot to reinstate the Pretender.
1723	Pope's edition of Buckingham's *Works*, seized by Government on suspicion of Jacobite passages. Pope appears before House of Lords as witness at Atterbury's trial.	Atterbury found guilty of Jacobitism and exiled. Bolingbroke pardoned and returns for brief stay.
1725	Pope's edition of Shakespeare in 6 volumes. *Odyssey*, Vols I–III.	Bolingbroke returns from exile and settles near Pope at Dawlay Farm.
1726	*Odyssey* IV–V. Swift visits Pope. Friendship with Spence begins.	Bolingbroke begins *The Craftsman*. Theobald's *Shakespeare Restored*. Swift's *Gulliver's Travels*.
1727	Pope-Swift *Miscellanies*, I–II. Swift's second visit to Pope.	Death of George I. Accession of George II.
1728	Pope-Swift *Miscellanies*, III, incl. *Peri Bathous*. *The Dunciad*, in 3 Books, with Theobald as hero.	Gay's *Beggar's Opera*. The War with the Dunces reaches a peak.

1729	*The Dunciad Variorum.*	Swift's *Modest Proposal.*
1731	*Epistle to Burlington.*	
1732	Pope-Swift *Miscellanies,* IV.	Death of Gay. Hogarth's prints of *The Harlot's Progress.*
1733	*Epistle to Bathurst. Imitation of Horace, Satire II, i. An Essay on Man,* Epistles I–III. (June) Death of Pope's mother. Pope becomes more committed to the Patriot opposition.	Walpole's Excise Scheme defeated. Bolingbroke's 'Dissertation upon Parties' appeared in *The Craftsman.*
1734	*Epistle to Cobham. Essay on Man,* Epistle IV. *Imitation of Horace, Satire II, ii.*	
1735	*An Epistle to Dr Arbuthnot. Epistle to a Lady.* Pope's *Works,* vol. II. Curll's edition of Pope's letters. Prince of Wales visits Pope at Twickenham.	Death of Arbuthnot and Lord Peterborough. Bolingbroke returns to France. Hogarth's *Rake's Progress.*
1737	*Imitation of Horace, Epistle II, ii.* Authorized edition of Pope's letters. *Imitation of Horace, Epistle II, i.*	Death of Queen Caroline. Prince of Wales heads Patriot opposition. Crousaz attacks *An Essay on Man.*
1738	*Imitation of Horace, Epistle I, vi. Imitation of Horace, Epistle I, i. Epilogue to the Satires.*	Bolingbroke returns from France and stays with Pope at Twickenham. Dr Johnson's *London.*
1739	Spends winter with Ralph Allen at Prior Park near Bath.	Warburton's *Vindication of the Essay on Man* defends Pope against Crousaz.
1740	First meets Warburton. Refurbishes his grotto.	
1741	Publishes *Memoirs of Martinus Scriblerus.* Works closely with Warburton on revised edition of his poems.	Handel's *Messiah* receives its first performance, in Dublin.

1742	*The New Dunciad* (i.e. Book IV).	Walpole resigns.
1743	*The Dunciad in Four Books*, with Cibber replacing Theobald as hero. Pope's health deteriorates.	
1744	(May 30) Pope dies at Twickenham.	

Further Reading

Primary Texts

The standard edition is *The Twickenham Edition of the Poems of Alexander Pope*, general editor JOHN BUTT, 11 vols, (Methuen, 1939–69):

I   *Pastoral Poetry and An Essay on Criticism*, ed. E. AUDRA and A. WILLIAMS, 1961.

II   *The Rape of the Lock and Other Poems*, ed. G. TILLOTSON, 1940, revised 1962.

III, i *An Essay on Man*, ed. M. MACK, 1950.

III, ii *Epistles to Several Persons*, ed. F.W. BATESON, 1951, revised 1961.

IV   *Imitations of Horace*, ed. J. BUTT, 1939, revised 1953.

V   *The Dunciad*, ed. J. SUTHERLAND, 1943, revised 1963.

VI   *Minor Poems*, ed. N. AULT and J. BUTT, 1954.

VII–X   *Iliad and Odyssey*, ed. M. MACK, N. CALLAN, R. FAGLES, W. FROST, and D. KNIGHT, 1967.

XI   *Index*, ed. M. MACK, 1969.

These definitive texts have been conveniently condensed into one volume in *The Poems of Alexander Pope*, ed. J. BUTT, (Methuen, 1963).

The earlier prose writings of 1711–20 have been collected in *The Prose Works of Alexander Pope*, ed. N. AULT, (Blackwell, 1936). The later prose is being edited by Maynard Mack and is expected soon. The standard edition of the letters is *The Correspondence of Alexander Pope*, ed. GEORGE SHERBURN, 5 vols., (Clarendon Press, 1956). The headnotes to each year's letters in this edition provide a useful supplement to the biographies mentioned below. Pope's reminiscences about his life are recorded in Joseph Spence, *Observations, Anecdotes and Characters of Books and Men*, ed. JAMES OSBORN, 2 vols., (Clarendon Press, 1966).

Biographies

The best short life of Pope is still that by SAMUEL JOHNSON, originally published in *Lives of the English Poets*, 1779–81, available in the Everyman's Library edition (Dent, 1925). The most authoritative life is GEORGE SHERBURN, *Early Career of Alexander Pope* (Clarendon Press, 1934). An account of the later career is still needed though R.W. ROGERS, *The Major Satires of Alexander Pope* (University of Illinois Press, 1955) goes some way towards filling that need. BONAMY DOBRÉE's study *Alexander Pope* (Sylvan Press, 1951, Oxford University Press, 1963) is a useful brief biography that is also a

critical introduction to the poetry. MARJORIE HOPE NICOLSON and
G.S. ROUSSEAU, *This Long Disease, My Life* (Princeton University
Press, 1968) is a specialized treatment of Pope's illness and his
relation to eighteenth-century science, and for purely human
onslaught upon him see J.V. GUERINOT, *Pamphlet Attacks on Alexander
Pope 1711–1744*, (Methuen, 1969).

Criticism

One of the best introductions to Pope for the new reader is MAYNARD
MACK's essay 'Wit, and Poetry and Pope', reprinted in *Eighteenth-
Century English Literature*, ed. J.L. CLIFFORD (Oxford University Press,
1959). The most sensitive and subtle full length study of Pope's
poetry is REUBEN BROWER, *Alexander Pope: The Poetry of Allusion*
(Clarendon Press, 1959). Two other good general books on Pope
that also contain penetrating analyses of the poetry are THOMAS R.
EDWARDS, *This Dark Estate: A Reading of Pope* (University of Cali-
fornia Press, 1963) and GEOFFREY TILLOTSON, *On the Poetry of Pope*
(Clarendon Press, 1938).

The twentieth century has seen a great revival of interest in Pope's
poetry and this is no place to attempt a survey of even the best of all
that has been written about him. For further help with individual
poems the introductions to the respective volumes of the Twicken-
ham edition provide good starting points. IAN JACK, *Augustan Satire:
Intention and Idiom in English Poetry 1660–1750* (Oxford University
Press, 1952) has detailed analyses of both *The Rape of the Lock* and
The Dunciad, and the respective volumes in the Studies in English
Literature series, J.S. CUNNINGHAM, *Pope: The Rape of the Lock*
(Edward Arnold, 1961), and H. ERSKINE-HILL, *Pope: The Dunciad*
(Edward Arnold, 1972), provide further cogent evaluations of these
two poems. The most important and far ranging study of *The
Dunciad* is AUBREY WILLIAMS, *Pope's Dunciad: A Study of Its Meaning*
(Methuen, 1955).

The shift of focus in recent times from the earlier to the later
poetry as the greatest period of Pope's achievement has been accompanied by two books that merit special attention: PETER DIXON,
The World of Pope's Satires (Methuen, 1968) relates the *Imitations
of Horace* and *Epistles to Several Persons* to their contemporary setting;
and MAYNARD MACK, *The Garden and the City* (Oxford University
Press, 1970) crucially extends our understanding of Pope's later
poetry. Mack's book seems to me the most important study of Pope
written since that of Brower.

Finally there are three anthologies that should prove specially
useful. *Alexander Pope: A Critical Anthology*, ed. F.W. BATESON and
N.A. JOUKOVSKY (Penguin, 1971) collects a wide cross section of Pope
criticism from his own time to the present day; *Writers and their*

Background: Alexander Pope, ed. PETER DIXON (Bell, 1972) presents a series of scholarly articles on the intellectual and social background to Pope's poetry; *Essential Articles for the Study of Alxander Pope*, ed. MAYNARD MACK (Cass, 1964) brings together a mass of critical articles that would be otherwise difficult to obtain.

Background Studies

Intellectual History:

BASIL WILLEY, *Eighteenth-Century Background* (Chatto & Windus, 1940) is the most useful introduction to the philosophical inheritance and beliefs of Pope's time. LESLIE STEPHEN, *History of English Thought in the Eighteenth Century*, 2 vols (London, 1876–80) is still indispensable. A.O. LOVEJOY, *The Great Chain of Being: a Study of the History of an Idea* (Harvard University Press, 1936) is a detailed treatment of one particular aspect of the eighteenth-century inheritance that has particular relevance to Pope. The best treatment of the philosophical background to Pope's poetry generally is Maynard Mack's introduction to the Twickenham edition of *An Essay on Man* (Methuen, 1950).

Social and Political History:

Perhaps the best starting point here is A.S. TURBERVILLE, *English Men and Manners in the Eighteenth Century* (Oxford University Press, 1926; reprinted 1957). This is an illustrated guide to the social, political and religious scene. G.M. TREVELYAN, *Illustrated English Social History* vol. 3 (Longman, 1952; Penguin, 1964) has a chapter of a similar nature on Defoe's England. DOROTHY GEORGE, *England in Transition* (1931, Penguin 1953) provides a third picture of life in England during Pope's time. A.R. HUMPHREYS, *The Augustan World* (Methuen, 1954) is especially useful to students of Pope because it relates the social, political and religious scene to the literature.

For further study of England's capital city J. Strype's edition of STOW'S, *Survey of London and Westminster* (London, 1722) is invaluable if it can be obtained. Of modern books GEORGE RUDE, *Hanoverian London, 1714–1808* (Secker & Warburg, 1971) is the most lively account of the political and social life of the city, while JOHN SUMMERSON, *Georgian London* (Pleiades Books, 1945; Penguin, 1962) is a superbly detailed study of London's architecture and includes many plates and diagrams. The most important study of London as it concerns Pope's poetry is undoubtedly PAT ROGERS *Grub Street* (Methuen, 1972).

The most useful book to supplement A.S. Turberville and Dorothy George with regard to political life in Augustan England is J.H. PLUMB, *The Growth of Political Stability in England, 1675–1725*

(Macmillan, 1967; Penguin, 1969). For further material see DEREK
JARRETT, *Britain 1688–1815* (Longman, 1965). ISAAC KRAMNICK,
Bolingbroke and his Circle (Harvard University Press, 1968) is especially
useful in this context since it discusses Pope's relationship to the
Tory opposition to Robert Walpole.

Literary criticism:

SCOTT ELLEDGE's edition of *Eighteenth Century Critical Essays*, 2 vols
(Cornell University Press, 1961) is the standard source for any
student wanting to delve further into the literary beliefs and
viewpoints adopted by Augustan writers. A useful concise discussion
of eighteenth-century critical ideas will be found in the relevant
chapters of W.K. WIMSATT and CLEANTH BROOKS, *Literary Criticism:
a short history* (Vintage Books, 1957). The most thorough historical
treatment of the subject is J.W.H. ATKINS, *English Literary Criticism:
Seventeenth and Eighteenth centuries* (Methuen, 1951).

The Kindred Arts:

JEAN HAGSTRUM, *The Sister Arts* (University of Chicago Press, 1958)
discusses the tradition of literary pictorialism and English poetry
and devotes a whole chapter to a discussion of this tradition as it
affects Pope's poetry. W.K. WIMSATT, *The Portraits of Alexander Pope*
(Yale University Press, 1965) brings together all known paintings
of Pope and has many useful notes about Pope's connections with
contemporary painters. The best discussion of the relationship of
landscape gardening to Pope's poetry will be found in EDWARD
MALINS, *English Landscaping and Literature 1660–1840* (Oxford
University Press, 1966). For the student who wishes to learn more
about eighteenth-century sculpture MARGARET WHINNEY, *Sculpture
in Britain, 1530–1830* (Pelican History of Art, 1964) is invaluable
and contains a fine collection of illustrative plates. James Sambrook's
chapter on 'Pope and the Visual Arts' in *Writers and their Background: Alexander Pope* (see under 'Criticism' above), pulls some of
these various threads together. Since Pope's circle frequently encountered Handel and his music a final study of the arts in Augustan
England is the detailed and instructive *George Frideric Handel* by
PAUL HENRY LANG, (Faber, 1967).

General Index

Index to Pope's Works